Binge Birding
Twenty Days with Binoculars

Nancy Grant

Binge Birding
Twenty Days with Binoculars

Nancy Grant

*A Solo Road Trip
from the Ohio River Valley
to the Texas Gulf Coast*

For
Jenn and Matt

Table of Contents

Becoming a Birder

When I started looking at birds more carefully I was delighted with each new find. The more I looked, the more I saw. Gradually, I began to think of myself in a new way—I was becoming a birder. And then I discovered something surprising.

Being a birder is much more than looking at birds. It's more than knowing the name of a particular kind of bird or recognizing its song. It's more than lists. It's more than pretty photos.

Being a birder is the chance to join a global community and take part in a culture of curiosity that extends far beyond traditional field guides and today's speedy identification phone apps. So much of birding lore is passed along from person to person. You're probably discovering this, too. Maybe you've joined a social media group devoted to the birds in your state. Perhaps you've started going on Saturday morning walks sponsored by a local bird club. These opportunities to meet and exchange ideas with other people who are also fascinated by birds adds depth and richness to life. And it's so much fun! I call it birding the friendly way.

If you want to know more about any of the birds I encountered during my travels, the best place to start for accurate, easy-to-read, up-to-date information is *www.allaboutbirds.org*, the free website maintained by the Cornell Lab of Ornithology. The information there is presented clearly for birders of any level of experience. You can look at photos and range maps, discover interesting facts, and listen to bird songs and calls.

When I began my birdwatching trip in April 2017 I did so thinking only of a vacation. As I posted photos on social media each day I realized that a lot of people dream of taking such a road trip. Their comments inspired me to write this book and share the fun of my adventure with other curious folks.

As a working journalist and researcher for more than thirty years, and a field naturalist in my spare time for more than twenty years, I am in the habit of taking meticulous notes. I double-check, and then check again just to make sure. I ask questions and dig for answers, learning along the way. This account of my travels is based on my daily field notes and is accurate to the best of my ability.

The names given here of the people I met along the way are different from the names I jotted down in my notebook. I've changed them to protect the privacy of those individuals.

The restaurants, hotels, and other businesses I describe are open to the general public. I have received no compensation from anyone for mentioning these places by name. The parks and refuges I visited are also open to the general public, although their visiting hours may change from season to season.

As for the birds, the names in this account are the accepted common names in use at the time of my observations. I've included the two lists of birds that I prepared after the trip, one in the order of their discovery, and one arranged in scientific groupings.

I traveled alone, but I've written this book so that you can come along for the ride.

Let's go birding together!

Nancy Grant

CHAPTER ONE

Roadside birding
in three southern states

Flexible plans, travel glitches, clicking off the miles

There he goes, red wings flashing in the morning sunlight, flying up to perch on the roof peak of my house. I stop what I'm doing, again, to watch my favorite cardinal as he whistles his song, even though I know perfectly well what he looks like and could easily just listen.

"What cheer, what cheer, what cheer," he sings, and then adds a long string of "purdy, purdy, purdy," as he looks east, then west, north, then south, searching for any rivals. He draws himself up to his full height, all six inches of feathered importance, and sings again. "Purdy, purdy, purdy."

He's on high alert this sunny spring morning here in Kentucky at my farm near Louisville. And he should be. Other cardinals live in the brushy thickets on neighboring farms. The next closest cardinal lives a few acres away on the other side of my south fenceline. When my rooftop percher pauses his singing, we both listen for the neighbor's song to ring out in response.

And there it is, piercingly loud, carrying crisply over the greening fields. "Whoit chew, whoit chew, whoit chew," and "birdy, birdy, birdy." Their voices are similar yet different, and for now, this is just a vocal duel, variations on the same theme: I live here and don't you forget it. If the other male would venture over here there'd be a flying chase, for sure.

The bird on my roof peak looks around again and sings another string of whistling notes, "What cheer, what cheer, what cheer." He's a red bird, the reddest red, a solid, rich, brilliant red, except for the black feathers that outline his orangeish-red bill. His red crest is raised, the point of feathers giving his head a jaunty look in the April sunlight.

This handsome singer and his mate live here year-round, and we all know each other well. He's keeping a careful eye on me, to make sure that I am not going anywhere near his mate. Her feathers are a soft beige with paler red accents at the tip of her crest and along her wings and tail, and she has a knack for slipping into leafy bushes and disappearing. She's out of sight just now, hunkered down in the vine-covered shrubs in my east garden, but she whistles and chips back from her hiding place to let him know where she is.

I know where she is, too, and exactly where she's building her nest this time around. It's in the small holly tree on the north side of the house. I wonder when she'll lay the first egg? Does she already have one or two in the little cup-shaped nest of twigs?

But enough of that. I can't keep stopping to wonder about my local birds or I'll never get on the road on time.

My travel plan is simple. Drive down to the Texas Gulf Coast and look at birds. Eat fresh seafood. Look at birds. Stay in nice hotels. Look at birds. Camp for a few nights. Look at birds. Maybe go horseback riding on the beach. Look at birds. Then drive back home. Look at birds everywhere.

That's all there is to it.

But before I can do any of that I've got to finish packing the car. I need to get all the stuff I've dragged out onto the front walkway into my car, and do it so that I'll have easy access to what I need when I need it, without having to root around through unnecessary items.

My car is not a sedan, but an SUV, a Ford Explorer with eighty thousand miles on it already and lots of room inside. I travel a lot, but this will be the longest solo journey I've tried so far. I look at the piles again: duffle bag; big rolling suitcase; my tent, bedroll, and camping gear, including my camp kitchen; beach tote bag; two small insulated rolling coolers; snacks and bottled waters; a windbreaker and a soft black velour zip jacket; two kinds of folding chairs.

I'm going to Texas with an open-ended goal, to see as many different kinds of birds as I can find, and to learn something about the habitats and lifestyles of the new ones. I get such a thrill when I can identify a new bird, when I can match up the field marks with a name and understand what the bird I'm looking at is doing, why it's where it is right now.

Every night for the past week, I've fallen asleep thinking about how to stow all of this in the most logical and easily accessible fashion. Last Saturday I tested part of my plan with empty storage bins—it seemed to work okay—but today is the real deal, with the bins full, plus all the other stuff I need.

When I was dragging all this gear out here after breakfast, the Blue Jays were just minding their own business over in the north fenceline, calling "queedle, queedle, queedly-do" softly back and forth to each other. But they were also watching me, as they always do. Every time I come outdoors they follow me around with their eyes, checking to see whether I'm going to pull weeds in the garden or take a walk or get in my car. If I get too close to them or do something noisy and unexpected, they dash away in a flurry of blue and white and black.

Now they're screaming and jeering, "jaaay-jaaay-jaay." What is going on? Where are they? Oh, I see, they've flown down by the little stream that runs through my left woods and they're shrieking again and again, their raucous calls overlapping, getting more and more agitated. Something's bothering them, but it's not me. I can't see anything special down there, and I really don't have the time to take a closer look. I need to keep loading the car.

My big suitcase goes flat on the back seat behind the driver's seat, then I plop my duffel bag on top of that. The duffel will go in with me to my hotel room every night. As I need fresh clothes I'll add them from the suitcase, but it will stay in the car most of the time. On the other side, behind the passenger seat, I can just barely squeeze the empty laundry hamper upright, wedged against the base of the back seat. There's room for two tote bags over here, too. So far, so good.

Argh. My plan for the liftgate section is not going to work. This bin of camping gear is going to have to go sideways instead of crossways so there'll be enough room for the collapsible chairs in bags in the center. Now I'll have to shift more things. The aluminum folding chair can go over here, then the red-and-black plaid stadium blanket over that, then the folding camp stool flat on top. Pile more tote bags over that. At least I got the spot for the coolers right—they fit just fine at the far back by the liftgate.

The trick to packing such a mixture of stuff is to place things so they won't squeak or rattle, or shift going around curves or up and down hills. Or crash forward if I have to make a sudden stop. Now that everything's packed in the back, I can cover it all with the old striped comforter that's part of my camping gear, shut the liftgate, and close the back doors.

I walk around to the front and sit in the driver's seat to check that I still have clear sightlines in the rearview mirror. Yes. And in the side mirror I can see the female cardinal poking around for something to eat in the weeds growing up through the gravel next to my wheelbarrow. She flies off as soon as I walk back around the car.

There's only one item left on the walkway—a plastic laundry basket that goes on the front passenger seat. It has nothing to do with laundry—it's my mobile birding center, information hub, and traveling office, and needs to be within easy reach at all times. It's filled with all my travel essentials: my best binoculars, paper maps, bird field guides, a yellow rain poncho, bird checklists and identification charts, my favorite ball cap, a folder with all my hotel and campground reservation confirmations, two books about Texas birding hotspots, blank notebooks, spare car key on a lanyard, a plastic cup filled with pens, scissors, tape, and paperclips, plus this year's official Texas State Travel Guide, my digital camera with zoom lens—and a big bag of M&Ms.

When I brought the basket outside earlier it was only half full, but now that I've been adding items to it from my staging area inside the house, it's too heavy to pick up. Another delay. Take out the books, put the basket on front seat, put the books back in, shut the door. It fits!

§

For my last lunch at home some cheese on a slice of bread and a gulp of cranberry juice will have to do. I scarcely taste it anyway, because I'm still going over last-minute notes at the kitchen table. I scribble yet another reminder for the cat sitter, then check over all my "to do" lists one final time. Done! I tear them in half and throw them away. Now it's time to say goodbye to my three kitties, lock up the house, and get going.

At my car I put my cell phone and reading glasses in the cup holder in the center console, then settle into the driver's seat. I am so keyed up after loading the car, and so eager to get on the road, I have to make a conscious effort to relax. I take a very careful deep breath and turn the key to start the engine. While waiting for all the electronic displays on the dash to materialize I take a few more carefully measured breaths, in, out, in.

The start of a trip is always exciting, filled with high hopes for good travel karma, good wishes that plans will work out right without too many glitches. Now I need to calm down and get into driving mode. Everything is going to be fine. And if I've forgotten something, well, I can just buy it down the road. Oh, yes, there's my wallet with three credit cards and some cash. I give it a quick pat for good luck.

While I set the controls for the air conditioning and check how the air's flowing from the various vents, I look out over the hood toward my front hayfield and the woods. Spring is well in progress this first week of April in my part of the Ohio River Valley. The short grasses and clovers closest to me along the gravel drive are gleaming a fresh emerald green. Out in the sloping front hayfield, the grasses and wildflowers and clovers there are shooting up taller and taller, opening fresh leaves to gather the energy in the sunshine. Strands of silk from ballooning spiderlings wave and shimmer from the tops of some of the plants like bits of silver thread floating in the very light breeze.

At the bottom of the hill, down by the stream, the shrubby layer of understory plants is already a rich green, too, and fresh leaves are unfurling on the vines. A few of the trees, though generally still bare of leaves, are beginning to show color, with tiny flowers that give the tips of their twigs a pinkish cast or narrow slivers of unfurling leaf buds that show a sort of washed-out chartreuse. I know that fresh, tiny little caterpillars and other insect larvae that I can't see from here are creeping about, munching on the emerging leaves everywhere.

To the north of me in Indiana and Ohio the land is gradually greening up, too. But I am heading south today. Driving this direction in April puts me out of sync with the patterns of the natural world, because I'm about half a year late. Many birds flew south last autumn as their preferred foods became scarce and open waters froze over solid. My plan is to get to the Gulf Coast right about the time the migrating birds are beginning to move north again, and then I'll be in sync with their movements and the greening up of the continent.

Of course, the land I drive across will not be empty. There are full-time, year-round resident birds in all the states I'll visit. In each one there are different combinations of birds to see, depending on the season, with some living in a place all year, and then a varying mix of migrants coming through at different times. The migrating birds move up and down across the continent in distinct patterns, with some species arriving in a particular spot just for the winter, or just for the summer, or only briefly because they are just passing through in one direction or the other on their way somewhere else completely. Because their movements follow predictable routes at predictable times, traveling in April should give me the most opportunities to see the greatest variety of birds wherever I am.

I take yet another deep breath and reach into the laundry basket for my travel journal. That makes it sound a lot fancier than it is—it's just a common, mass-produced, spiral-top steno pad. Not leather-bound, not made with handcrafted paper, just a totally practical, familiar part of my life wherever I am. I've filled hundreds of them with nature studies and work notes over the decades. The pages have wide-ruled lines and are tinted faintly green, very easy on the eyes, which is especially nice when writing in bright sunlight. I only write on the front side of each page, leaving the reverse side for extra notes later.

Wait. What is that? Whose shadow is that moving in a sort of wavy circle over the grasses?

I look up and see one of the regular local hunters, a Red-tailed Hawk, riding a thermal, a rising column of warmer air that gives the bird extra lift without the need of wingbeats.

Is this what the Blue Jays were so irate about earlier? It's a never-ending battle between these two species, the hawk looking for food, the Blue Jays worried they might be the next meal. Red-tailed Hawks usually hunt mice and other little grassland creatures, but a bit later on in the season, a small just-hatched Blue Jay nestling might be a tasty snack for an adult hawk to eat on the spot or take to feed to its own nestlings, and the jays are taking no chances. Whenever they find a hawk, they'll set up a racket to let these predators know they're watching their movements. This hawk is in no hurry to leave, but soars gently on, using invisible currents of air to move across the fields and out of my line of sight.

I turn back to my notebook and write "My Great Texas Birding Adventure" on the first page. That's what I'm hoping for, a great adventure—but I'm a long way from Texas right now. This notebook will be like a ship's logbook, a place to record the mileage at every stop, make notes about the weather, traffic conditions, and keep track of all my expenses. During breaks, I'll jot down descriptions of meals, people I meet, observations about the changing scenery, whatever I think of or notice. But mostly, my journal will be a place to write down what I find out about the birds I see and where they live.

When I'm exploring on foot, I'll use one of the smaller, pocket-sized spiral notebooks (also cheap, and easy to buy anywhere) to record the bird species I see while I'm out in the field. When walking, it's so much simpler for me to write the old-fashioned, pen-on-paper way instead of trying to type things on my phone's tiny keyboard. And with a real notebook I can make sketches or draw little maps, anything that will help me remember what I'm seeing and doing. At night I'll tear out the little pages and tape them onto the reverse side of that day's notes in the larger travel journal to keep everything in one place.

All the digital displays on the dash are ready. I reset the onboard digital computer system's value for the trip mileage to zero and turn on the headlights.

I wanted to get away about one o'clock and I've done well— I'm finally putting the car in gear at twenty past. Time to focus on driving.

§

While planning this trip I've resisted the urge to make a guess about how many bird species I will find. I'm not aiming for a particular number, and this trip is not part of a Big Year contest or challenge to accumulate some enormous number of species seen. I'm not doing anything competitive at all. I want to be satisfied with whatever the total is, not comparing it to some previous expectation. I'll review my daily field notes whenever I have the time, but I'll wait until I get back home to make an exact list of all the bird species I see. The final numbers will be a surprise.

And I've resisted the urge this morning to make any official notes about the birds I've seen while I've been packing my car. It just wouldn't be fair to start a trip list while I'm still in my own driveway. But as soon as I'm on the road, every wild bird I see will go on the list.

Pulling out onto the pavement, I'm thinking about the way the various bird species move across the land. Although the areas covered with fresh green growth are expanding northward as spring advances across the continent, the colors on the range maps in field guides tend to follow a different scheme. Red or pink means a bird's breeding range, which usually occurs in summer. Blue means winter, and purple indicates the places where a species lives year-round. Migration routes are shown with a rich, deep yellow. For the few bird species that use different paths moving south and north, one route is pale yellow, the other pale green. Dots of various appropriate colors indicate exceptions or strays that occur outside the usual areas.

In my imagination these swaths of solid map colors ebb and flow as each species moves around, but not like the rigid shapes inside a kaleidoscope. The leading edge of where the majority of a particular species is right now is a wavy line, with birds poised all along it ready to move again as soon as conditions are right. I am so eager to see them, to make the lines on the range maps come to life.

I'm only half a mile from home, just getting up to speed on the little country road that leads over to the highway, when I see my first official trip bird, a Red-tailed Hawk, its brick-red tail fanned out at just the right angle to the sun so I can admire it. It's probably the same individual whose shadow I noticed just before I left home—these raptors have large territories and are year-round residents here. The hawk moves forward with slow, deliberate wingbeats, scanning the fields below. The lifestyle of these hawks depends on two different kinds of habitats—tall woods for their bulky stick nests, then grassy fields where their keen eyesight and forward-focusing eyes help them hunt for mice or voles, or other small prey like unguarded fledgling songbirds, to pounce on, feet first. The hawk soars higher, then tilts to the right to curve away from me.

During the winter months, additional Red-tailed Hawks from farther north move into this part of the Ohio River Valley to hunt. They tend to perch on light poles above the highways where I'll soon be driving. With no need to find nesting sites during the winter months, and wary of intruding into the established territories of the resident hawks, the cold-weather visitors often hunt along the grasses of highway medians and shoulders, and in the centers of exit and entrance ramp exchanges. The design of the interstate highway system suits them well, and the trees along the nearby fences and in the yards of older subdivisions provide great nighttime roosting spots. But I don't expect to see many hawks perched on light poles on this trip, as most of the visiting winter hawks have already flown back north to return to their own home territories for the summer breeding season.

Aha, so far no annoying noises from inside the car—but I've only driven a little over six miles. My first stop's right here at the local gas station to top off my gas tank. After writing down the tiny little number of trip miles so far and the cost of the gas, I cue up one of my favorite playlists, featuring big and bold marches. Tunes by John Philip Sousa and Henry Fillmore can keep me company for this first stretch of driving.

This afternoon's drive should be easy. I'm on familiar roads, driving south and west through suburbs and light industrial areas. When I get to I-65, I'll turn due south toward Nashville, Tennessee. I don't need GPS for this segment, and I don't need to look at any of the paper maps in the laundry basket, either.

As I keep track of the positions of the cars and trucks ahead and behind me, I'm also watching the shoulders on each side of the highway and scanning the sky far ahead for birds. When I first started studying birds, I couldn't tell one big roadside bird from another, or figure out what kind of bird was circling overhead. I had to look and look, and look again. But familiarity eventually leads to recognition.

I've been studying birds for about twenty years now, casually at first, then getting much more deeply involved during the last ten years. More than nine hundred species of wild birds are known to live some part of their lives in North America north of the Mexican border. I am most familiar with the birds in the eastern portion of the United States, especially those in the Ohio River Valley. I've done a lot of exploring up, down, and for many miles on either side of the river in Indiana, Ohio, and Kentucky, but I've also gone farther away several times to study birds as far south as Florida and as far north as Lake Erie.

As I begin this birding adventure, my life list stands at two hundred twenty-five wild bird species observed in North America. Not a lot, but it's sure been fun finding them, and I hope to add plenty of new lifers on this trip. But I'm not going to chase rarities, and I do not have what's known among birders as a "target list" of species that are the sole reason to go to a particular place. I don't have any must-see birds in certain areas. I've learned the hard way that if you go out looking for Awesome Bird, and you do not see it, then you're disappointed and your day goes flat—never mind that you saw twenty-seven other really amazing birds. So I don't do that.

Oh, sure, I would like to see that jay that's a different color from the ones at home, and there are some woodpeckers that would be interesting to find, and a hawk that—nope, I'm not going to start making wish lists! I'll have a good time no matter what birds happen to be wherever I am on any particular day. The weather and the wander factor and pure chance will all play big roles, and that's just fine with me.

What's that up there? It only takes one glance for me to know immediately who that dark bird with a wide wingspan is, the one cruising above the hills with the merest, most subtle shifts of its long, black wings. It's a Turkey Vulture. Turkey Vultures are hunters, too, like the hawks, but instead of live prey they're looking for dead things to eat. As carrion specialists, their senses are developed not to detect the motion of tiny creatures scampering among the grasses but the odors of decaying flesh anywhere and everywhere. Scientists have done some clever experiments to show that Turkey Vultures have a highly developed sense of smell that seems to play a larger role in finding food than sight does. They cruise along in the sky above the fields, checking above highways, country roads, anyplace with speeding cars, sniffing and looking for roadkill. Cars and trucks colliding with wildlife sure have improved their chances of finding a meal.

§

So far, there are still no bothersome noises from the back of the car as I go up and down hills and around curves on this stretch of interstate—but I've got a problem in the front seat. The laundry basket is bigger than the passenger seat, and it extends slightly beyond the front edge, just as I knew it would. But instead of staying level, the way it was when I loaded the car, now it's tilted toward the floorboard, and it's in danger of tipping completely over and spilling its contents all over the place. I hadn't counted on the weight of the books versus the thinness of the plastic bottom of the basket. It's not sturdy enough to hold its shape, and gravity is taking over. This is not good. I'm going to have to make an adjustment, and soon.

I've planned this first section of my trip to go easy on the miles, to give myself time to settle in comfortably. I like driving, and the first day out on a road trip should be fun, with no unnecessary pressure. And I'm going easy on the time behind the wheel, too. Although I crossed out of the eastern time zone into the central time zone a few miles back, I have not reset the digital clock on my dash, or on my cell phone. For safety and alertness, I need to keep track of my accumulated time at the wheel based on the time where I woke up this morning.

After a little bit less than two hours on the road, I'm taking my first break in Smith's Grove, Kentucky. I don't drink real coffee, but when I'm traveling, sometimes I like to stop for a special treat, a cup of McDonald's decaf with three creams. It has absolutely no effect on my brain, but it sure smells and tastes good. And besides that, McDonald's bathrooms are usually clean and well-lit.

I stand by my car sipping my warm cup of decaf for a few extra minutes to stretch my legs, and watch as some House Sparrows hop around in the rather scraggly bushes at the edge of the parking lot.

House Sparrows are ridiculously easy to find, so this is no great feat of birdwatching. Intentionally, though wrong-headedly, these sparrows from Europe were set loose in New York City in 1850. They rapidly expanded throughout the continent, reaching California by the early 1900s. To supplement their natural diet of seeds and insects, they tend to hang around places where human food crumbs are easy pickings, just as they do in their native Europe. They'll build their messy nests almost anywhere—wedged in under house eaves, in the crooks and crannies of neon signs, gutters, you name it. They can be a nuisance and they're often aggressive toward native birds.

But the males are handsome in a simple, eye-pleasing way, with a black bib and chestnut brown shoulders. Their bold approach and insistent "cheep, cheep, cheep" sounds like something out of a cartoon, but it's pleasant to hear right now, rising above the noise of all the semis and cars whooshing past on the highway. Many American birders scorn these non-native birds, but they'll go on my trip list just the same as all the other birds that live freely in the wild. It's not much of a list so far, only three species, but it's a start.

I put my almost-empty coffee cup on the hood of the car, then carefully open the passenger-side door to try to figure out how to solve the sagging laundry basket problem. It needs a prop, but what? It must be firm, but considering that it will be underneath the heavily laden basket, it has to be something I won't need quick access to anytime soon. I study the situation for another minute. The empty spare cooler should be just about the right size and shape, so I get it out of the back, move a few things around to fill in that gap, and take it around front. Yes, it will fit on the floorboard, and the front edge of the basket can rest on its top. It's off by an inch or so, but close enough to give the bottom of the basket the support it needs. It's not perfect, but it will have to do. My decaf's cold by now, so I toss it in the trash and get in my car to head on down the road.

There, just up ahead, I see the distinctive shape and flight style of a Great Blue Heron. It is a great big bird—if it were standing on the ground, its eye would be almost level with my shoulder. But it's flapping steadfastly along above the highway, long legs stretched out behind, head drawn back above the s-shaped curve of its long neck, making the bird look weirdly out of proportion. Its big wings—almost six feet across from tip to tip—cut through the air just fast enough to keep it moving forward, flying east to west over the interstate. It's probably heading for a favorite farm pond to hunt for a fish or perhaps a water-filled roadside ditch to look for frogs.

The Great Blue Heron's hunting style is very different from the hawk and the vulture I saw earlier. This giant wader's approach is sedate and extremely patient—stand perfectly still in the shallows, peer into the water below minute after minute after minute, perhaps for a quarter of an hour or more, then strike in a flash with that long bill to capture a meal. I have a special fondness for Great Blue Herons—they're so tall and so elegant. And we like the same kinds of food, although I prefer my fish or frog legs cooked, not alive and still wiggling.

§

A few miles on, a couple of crows fly with much faster wingbeats, dashing over the highway in the other direction. When I began studying birds I thought a crow was a crow, and that was that. Noisy, bold, all black.

But that isn't the whole story. North America has two main species of crows with slightly different lifestyles, habitat preferences, and voices, plus a third species that occasionally wanders north into Texas from Mexico, and a fourth species that lives along the upper northwestern coast of the United States and Canada. They all look almost exactly alike—solid black—but here in this part of Kentucky, I'm safe to count these as American Crows even though I did not hear them. It's the only logical choice.

In my handwritten field notes I always write the name of a bird species in all caps so it stands out on the page, and I often use a kind of personal shorthand when I'm in a hurry. When I type up my field notes at home I use lowercase when I'm referring to a general group of birds, then normal capitalization when I mention the full common name of a particular bird species. I'm following that same system here. It's nice and neat that way.

I don't use Latin binomials, the scientific names for birds, in my field notes very often. I don't have all that many of them memorized, and usually have to look them up when I get back home, but this is one I do know by heart. The American Crow is known as *Corvus brachyrhyncos*. It's customary to write these names in italics because they are in Latin, not English. I won't use scientific names much on this trip, except when I really must do so to help remember a point. Adding any Latin bits to my notes as needed is something else I'll do when I get back home.

This is such a lovely afternoon for driving, with blue skies and some small, puffy white clouds here and there. Traffic's been steady, but moving at a good pace.

Kentucky's in my rearview mirror now—I've crossed the Tennessee state line and I'm right where I want to be to stay on track with my very loose schedule.

§

A road trip to Texas was not my original plan for this year. Last December, when plans to drive to Florida with friends after the holidays fell through (we were going to go to a dance weekend, with birding on the side), I decided to just stay home. But after my January birthday came and went, I was still restless. I wanted to go on an adventure, give myself a treat of some sort. I puzzled over and over again. Where to go, when to go, and what to do? I'd be traveling on my own, so I could do anything. Well, within a budget, of course. Nobody to share expenses with does make a difference, but I wasn't going to scrimp, either.

How about changing directions? Instead of going southeast to Florida, why not drive southwest to Texas and explore the other side of the Gulf of Mexico? Going solo would mean no one to share the driving with, so I'd have to set up the trip with a pace of reasonable distances to cover during any particular day. It would be roughly a thousand miles of driving just to get from my house in Kentucky to the Texas state line. How could I make this work? Would a vacation of about three weeks give me enough time to get there and back without rushing?

I've been in many parts of Texas on other kinds of trips over the years, before I started studying birds so intently, and I have vivid memories of how far apart things are in that enormous state. I knew that once I got to the state line, I would need to choose a region, instead of trying to go all over the place.

What if I drove all the way down the coast? I'd probably see many of the same shore birds I recognize in Florida—and maybe I could finally sort out some of the ones I don't know so well. And then if I went all the way south to the Rio Grande and the Mexican border I'd probably find new birds that live just in that region. Oh, and if I timed things right, I should be able to see the first waves of migrant songbirds heading back north. That was it—I decided to make it a coastal birding trip, nothing too far inland, just focus on the shore areas.

In early February I started shifting around project deadlines and other responsibilities at home so I'd be free to travel in April, and began my trip research. I discovered that the kind of trip I had in mind is not only possible, it's popular. It's so popular the Texas tourism folks call it the Great Texas Coastal Birding Trail, and they have maps and brochures to help birders explore the various sections. There are hundreds of locations to look at birds, all numbered and described with GPS coordinates, so many places to explore that the trail is divided into three big chunks along the upper, middle, and lower Gulf Coasts. Could I see all of them?

I sent away for the free stuff from the tourism department, bought two books about places to go birdwatching in Texas, and joined a social media group devoted to the birds of Texas to learn more. I'm in many other birding groups focused on individual states, and I've found that local folks are really generous about sharing tips about good birdwatching sites in their areas. And the photos are amazing! Feather details, close-ups of talons, gleaming eyes, action photos of birds hunting and mating and caring for youngsters—the kinds of images that feed a birder's dreams.

As soon as the books arrived, I started putting purple sticky notes on the margins of pages describing the parks and wildlife refuges that I'd like to visit. I spread out paper maps on the floor of my office, then used Mapquest and other internet tools to calculate mileage and driving times on my desktop computer. When I got conflicting answers, I cross-checked things with Google maps on my phone.

By the first week of March, I had enough information to make a tentative day-by-day itinerary. I picked today, Tuesday, April 4, 2017, as my starting date, and I have three full weeks to get all the way to the Rio Grande and back, looking at birds everywhere along the way. I've chosen a few widely scattered cities and towns to use as bases in the upper, middle, and lower sections along the four hundred fifty miles of the Texas Gulf Coast.

Just a few weeks ago I began making hotel and campground reservations, but only for the southbound section of the trip. Although I have places to spend the night, I haven't made detailed plans about exactly where to go birdwatching in the areas I will be using as bases. I'll decide on that when I get there. I've allowed ample time for weather glitches and spur-of-the-moment decisions based on what the birds are doing in whichever direction I'm traveling. For the return north, I will trust to luck, so I have no advance reservations for that final segment of the trip. As I head home I'll decide where to stay on a day-to-day basis. It's a very flexible adventure plan, designed to be stress-free and fun.

§

My first bird in Tennessee is another familiar one, a Black Vulture. They have shorter, wider wings than the other kind of vulture I saw earlier, and white feathers at the tips. When I was trying to memorize this difference years ago, I had to recite over and over again to myself "Black Vultures have white wing tips." And I had to get rid of the notion that they're buzzards. That's one of their common names in the United States, but it can cause confusion in the global world of birds, where the word "buzzard" refers to a completely different group of birds that do not live in North America.

Here on the northern outskirts of Nashville, even though it's well before typical rush hour, the traffic is already bunched up and slowed down. It's the usual problem in most large cities—too many vehicles going the same places at the same time, not enough lanes. Stop. Start. Stop, go forward a little bit, over and over and over for a couple miles, but it's only a brief delay. I had allowed for this sort of thing when I made plans to meet my cousin for dinner tonight in Franklin.

South of Nashville I know which exit to take for Franklin, but as soon as I do, I pull into a parking lot to set my phone's GPS for the location of the restaurant where we're going to meet. Throughout the trip I'll be using highway signs, printed maps, and GPS in whatever combination I need for wherever I am. And sometimes I'll just set out on my own to wander around to see what I can discover by chance.

I've found a place to park on a side street, and since I'm here a little earlier than expected, I'll have about an hour to meander on foot and explore the town before dinner. As comfortable as my car is, I'm glad to stand up and walk around—and with more driving to do after dinner, it's best to take advantage of the opportunity to move around while I can.

Amid the mature trees in this historic Southern town, the late afternoon sunshine highlights some cardinals dashing about. Their proper common name is Northern Cardinal, although I do not know of any other kind with a direction in the name. I never write all that down—cardinal is enough for my notes and in everyday conversation. There seem to be two males and two females—yes, now I have all four of them in view at once. There's a territorial dispute in progress, and they're chipping excitedly to each other as they fly from tree to shrub to tree, not singing, just chipping.

The old houses on these blocks have little square grassy lawns between their front porches and the sidewalks, plus gardens and weeds and shrubs and mature trees on all sides, good places to find seeds and insects to eat. I suspect that one pair of cardinals already has nestlings hidden in one of the shrubs. They'll need a steady and abundant food supply, and the parents won't want to share their turf with other hungry birds. That's what all the chipping is about, a bird shouting match. This is our place—get out!

Walking along toward the main street and center of the business district, I see a handsome gray Northern Mockingbird. There aren't any other kinds of mockingbirds named for a different region, and they live throughout the eastern United States, so I don't know why they're called that. It's a quirky detail, just like the name Northern Cardinal. I don't make up the rules about bird names, but I do have to follow them for clarity. From a perch about ten feet above the sidewalk, the mockingbird sings an impressive repertoire of songs copied from other birds. He darts down to the ground to poke in the grass in front of a handsome brick house for an insect, showing his white outer tail feathers and the big patches of white on his wings.

I've known cardinals and mockingbirds since I was a child. These two native birds like living near humans in cities and towns, and around homes in the suburbs and in rural areas. But unlike the

House Sparrows, they don't beg for food or eat human leftovers. They simply are very much at ease going about their normal lives amid buildings and traffic and other human activities. They're not tame, but they're not overly skittish, either. Many can be approached within ten feet or so for a better look. No need for binoculars.

My idea of shopping goes along the lines of, if you see a candy store, go right on in. And here's one now. Kilwin's is based in Michigan and well-known for fudge, but I'm looking for something else. The glass cases are filled with plenty of pretty treats and I take my time looking them over. So many to choose from—chocolate-covered pretzels and a square of pecan toffee bar will be nice snacks for tomorrow.

Back on the sidewalk, I turn the corner and there's cousin Rick, waiting for me outside the restaurant. I'll put birdwatching on hold for a while.

§

Dinner at Puckett's was fun. It's definitely local, an old-fashioned kind of place that's also part grocery store, bakery, and catering company, with live music, too. The layout of the building is quirky—to get to the restrooms I had to walk through part of the kitchen and past racks of freshly baked bread. While catching up on the news with my cousin and his wife and their grandson, I sampled my first local beer of the trip from a brewery with a funny name, Turtle Anarchy. The IPA I chose, Another Way to Rye, paired very well with my dinner, a dish called Piggy Mac— smoked dry pulled pork topped with macaroni and cheese, served in a small iron skillet.

Now, as I stroll along the last block back to my car, some noisy European Starlings fly across my path. They're one of the most familiar bird species anywhere in North America. They're everywhere. But they don't belong here. Since their deliberate but ridiculously inappropriate introduction in New York, just as wrong-headed as the House Sparrow's release, they, too, have spread across this entire continent with astonishing speed.

Even people who don't normally pay any attention to birds take notice when starlings gather in huge flocks in the fall and winter months. They swirl through the air by the thousands, forming patterns that resemble schools of fish, but up in the sky instead of in water. Watching them wheel and shift the shape of their huge aggregations, seemingly in perfect unison, is captivating.

But closer to the ground they're a noisy mess where they roost, squeaking and squawking, and leaving streaks of droppings. This time of year they disperse into much smaller groups, and indeed, there are only two birds in front of me, probably looking for someplace to build a nest. They'll stuff twigs into any appropriately sized natural cavity in a tree, but they will also use exhaust vents and other openings in people's houses, as well as nest boxes meant to help native birds. But they're wild birds, and they will go on my trip list.

Several American Robins are nearby singing in the remaining daylight. Their song is often represented in human speech as sounding like "cheerily, cheer-up, cheery-o" or various other combinations of those words. That's close enough. I'm certainly cheerful on this first day of my adventure, so their singing makes the perfect send-off for me as I get back into my car to head farther south.

Although I've driven on this section of I-65 many times, I've forgotten how quickly the area changes from suburbs to sparsely populated rural countryside, with the exits few and far between. The farm fields with creeks and ponds and the woodsy sections bordering the road would be great habitat for owls, and this is just the right time of the evening to listen and look. But as the sun sets tonight, I am not hunting for birds—I am looking for a hotel. My first definite hotel reservation isn't until Thursday in Texas, so tonight and tomorrow night will be a matter of stopping wherever seems practical.

As dusk deepens, I cross the Alabama state line and have to drive much farther after full dark than I intended to on this first day. I've tried a lot of different hotel chains over the years, and right now I have two favorites, places that are consistently clean with a high level of friendly service. Whichever one comes along next will be fine. Finally, I spy a sign for a Holiday Inn Express and take the exit for Athens.

When I pull under the covered portico at the hotel, already slightly beyond being mentally and physically ready to stop driving, I'm not paying all that much attention to what is in front of me. In fact, I don't think anything at all about the pile of lumber and other construction materials in the parking lot. So it's a complete surprise when I walk into the lobby to inquire about a room and see that the front desk is nothing but a cheap portable exhibit hall table with cloth skirting pinned around it.

"The hotel is in the middle of a complete remodel," the clerk tells me. "But we do have rooms available. What would you like?" I stand there blinking, and thinking over my options. I really do not want to drive any farther tonight. I ask about breakfast, one of the reasons I like this hotel chain. "Oh, don't worry, yes ma'am, there will still be a free hot breakfast as usual, only it will be served down the hall in the conference room." As I look around that seems to be the only location available. The typical central great room and gathering room combination doesn't exist right now. Everything is stripped down to bare studs and raw concrete, and all of it covered with clear plastic sheeting hung from the ceiling to the floor.

At this point I don't care, so I check in and go upstairs to my room. It's already been remodeled, with trendy light fixtures and a kind of center-of-a-big-city loft vibe to the decor, even though it's on the outskirts of a rural town with a population of only about twenty thousand people. I like it.

§

It only takes me a few minutes to get settled in a hotel room. I have a standard routine that I follow wherever I am. Check the "in case of fire" map on the back of the door. Spread a hand towel from the bathroom out like a kitchen placemat on the top of the chest of drawers near the TV, then put all the things from my pockets plus the room key on it. Nice and neat, and against the white background everything is easy to see and keep track of. Spread out my other personal items on the counters in the bathroom, and I'm done.

Now I can relax, change into loungewear (fancy name for a pair of old comfy sweatpants and a soft plaid flannel shirt), lay out my clothes for tomorrow, catch up with writing today's travel notes, and review my travel route.

I've sent out my daily "birder to base" text to my daughter and the two other people who are keeping track of where I am as I travel, and a text to the cat sitter. Now I can indulge in one of my favorite indoor birding activities—checking on all the latest bird news and photos on social media.

I enjoy seeing all the great photos, and finding out about which species are displaying for prospective mates, which ones are singing, which ones are flying north, which ones have begun nests—so much is already going on all along my travel route. But what the birds did today in one place is no guarantee that they'll do the same thing there tomorrow or the next day, or whenever I happen to get to those particular spots. I have to be satisfied tonight with studying the photos of the ones I don't see at home, try to memorize their field marks, and keep my fingers crossed that I will get good looks at them later when I get to Texas—and that I'll be able to recognize them when I do.

§

It takes less than a minute to count up today's list of bird species—only ten, and two of them are not native—but that's about what I expected, considering that I spent my time either barreling along at seventy miles per hour or walking around in busy human habitats. All were easy to find, quite common and widespread in the eastern United States. Their bills are different shapes, what they eat and the ways they search for that food are different, but they all have one thing in common.

Feathers. It's what makes them birds. No other class of animals have such things, and they are fascinating. Not just the colors, but also their shapes and functions. The most noticeable ones are the outer layers, the body feathers and the flight feathers on the wings and tail. But there are other kinds of feathers elsewhere, including the layer of down nearest the skin, as well as plumes and bristles and other shapes, each with their own purpose and function. I hope I get a good, close-up look at some on this trip.

I drove only two hundred eighty-seven miles today, which is right about what I expected and wanted to accomplish. Reviewing my notes, I'm thinking about the geography of where I've been today. The little stream at the bottom of my front hayfield flows into a small creek that joins another slightly larger one, then into a much bigger creek called Floyd's Fork, and eventually into the Salt River, the first major river I drove across this afternoon. The Salt River then flows mostly westward and on into the Ohio River at a spot far downstream from Louisville. I started out at an elevation of about six hundred fifty feet above sea level, and my route so far has been up and down through many valleys and across various sizes of streams and rivers.

The Ohio River Valley is a vast watershed, draining more than two hundred thousand square miles, making it the largest tributary of the Mississippi River. The rain that falls on my old farm takes a very long, wiggly, downhill route to reach the Gulf of Mexico. But I'm not thinking so much about the physical features of the land I'm driving through. I'm thinking about the airspace above it.

Birds on the move tend to use the same wide corridors for their travels, and there are four of these major flyways over North America. This section of the continent that I'm driving through now is the Mississippi Flyway, and it extends from the coast of the Gulf of Mexico all the way up to the farthest reaches of the northeastern half of Canada. The Atlantic Flyway lies to the east, and the Central Flyway and Pacific Flyway are over towards the Rocky Mountains and beyond.

Today I drove across the Salt River and the Green River in Kentucky, the Cumberland River in Tennessee, and tomorrow, here in northern Alabama, I will drive over the Tennessee River, which is the largest tributary of the Ohio River. So today, even though I've traveled in three states, I'm still in the same watershed where I began. And I'm still in the Mississippi Flyway. Everything looks and feels familiar. That will start changing tomorrow as I drive farther south.

The birds don't know the names of the states or the rivers or the towns; as they fly over the land they're looking for the kinds of food their bills and feet and eyesight can help them catch. They also need water to drink and a place to find shelter from storms and safety from predators. So what's important to them is habitat, not names or human boundary marks. The fresh water available year-round here in the heart of the continent feeds all these streams and rivers—and trees.

In the broadest terms, I've been driving through forests. Well, forest remnants and pockets, because most of this part of North America has been logged and the landscape changed in other ways to suit humans. Where I've been driving today includes various combinations of southern hardwood forest trees, a few evergreens such as eastern redcedars, plus native shrubs, vines, grasses, and wildflowers, with exotic ornamentals thrown in, courtesy of human gardeners and carelessness. The birds I've seen today are year-round residents and generalists, able to find what they need in these habitats—but soon I'll be in different ecosystems and have the opportunity to see birds who prefer the unique features of those other zones.

To do that I have a lot of miles to cover tomorrow, so I'd better get some sleep now. The last part of my evening routine is easy. I pull the wall charger for my phone out of the boldly patterned black-on-red zippered pouch I keep it in (so bold it's impossible to leave behind when preparing to check out the next day) and put them both on the nightstand along with the LED flashlight that I always carry with me. I plug in my phone, reset its clock to local time, make a note to reset the digital clock in the car in the morning, then turn out the lights.

And then turn the lights back on again.

The hotel room's microwave, with its gleaming digital clock, is on a cabinet directly across from the bed, right where I can catch glimpses of it through my half-closed eyelids. I take the little pad of hotel notepaper I just wrote on, open it like a book, place it so that half is on the top of the microwave, then let the other half hang down over the edge to block the shining numbers. Back to bed, again, this time with all lights out for real. I have a lot of driving to do tomorrow, and more birds to find.

###

CHAPTER TWO

On to Mississippi, Louisiana, and Texas

Birding by ear, a boat ride, finding lifers

Wherever I am, I wake up hungry. But first things first—before I eat breakfast I always take a short walk. It's already past sunrise here in northern Alabama, and the local birds are active as I stroll around the hotel parking lot.

The resident Northern Mockingbird trills a string of imitations of other birds' songs, then a Barn Swallow races past me in an elegant arc before swerving in a split-second pivot. I turn this way and that, watching as half a dozen other swallows swoop through the air. This is a bird of open country, a bird that eats insects on the wing, with a tiny bill but a large, gaping mouth, perfectly suited to its food-gathering strategy. In rural areas they appear almost magically above folks on riding mowers and tractors, to crisscross through the air, snatching at the bounty of insects this human activity stirs up. But they also fly through natural insect swarms over ponds and lakes, over hills or flat land, anywhere they can find tiny morsels to eat. Their legs and feet are not designed for walking—but they are masters of the air.

They don't sing, but they do make distinctive chittering sounds as they dash above my head. In English the sound they make would be spelled "veet" to rhyme with "feet." But in French there's a word that sounds just the same, but is spelled as "vite."

The French word means "quick," and that sure describes how these swallows fly. "Vite!" "Vite!" "Vite!" they chatter to each other as they chase insects above me.

Of the several swallow species in North America, this is the one with the most prominently forked "swallowtail" shape to its tail feathers. That, along with its rich blue back and rusty chin, make it easy to recognize.

And they make me smile because I've met my first returning migrants. These little guys spend their winters in South America and begin streaming northward over Central America in early March, reaching the United States in late March and early April. And here they are in Alabama already. This is a good way to start my day.

A couple of American Robins are prospecting for worms in the grasses at the edge of the pavement, singing cheerily to greet the day. Wait. What's that? Ah, yes. I turn toward the direction of the sound and watch as a perched Eastern Meadowlark sings "spring of the year" in its lilting fashion, then tries again, with a version that to my ears sounds more like "spring is sure here." Such a handsome bird, with a yellow breast accented with a black, v-shaped necklace.

I have learned, by careful effort, to bird by ear, to identify many kinds of birds by listening to their songs. But it didn't start out that way—I got interested in frog calls first. One evening I went to a program about the frogs and toads of Kentucky at the Louisville Nature Center. I listened to the stories the human speakers told, and then bought a cassette tape (yes, it was long time ago, tech-wise) to take home to listen to the various frogs' and toads' peeps and croaks. Oh, what a treat! And a revelation to me about a new way to enjoy being outdoors. Use your ears!

When I bought my first bird book in 1997, I wanted to learn what birds look like. I chose Roger Tory Peterson's *A Field Guide to the Birds: A Completely New Guide to All the Birds of Eastern and Central North America*, because a lot of people said I should. It's been considered a bible among birders since the first edition came out in

1934. Until that time, the most common method of identifying birds was to shoot them, then examine the dead specimens for field marks. Peterson's system revolutionized bird identification by using paintings to highlight significant field marks easily observed on living birds, near or far, with no need to kill them to study them. Birdwatching took off as a widespread hobby.

My copy is the fourth edition, copyright 1980—and it's in the laundry basket on the front seat of my car for this trip. As old as it is, it's still a lovely little book. The true-color illustrations are printed on top-quality, glossy paper stock in inks that don't smudge. The pages are sewn into the binding tightly, yet with enough flexibility to lie open flat.

All this is great for looking at birds, but listening? During my first years of birding, I scarcely paid any attention to the "voice" comments in the description of each species. The renditions of bird songs into English syllables seemed terribly clumsy to me at the time, and of little use.

Back then I thought that you had to see a bird to know who it is. I thought the information about songs was included only for the most dedicated scholars. Although the songs of cardinals and the shrieks of jays were part of the soundtrack of my childhood, as an adult it didn't occur to me that listening, instead of looking, as a means of identifying birds was not only possible, but completely acceptable. As I began to learn more about birds and their voices, at first I used sound only to help me identify birds that are active at night, like owls. But as I memorized more songs and started going on bird walks with more knowledgeable friends, I began to use song as a way to identify and locate daytime birds. Often, hearing the sound leads me to a glimpse of a bird perched on a branch, but sometimes, especially when the trees are fully leafed out, the song is the only clue I have that a particular bird is nearby. When that happens, I write (h) next to the name of the bird in my field notes.

"Ooo-woo, woo, woo, woo." I hear a quavering, plaintive sound. A sort of purring, slurred cadence of soft notes, all on the same pitch—there's a Mourning Dove around here, and pretty close, I think. This is yet another bird I've known since childhood, and one that's easy to find throughout most of the United States. Oh, there it is, at the edge of the next parking lot, its pale, grayish beige feathers so different from the bright yellow plumage of the meadowlark.

Walking slowly along to make my last turn around the building, I hear another familiar sound, but it's not very musical—just a few squeaky noises from a Common Grackle. These dark, shiny, native birds often gather in great flocks like European Starlings do, filling the sky with a jumble of screeches, squeaks, and squeals that can drown out all other sounds. But this bird only has three other companions and is more interested in finding something to eat than anything else.

§

During breakfast in the makeshift gathering spot, I check the regional weather forecasts—strong, possibly even severe, thunderstorms are predicted farther south this morning. I'm eager to get on the road, just in case of any weather delays.

At my car, I reset the digital clock on the dashboard to central time. I want something to listen to this morning that's perky and appropriate to this region, so I cue up my playlist of Civil War tunes. Saxton's Cornet Band and Old Towne Brass play marches and ballads and quicksteps with historically authentic instruments, and I enjoy humming along to those fine old tunes.

This is likely to be a very long day of driving, especially if I run into any of those big rainstorms. I am intent on covering as much ground as possible today. That's why I'm not going to stop at Wheeler National Wildlife Refuge. Instead, I'm making a mental note to try to visit on the way back home. Today I need to make as much progress toward Texas as I can.

But after only forty-five minutes on the road, I've decided to pull off at a rest stop for a restroom break. Knowing which rest stop to choose can be such a guessing game. Sometimes the highway signs indicating that a rest stop is coming up will also tell the number of miles until the next one—and sometimes they don't. I've passed one up before, only to find that the next one is closed for repairs. So I usually stop when I see one, whether or not I really need to at that exact time.

This is a quick stop, and as I get back on the road, light rain sprinkles begin to fall, but they don't last long. An hour later I stop again, this time to buy gas in McCall, Alabama. My car's driving range is around the four-hundred-mile mark, and the digital dash display gives me a continually updating estimate of the miles remaining until the tank will be empty. When it reaches only fifty miles to empty, it chimes. That's fine at home, where I know where all the gas stations are, but in unfamiliar territory I prefer to refill somewhere around the one-hundred-fifty- or one-hundred-miles-to-empty mark to be on safe side. After I top off my tank, I stand at the edge of the parking lot, drinking milk from my cooler and snacking on the chocolate-covered pretzels I bought yesterday in Tennessee. They're really good.

Although I drove through only light rain earlier, looking at the dark gray skies down the road, I think this would be a good time to check my phone for an updated weather forecast. Unfortunately, the NOAA weather radar for the area where I'm going is temporarily out of service. Oh, well, when I get back on the road I'll take my chances. Which isn't all that much of a gamble—if there are any urgent weather alerts active for any zip code as I travel through it, some very carefully coordinated technology will send an alert directly to my phone. I don't have to do anything special. I also hope I don't hear that weird sound today.

I'm not using the GPS on my phone today because I'll be spending the whole day on the interstate system. It's well marked and pretty much goof-proof. Just to make sure, though, I will look at my paper maps for a minute. I need to watch for the intersection of I-65 with I-59/I-20 to veer off from due south toward the southwest. I choose some fresh music to listen to, a mix of some good old-fashioned fiddle tunes with plenty of jigs and reels to keep me alert, and merge into the traffic.

A little over an hour later I need to take another break at the next rest stop, one that features an impressive stand of tall pine trees. The farther south I travel, the more changes I'm noticing in the vegetation, with a different mix of tree species, and much thicker suits of leaves on the trees. The native plant community here is known as Southern mixed pine-oak forest, with a different, less diverse mix of trees than in my home territory in the Ohio River Valley. I listen to yet another Northern Mockingbird for a few minutes, then notice a Blue Jay up in the branches. Some of his or her pals set up a noisy exchange of shrieks, and the lone jay dashes over to join them.

No rain here—it's sunny, breezy, and quite warm, already eighty-two degrees Fahrenheit. A long-sleeved shirt will be enough for today, so I peel off the sweater I've been wearing since breakfast, then get back on the road.

Shortly before one thirty, I cross the state line into Mississippi, the fourth state of my journey, and pull into the welcome center rest stop to make a quick search for my M&Ms. They've gone missing amid the books and maps in the laundry basket. Then I remember I have still have another treat from yesterday's candy store. The toffee square covered with chocolate and chopped nuts is delicious, just the thing to keep me energized. I put the car back in gear and merge back onto the highway. The road isn't very crowded here.

§

It's difficult to locate small birds when driving at seventy miles per hour, so there's no telling what I've passed by this morning. But the two Canada Geese at the edge of a roadside pond are big enough to catch my eye as I zoom past. Canada Geese have two different lifestyles. Many do fly to Canada in the warm summer months to nest and raise goslings, then fly south again in great, long, v-shaped skeins to places with open water to spend the winter months. But there are others who prefer to stay in the warmer parts of North America for their entire lives, never going to Canada at all, swimming around on freshwater lakes and large ponds year-round. Since there are only two by the farm pond, my guess is that they are local geese, not part of a migrating flock.

Today is all about clicking off the miles, so my lunch stop is nothing fancy. I've been watching the little blue highway signs before each exit and have pulled off here because it says there's a Subway shop. It's inside a small country gas station and has a couple of tables with benches. But I'm eating my six-inch turkey sub standing up by the hood of my car in typical birder fashion. I really don't want to sit right now. I swish the sandwich down with some of the cranberry juice I brought from home and listen for any birds. Nothing. Instead I watch some pretty yellow butterflies darting about in the nearby bushes. I take a few extra minutes to stretch my arms on the way back from the trash barrel, then get in the car. I've cued up some high-energy brass band music and I'm ready to get back on the interstate.

Ever since I skirted the hills around Birmingham earlier today and turned southwest on I-59, and on through Tuscaloosa, I've been in a watershed separate from the Mississippi River. The rain that falls here eventually finds its way to the Mobile River and straight to the Gulf of Mexico. As the land gets flatter and the vegetation changes yet again, I cross the Pearl River, which also drains directly into the Gulf of Mexico. At four thirty I enter Louisiana—state number five of my trip. The farther southwest I drive, I will eventually cross a slight ridge and re-enter the Mississippi River's drainage area for a while as I get closer to sea level.

I'm stopped again, this time at the Louisiana welcome center near Slidell, to take a much-needed walk and stretch my arms and legs. I'm quite surprised to see a large outdoor map of the state with a painting of a Brown Pelican on it. I associate that bird more with Florida, but I've found out that it is, indeed, Louisiana's state bird. But there are no live pelicans of any kind visible as I walk around all the concrete paths among the picnic tables, carefully avoiding the puddles from heavy rain that fell before I got this far south. Apparently I have dodged the worst of today's rainstorms. In the bright sunshine, long streamers of Spanish moss dangling from the trees sway in the brisk breeze. That moss is an indicator that I am in a different forest type, and I can expect to see some different kinds of birds very soon.

I've checked my paper maps yet again, and it's a good thing I did—the turn west onto I-12 that will take me well above the traffic in New Orleans will be the very next interchange. I'm not at all tired now, but I do need to start thinking about how much farther I want to go before dark, and what town might be a good place to stop for the night. I'll check on distances again in two hours.

On the road again, and when I make the turn to go what I thought would be due west, I am surprised to see that my car's compass says I am really heading northwest. But now I remember how big Lake Pontchartrain is and understand why the road has to swing that direction.

I know there are good arguments about keeping highway billboard clutter to a minimum, but I really appreciate the information they give as I drive along. I always keep an eye open for signs advertising large truck stops where I know there will be lots of people around and clean bathrooms. There's one coming up in Denham Springs, Louisiana, so I'll top up my gas tank.

Mission accomplished, I'm back on the road again, but thinking about stopping for the night soon.

The land is getting flatter and flatter as I head due west through Baton Rouge. I drive over a very steeply arched bridge across the mighty Mississippi River and realize at the top of the bridge that I've had exactly enough driving for one day. As the light fades I decide that I'd better find a place to spend the night, and quick.

What I didn't realize when I made my decision is how sparsely populated this section of Louisiana is, or why. I'm driving through the Atchafalaya Swamp Basin, a huge wet region that's larger and much different from Florida's Everglades, the only other major southern swamp I've ever visited. This basin has two kinds of woods, bottomland hardwood forest and alluvial, that is to say watery, hardwood swamp habitats where standing water is the norm. Water stretches out in both directions from the highway—there's no dry land to build a town on!

This is very different from the upland forests I know so well. Where I live in the Ohio River Valley, somewhere between forty and fifty inches of rain will fall in any particular year, but because of the hills, water that isn't absorbed into the soil quickly drains away. But here the land is flat and scarcely more than twenty feet above sea level. The average annual rainfall here is about sixty inches, and water pools and ponds and stays around for a long time. I do not know how this affects the birds. How the highway department ever built this section of the road is a mystery to me, because it doesn't seem like there's anything to keep the pilings from sinking down, down, down into the brown water and mud.

I'm grumbling to myself, "where's the next town?" as the miles click past, and then, after another very long, flat bridge over an immense bayou, I come to Henderson, on the outskirts of Lafayette. It's still daylight, but just barely, as I pull into the parking lot of another Holiday Inn Express. I am ready to quit for this day.

§

In the parking lot I meet my first road trip cat, a gray tabby with longish fur, a white bib, and four white paws, quite similar in appearance to one of my cats at home. At the front desk the clerk tells me that she's the resident hotel cat. Instead of merely roaming the parking lot, she also comes inside the lobby to greet guests. She even has her own special name badge instead of a metal tag, proclaiming her as the welcome ambassador. Her name is Momma, and she's beautiful. And seeing her makes me miss all three of my kitties!

In my room after spending ten hours on the road, I plop my duffel bag on the luggage rack, splash some water on my face, and then come back downstairs. I can leave my car where it is and walk to dinner tonight, and that's a real plus.

I amble diagonally across the parking lot to Landry's, the restaurant the desk clerk recommended. When I am traveling by myself with no family members or business associates to meet, I still look forward to the dinner hour as a social time—I just don't know ahead of time who my companions will be or what we'll chat about. The best solution is to sit at the bar and strike up a conversation with the bartender, and then see what happens. If nothing interesting turns up, I can usually count on at least one big-screen TV with some sort of sports, and this time of year there will be baseball games to watch.

The bartender tonight, a young woman, pours me a glass of Chardonnay and I begin to think over the day's adventure, which was actually rather tame. I didn't see many birds (maybe eight kinds?) and all were very familiar ones at that, birds I could have just as easily seen if I'd stayed at home—but I've driven five hundred twenty-eight miles today! The interstate highway system is phenomenal and plays a huge role in my ability to travel alone over great distances so comfortably. Getting back to birds, the first Barn Swallows of the year are the highlight of this day.

As I chat with the bartender about my trip, a tall fellow comes in and sits on a barstool to my left and joins in the conversation. Turns out that although he lives in Texas, Barry's work in the swimming pool business often means he travels through this part of Louisiana. I'm in Cajun country now, and he recommends a visit to the Cajun shop in between this restaurant and the hotel—but the shop's closed this time of night.

Since I haven't done anything much all day but sit in my car, I order a very light dinner from the appetizer menu. My first seafood of the trip is a delicious concoction called Firecracker

Shrimp, big plump ones, coated with tempura batter, fried, then brushed with a sweet chili glaze, not too spicy but just right, and served on a bed of lettuce. Although the restaurant has many local touches in the decor, it is part of a national group operating several different kinds of restaurants with different themes throughout the United States. I like this one. I order another glass of wine and some soda water as the three of us chat at intervals. I'm kind of following a baseball game on the TV to the left. This is opening week, and although I'd like to know the score in the Cincinnati Reds game, I'd rather talk with people.

A while later, as I walk back to my hotel, pleasantly sleepy, I catch a glimpse of a solid black cat slipping around the corner of the Cajun arts and crafts shop, another reminder of my cats back home. In my room I check for a text message from the cat sitter — yes, they're fine — and then do a rush job of getting settled in for the night. I think I'll be asleep the minute I turn out the lights.

§

This Louisiana morning is breezy and pleasant, with clear, sunny skies overhead as I take a short stroll around the hotel parking lot. When I return to the lobby, the hotel cat is sitting contently on a stack of today's newspapers on the front desk counter. She has her front legs folded under her chest to sit in the meatloaf position that my kitties also enjoy when they have something not too serious to think about. I speak softly to her, give her a gentle stroke on the head, and go into the great room for breakfast.

I only have about a hundred and thirty miles to drive to get to the hotel room I have reserved in Texas for tonight, so I'm free to do as I please here this morning before I move on.

Last night on my way to dinner I'd stopped for a few minutes to look at the things for sale in front of the place called the Louisiana Marketshops at the 115, which is the number of this exit on I-10. It's the place Barry, the guy I chatted with last night, said would be worth my time to visit. The metal garden silhouettes of herons, clever sayings on old wood about Cajun life, some knick-knacks in the shape of a fleur-de-lis—which is also the emblem of my hometown—and other curiosities look quite intriguing in the morning sunshine. After checking out of my hotel room, instead of getting directly back on the highway, I drive fifty feet across the asphalt, park, and walk up the steps to the front door of the shop.

The woman at the counter explains to me that, although the place is part flea market and antique mall, many of the booths also showcase the work of contemporary local Cajun artists, artisans, and other crafty, creative people. She invites me to take my time as I wander through the various rooms. The place is much larger than it looked from the front and is filled with paintings, textiles, photographs, and more. The display case that catches my eye contains old and new full-size duck decoys. Some have enormous price tags, which is not at all surprising, since that's the reason I stopped adding to my collection years ago. But there is one little hand-painted carving about four inches long and two inches high that I pause to study carefully.

Back at the front counter, I tell the woman of my interest in the small carving, and she walks with me through the crowded aisles to open the case. One of the upper shelves has a sign with the artist's name on it, and she tells me his story—he'd been carving all his life, right up to a few weeks before he died last year at age ninety-two. She doesn't have much of his work left but would be happy to show me anything in the case.

The minute I hold the little stylized Wood Duck in my hand I know it will be going home with me. I like the painted design, so accurate in its rendering of the field marks, yet with some subtle artistic exaggerations, and I like the man's story. Back at the front counter I happily pay the fifteen-dollar asking price as she wraps the little gem in tissue. I have my first souvenir of the trip. I don't know if I will see any Wood Ducks while I'm traveling, but that doesn't matter because I see that species often enough in other places at home. I like this one, and I'm sure I will enjoy this beautiful little piece of Cajun craftsmanship for a long time.

As the two women at the counter tell me more about the purpose of their marketplace, and as I explain my birdwatching trip, one asks, "Have you been out to any of the bayous or the lake to look around? There are lots of birds out there." My original plan for this day was to drive on into Texas and get started exploring there this afternoon, but now that I think about it, why not see what Louisiana has to offer? My hotel room in Texas is guaranteed for late arrival, so I don't need to rush. The other woman begins talking about a local fellow who has a business taking people out on his boat over on the bayou. She finds one of his advertising placards in the rack by the front door and encourages me to give him a call.

§

A short while later I have it all arranged. Danny will be available later today and the woman who answered the phone quoted me a very reasonable price for a two-hour excursion. "Meet him in the parking lot off Rookery Road at Lake Martin at one o'clock," she said. "Look for the red umbrella."

With that settled, I drive under the highway overpass onto a little country road, with my GPS programmed to take me to the historic district of Breaux Bridge, the nearby town. I park my car on the street, then stroll around on uneven sidewalks among the few blocks of old wooden buildings, built in a style similar to what I saw decades ago in New Orleans. In a shop window I see an advertising poster and discover that Breaux Bridge is the Crawfish Capital of the World. Indeed, if I could be here the first weekend in May, I'm sure the Zydeco music and food at the annual Crawfish Festival would be fun and entertaining. And that gives me an idea for lunch.

At Chez Jacqueline, a tiny little place specializing in French and Creole and Cajun food, I order a crawfish po'-boy sandwich to go to be sure I get to the lake on time. Everything is cooked to order in the back, so I spend the waiting minutes at one of the tables in the front, catching up with the world back home via social media. And checking for the latest bird sightings in Texas.

When my sandwich is ready, I pay for it, get in my car, and ask my phone's GPS app to take me to Lake Martin.

There's Danny standing by his pickup truck and the red umbrella, with his shallow-bottomed boat already off the trailer and waiting in the water. He's quite concerned that I plan to eat my lunch standing up by the hood of my car, but after yesterday's long drive it's what I really want to do. He thinks the nearby picnic table would be better, but I will stand. Compared to yesterday's rather sketchy birder's lunch, this meal is deluxe. The po'-boy is heaped with perfectly fried and deliciously tender crawfish and shredded lettuce, with a little cup on the side filled with extraordinarily spicy remoulade sauce. Flavorful and definitely completely local, it's delicious.

§

While enjoying my lunch, standing on dry ground, I hear, then see, a familiar bird—another bright red male Northern Cardinal in the trees at the edge of the gravel parking lot. These birds are really widespread, happy to live in just about any place with trees and shrubs, the more seeds and berries and bugs, the better. Then an Eastern Towhee calls, trying to entice me to "drink your tea-ee-ee." I don't drink tea, but between sips of water, I keep looking and see the familiar flash of brown and black as he flies deeper into the shadowy green leaves. While I've been thinking about the different mix of trees in the regions I've been driving through, what's important to an Eastern Towhee is not so much the trees, but the brushy undergrowth. This bird species prefers low, shrubby areas with plenty of leaf litter to scratch through, looking for insects to eat. It will stay on the edges of the swamp, I think, and not venture into the waterlogged sections.

After I finish eating, I get my binoculars out of the laundry basket. A birding pal at home refers to them as Hubbles, after the gigantic telescope. They are kinda big, seven and a half inches from back to front, and seven inches across at the widest point, a bit clunky by today's standards, but I like them. They're Nikon 10x50s, which means that what I'm looking at seems ten times closer than it really is, with two-inch-wide (fifty millimeters) lenses at the far ends of each of the tubes. This gives them great light-gathering capacity, which will be important today in the swamp, and the big field of view is good anywhere and everywhere. They're a bit heavy, but I've had them for so long I know just how to arrange the strap around my neck to get the most comfortable fit against my shirt collar. I also pick up my camera and a small pocket notebook, plus a ballpoint pen.

Danny, a big, sort of burly guy with an ample beard, gives me a firm, steadying hand as I step into his boat. No one else is expected this afternoon, so I have my choice of the half dozen seats. I settle down amidships, ready for a private tour of the cypress-tupelo swamp, but not knowing what to expect.

Danny steps in behind me and gets settled at the motor to steer us away from the landing. The water isn't very deep and would only come about half way up our shins if we were to climb out of the boat. But that would be a very bad idea—too many alligators live here.

Lake Martin spreads out over nine hundred fifty acres, and we want to get started exploring right away. We surge forward into what is, to me, a confusing bunch of bald cypress trees, their knobby knees jutting up out of the water. Not at all confusing to Danny—he knows the individual trees well, and he picks a route he thinks will give us plenty of birds to look at.

When I tell him about my plan to drive all the way down the Texas Gulf Coast in search of birds, he likes the idea a lot, and begins telling me about some of his travel adventures. Born and raised nearby, he's worked on oil rigs out in the Gulf and travelled for fun through many states on a motorcycle. He likes adventure, but with a three-year-old son now, he's working hard to make his boating business a success so he can stay closer to home. He already has a lot of bird photographers as regular clients, and he is eager to help me see a lot of birds.

My goal isn't spectacular photos. I carry a good, general-purpose Nikon D90, an early digital camera with features I still like. I keep a Nikon 18–105 mm telephoto lens on it, which gives me a lot of options. The lens is lightweight and when fully extended it's still only about six inches long, so it's easy to control for hand-held shots.

I admire other photographers who have lenses three, four, even five times as long and that cost more than my car; the feather details they get are stunningly beautiful. Sometimes I get lucky to be in just the right spot to get good quality close-ups of a bird, but that's not my main concern. For my kind of birdwatching I only need enough detail in my photos to support the identifications in my field notes, plus general views of habitats. Although the camera and lens are capable of autofocusing, I do not use that feature, preferring to set up my shots manually. The lens cap is off, and I'm ready for whatever happens next.

As we glide along in and out of the dappled shade, several male Red-winged Blackbirds fly by, flashing their trademark red epaulettes. This is a bird that's oh-so-easy to find anywhere in North America where there's standing water, whether it's a farm pond, a roadside ditch surrounded by cattails, or a swamp like this at the edges of Lake Martin.

We spot a black-and-white Osprey, also known popularly as a "fish hawk," sometimes as "sea hawk" or "fish eagle" because of its hunting style. Similar in size and body build to the Red-tailed Hawk I saw on the first day of my trip, this hunter also plunges feet first to capture prey—but instead of cruising above grassy fields, it hunts over open water to grab live fish. When it's successful, it almost always uses its talons to turn the fish so its head points in the same direction as its own, reducing wind turbulence as it flies away with its prize to eat later on a perch in the treetops or to feed to its mate or youngsters.

Moments later I notice a group of Tree Swallows, which have shorter tails than yesterday's Barn Swallows. They swoop and jink over us, searching for insects above the water, flashing their metallic blue upper sides then giving me a view of their white underparts. They've spent the winter months here and soon will leave to fly north. Some will only venture a short distance, but others will go as far as northern Canada.

A bit farther away, a Mallard drake swims sedately, the sunlight making his green iridescent head feathers gleam. This might be one of the most easily recognizable species of waterfowl in all of North America, often seen paddling around on city park lakes, as well as in wilder habitats. An Anhinga, a bird I know from Florida, sits on a stump, holding its wings out to dry. Unlike dabbling ducks like Mallards, these diving birds' feathers don't shed water easily. After they've been fishing completely submerged under water, when they come back up they need to let the water drain off and let their feathers dry out.

We pause to look at a large basking alligator from a safe distance, then come upon a Snowy Egret, the medium-sized, white wading bird whose feet look like golden slippers, a very pretty bird that I also know from many visits to Florida. On another partially submerged log we find some baby alligators basking with their already-quite-toothy jaws wide open in the warm sunshine. They're definitely worth a photo, and I take several.

As we turn and curve among the trees in ways that make absolutely no sense to me, but are perfectly purposeful to Danny, we find a mature Black-crowned Night-Heron standing stodgily amid some floating vegetation to our right, intent on finding a late lunch. Of course, birds don't eat meals at regularly defined intervals—they eat whatever they can find whenever they can find it. Sometimes it's a case of little nibbles all day long from sunup to sundown, or even after dark. And if they miss a strike, they go hungry until they do have success.

I tell Danny how glad I am to see this bird relatively out in the open. At home, in a small park where I often go birding, they're extremely hard to spot amid the tangles of branches and leaves along a very narrow creek, with no way to get close for a better view. But here I can watch from Danny's boat with nothing to block my view of the bird as he focuses his ruby-red eyes on the water around his feet.

§

Danny and I chat quietly as he steers us along, and then I see something on the water that makes me look twice. Carroty orange bill, beige head, rusty orange breast. Then it stands up a bit taller to reveal black feathers below. "Isn't that a Black-bellied Whistling-Duck?" I ask Danny. "Yes, and there are some more near it. Look to the left a little bit," Danny answers. A common sight for him, but I am so pleased with myself to be able to put a name to it before he pointed it out—it's my first lifer of the trip! And I'm not even in Texas yet. What makes me smile even more is that I recognized it not from studying a field guide, but because I've been seeing photos of this bird on social media. Commonly called tree ducks, this species can perch on limbs. And they nest in tree cavities instead of on water, a strategy also used by Wood Ducks. I don't know much else about this species, except that they used to live year-round in Central and South America but are being seen more often farther north in the United States.

From time to time Danny cuts the motor and lets the boat drift forward on purpose to wedge its prow gently between two tree trunks so we can pause in one spot. At this resting point we look to our right to watch a Little Blue Heron striding through the shallow water, trying to stir up a potential meal. This one's a breeding adult whose head and neck feathers are not blue but a soft plum, almost maroon, color. A Great Blue Heron flies in from the left, navigating his large body, wide wings, and long legs through the towering trees with ease.

The words "great" and "little" in these two birds' names are relative—at nearly two feet tall, the Little Blue Heron would be a pretty big bird in most situations, but by comparison to its cousin it is small—the Great Blue Heron is twice as tall. And its cousin of almost the same stature, a Great Egret standing on another bit of exposed gravel, is like a white ghost bird amid the shadowy trees. As we look this way and that, the variety and colors of the birds— Green Heron (mostly brown and green), Great Egret (white), Double-crested Cormorant (mostly black)—visible around us, all easily identifiable to me based on long experience, keeps me busy jotting down names in my notebook.

A somewhat larger boat filled with a dozen people comes toward us noisily, and Danny says, just loud enough for me to hear, "I think we can find more birds in another area. Let's go."

To get us out of our watery parking place, Danny stands up and walks past me to go forward to pick up the long pole lying in the bottom of the boat. It has a flap of rubber or plastic about a foot long and a few inches wide attached to the end that goes in the water, to give the pole purchase on the soft, oozy mud below. He pushes, the nose of the boat scrapes free of the tree bark, we glide backwards a few feet, he pushes again with the long pole to swing us halfway 'round, and then he walks past me again and starts up the motor.

As we go deeper into the swamp I hear the rattling call of a Belted Kingfisher, another bird I know well from home, but I cannot find it in the openings between the large tree trunks. I am surprised to hear the murmuring coos of a Mourning Dove, too, because I think of it as a bird of dry woods and grasslands, not a swamp. It's a seed-eater on dry land, so perhaps it is just taking a flying shortcut to a better place to forage.

A few minutes later we glide near a miniature island in the swamp, a little bit of muddy ground and exposed gravel a few inches above the water and scarcely ten feet across, with short, leafy, green plants sticking up. Danny cuts the motor and gives me time to focus my binoculars on this different patch of vegetation.

"Hmm," I murmur, "I can make out that there's a sandpiper standing on the gravel, with a white eye ring and lots of white spots on its back, but I have a lot of trouble identifying sandpipers because I don't see many of them that often at home." Many shorebirds fly back and forth through the Ohio River Valley on their way to and from their northern breeding grounds, but they're hard to find and I don't have many of their field marks memorized.

In the softest voice possible from a man so big, Danny says, "Well, I usually see them alone," he pauses, then adds, "one at a time. You know, solitary," he says as a subtle hint. Aha, Solitary Sandpiper—and there are actually three of them poking around for food with their long, straight bills. We've only been out on the water for about an hour, and I've already found—quick count through my notebook—sixteen kinds of birds in this waterlogged habitat.

From time to time as we go further into the swamp we flush more Black-bellied Whistling-Ducks—and they really do whistle. It's their call, not an effect of wind through their wings like the sounds some other kinds of ducks make in flight.

Stop and start, stop and start, on we go, making slow, steady progress in search of birds amid the dragonflies and damselflies and the croaking frogs. As we make our way along past more cypress and tupelo, we catch a glimpse of a Red-shouldered Hawk through an opening in the tree canopy. When I first started looking at hawks, I often confused the two species with "red" in their names because sometimes you don't see the tail, or the shoulders either, all that clearly. But gradually I've learned other cues, and this one's buffy, rusty chest and legs made it easy to confirm the identification.

Another kind of dabbling duck drake, paddling gently at the edge of some reedy growth in the distance, a Blue-winged Teal, is easy to identify, not by the color on his wings, which at rest appear mostly brownish, but by the curved white line on his cheek. It's funny how often the name of a bird is not the same feature that makes it easy to identify in the field.

Then, much closer to us, we see a Yellow-crowned Night-Heron stalking prey. In the dim light of the swamp in this spot, the overall color scheme of this bird, gray and white, appears quite similar to the Black-crowned Night-Heron, but the body is slimmer, the legs longer. In the distance I hear the familiar, churring call of a Red-bellied Woodpecker. Its red belly is almost impossible to see as it forages on tree trunks at home, so when I can't see that, or its distinctive red and white head markings, I've learned to rely on my ears instead.

By now we are quite far from our starting point, very deep in the swamp, alone, and yet completely comfortable with each other even though we only met an hour or so ago. Murmuring comments every so often, but silent much of the time. Delighting in the wild creatures, completely focused on what we can hear and see in the trees and among the shadows. Sensing the world around us in an intense way. This languid afternoon, we might as well be the only two people in the world.

And then we come upon evidence of other humans — a series of signs warning us not to enter the section of the swamp in front of us. We are at the back edge of The Nature Conservancy's Cypress Island Preserve, and boats are not permitted beyond this point. In the distance there's a rookery, a collection of nests where many of the large bird species we've been watching this afternoon are raising their young.

Somewhat wistfully, Danny says, "We used to be able to go in a lot closer to the nests, but now things are different." We talk about the birds' need for privacy, and, considering all that we've already seen, I tell him I don't mind at all that there are places that are strictly for the birds now, no people allowed. We agree that we have no interest in breaking the rules, so we turn away and set out to try another spot.

At some point Danny must have looked at his cell phone because he knows that we've passed the two-hour mark for our excursion. "I'm on my own time now," he says, "but you don't seem to be in any hurry. What do you say to trying one more place before we go back?" I agree immediately and he steers the boat into an even more deeply shady section of the swamp. We find yellow floating booms marking off what probably had once been perfectly square sections of undergrowth, the study plots for an unknown scientific project. Danny thinks it might have had something to do with experiments to monitor and remove invasive plant species, as much of a problem here, deep in this watery realm, as it is on dry land in the other places I go birding.

He cuts the motor off once again, and we sit quietly in the dappled shade for a few more minutes, enjoying the views all around us. Underway again, he tells me that he's promised his little boy that Daddy will be home early enough for some play time before supper, so now we take as direct a path as possible through the huge trees to get back to the boat landing. Along the way I hear the plaintive call of a Fish Crow, a sound I recognize from Florida. It's hard to put it into the English alphabet, but a sort of complaining "uh-uh" is fairly close. It's a quite different sound from the slightly higher-pitched and brash "caw-caw" of an American Crow.

Near the landing, Danny notices some small black-and-white-and-yellow birds and cuts off the motor so we can drift closer to get a better view. This time I am the one with the answer—we've come across a small group of Yellow-rumped Warblers. These handsome and active little birds spend the winter in the lower half of the United States, often as far north as my place in Kentucky. When I tell Danny that people have nicknamed them "butter butts" on account of that distinctive yellow patch above their tails, he laughs. I have the idea that he'll be adding that to his well-practiced line of patter for the next group of casual tourists he takes out into the swamp. But he'll have to do it soon, because these little birds will be leaving this area to fly up to their summer breeding grounds in Canada any day now.

Back on solid ground, I've counted the bird names in my little notebook—twenty-two species, including my first lifer for the trip. When I tell Danny how much I've enjoyed birding by boat with him, he says, "I enjoyed it, too, and I hope you have a wonderful trip. Come back here anytime!"

§

As I settle into the driver's seat of my car, I've decided that I like Cajun hospitality a lot. My travel karma is solidly on the good side. I take a quick sip of water and get back on the road, ready to make the last miles glide by on my way to Texas.

I cross the bridge over the Sabine River and into Texas just shy of six thirty, with nine hundred forty-five miles on the trip counter. I am a really long way from home! I've been through five states to get here—but Texas alone is almost as many miles across as I've driven to get here. This first exit on I-10 is number eight hundred eighty, same as the mileage from the west side of the state to the east.

Back home, I had placed a purple sticky note next to the description of this exit in one of my new books, not just because it's the welcome center for westbound traffic, but because it's also the access point to Tony Houseman State Park and the Blue Elbow Swamp Wildlife Management Area, a well-known birding spot. But I've arrived after closing time for the visitor center and boardwalk, and I have to be content to walk around the parking lot for a few minutes. I can't see the swamp from here.

Very noisy, very bold, shiny, iridescent black birds are flitting around, hopping from the sidewalks onto the picnic tables, pointing their heads straight to the sky as they make a racket. It is one of the strangest bird noises I've ever heard, sort of an electronic whirring and wheezing. The general shape of the bird is familiar, but the tail feathers have me puzzled. They seem much too big for the bird's body, and they stick up and out in weird ways. Smaller, lighter-colored birds are among the dark ones, and I can't make out what they are, either.

Back at my car I get a field guide out of the laundry basket and turn to the section about blackbirds and grackles. Aha! The big ones are Great-tailed Grackles, another lifer! And the smaller ones are, too—the females are only about two-thirds the size of the males. In many bird species the female looks very different from the male, usually drabber so she's inconspicuous at the nest, but this is the first time I've seen such a difference in size, too. How nice to find them at my first stop in Texas. And how surprising that my first lifer in Texas is not in some remote wild place but in a busy interstate rest stop!

The field guide mentions that the sounds these birds make resemble the jumble of squeals when tuning into a radio station, and I think that's a good description. It sure isn't a musical song. I take some quick photos with my cell phone, and then set my GPS to get me to my hotel in Orange, Texas, only about fifteen minutes away.

Oh, too funny. This Holiday Inn Express is also being renovated this year. The front desk is quite proper, but other parts of the hotel are still being worked on, with signs by the elevator and elsewhere reminding guests to be careful in the construction zones.

This hotel is on a bit of land next to a one-way access road crammed up parallel to the interstate, with no restaurants in sight. After freshening up quickly in my room, I go downstairs and ask the desk clerk for advice. She recommends a place called Spanky's, a short drive away in the main section of town.

My GPS gets me there quickly, and I soon find out that the desk clerk was right about the food. The menu lists lots of good old-fashioned local fare, with lots of Tex-Mex, BBQ, and seafood options. I choose the BBQ ribs with baked beans and potato salad, and a Corona Extra. In the bar area I watch baseball on two of the twelve big-screen TVs while I eat, exchanging a few words with the woman on my left, but mostly I'm concentrating on enjoying my meal. It's noisy here, cheerfully so, and I'm hungry.

I've driven back to my hotel after dark without asking the GPS for help, and without missing a turn. At the hotel I walk around the parking lot for a little while, looking at license plates as

I often do—mine is the only one from Kentucky—and then go up to my room. After putting all my things in the usual places, I take a few minutes to look at my bird lists from today. Two lifers in two different states—good birding karma for sure. I'll be checking out right after breakfast in order to have ample time for a full day of activities tomorrow. I'm going to study my travel books for a few minutes to come up with some ideas, then I'm going to turn out the lights and go to sleep a bit earlier than usual.

###

CHAPTER THREE

Bayous, marshes,
and the Gulf of Mexico

Nestlings, swamps, and boardwalks

This morning the air is clear under mostly sunny skies with only a few clouds, good weather for a walk before breakfast. I've driven more than nine hundred fifty miles and what is the first bird I encounter? Another Northern Mockingbird singing in the hotel parking lot. I like mockingbirds. They live year-round at my place back in Kentucky. And when they begin singing in the spring they're fun to listen to as they string together long bursts of songs they've copied from other birds. It's a cheerful mix, and a nice way to greet the day here in Texas.

After a quick breakfast at the hotel, I gather up my things and check out to get an early start on the road. On my way to the interstate ramp I spy some city birds, a little group of Rock Pigeons, the latest name for the same birds I've known over the years as Pigeons, Feral Pigeons, and Rock Doves, as the people who make up the rules for bird names change the common name for *Columba livia*. They're fluttering around on the side of an overpass, jostling for a perch on the concrete, and I feel as though I might as well be in New York or downtown Louisville or Cincinnati instead of in Orange, Texas.

The funny thing about this morning is that when I get to the interstate I must use the eastbound lanes because that's the only way to return to the Tony Houseman area. Not only do I have to go backwards, I have to drive all the way across the Sabine River into Louisiana again, then turn around and retrace my route from late yesterday afternoon. The only access to the area where I want to be is from the westbound lanes of traffic.

As I pull into the busy parking lot at the welcome center rest stop for the second time, I see a lot of Great-tailed Grackles, perfectly and noisily at ease among the cars and trucks and the people walking back and forth. Inside the building, the folks at the Texas Travel Information Center show me around the racks of brochures and help me select the ones that will likely be most useful for birding. And they have more maps! A woman graciously offers to put my name on the plastic bag of free info I've gathered and hold it at the counter while I explore the boardwalk.

Although I've spent the first part of the morning going backwards, I'm really at the beginning. This is stop number one of the enormous Great Texas Coastal Birding Trail, in a section that some books call the East Texas Loop, others the Big Thicket Loop. The name doesn't matter to me, I just want to see a new habitat and find more birds.

As boardwalks go, this is a short one, roughly six hundred feet, but it is the only way for people without boats or hunting permits to see anything at all of the more than three thousand acres of the Blue Elbow Swamp Wildlife Management Area. There is no other access because managing the animals and plants is the priority here.

The Blue Elbow is the name of a deep hairpin curve in the Sabine River, and this swamp has many of the same kinds of trees, bald cypress and tupelo, as the swamp around the edges of Lake Martin that I enjoyed exploring yesterday in Danny's boat. In fact, I feel like I'm still in Louisiana instead of in Texas. Except there isn't much water to look at here today. I amble slowly along on the raised boardwalk, stopping every so often to read the excellent interpretive signs that explain the unique features of this habitat.

This swamp is rather dry just now because the water level fluctuates according to the rainfall patterns, and lately there's been very little rain. This area was heavily logged from the early 1800s until the mid-1900s. The loggers used that variable pattern of rainfall to cut timber in the dry months, then float it out to the river in the wet months. The damage they did to this complex habitat is still visible in the lines of ditches that run through the interior of the swamp. With so little standing water today, the section visible from this boardwalk seems more like an ordinary bottomland forest, not swampy at all. I hear a Northern Cardinal singing from deep among the trees, out of sight.

And I neither see nor hear any other birds at all during the next half hour. Birding is like that. There is no easy explanation for why a normally birdy spot will seem empty, although it's possible that a marauding hawk might have passed through just before I arrived. I use the word "seem" on purpose—I'm sure there are other birds hidden out of my sightlines in the brushy areas, just waiting to resume their normal behavior when they decide it's safe to do so. As I slowly retrace my steps back toward the building, a Great Blue Heron flaps over, going northeast. From this angle its feathers are a slate-y gray, not blue.

When I pick up my info packet inside the building, I mention to the guy at the desk that last night on my way to dinner I passed by a botanical garden and nature center, but I don't remember the name. Another welcome center host knows exactly what it is and finds the brochure for the Shangri La Botanical Gardens and Nature Center in a nearby rack. I'll look it over when I get out to my car.

§

Generally speaking, I avoid the artificial neatness of botanical gardens and their exotic cultivars. And I can't find anything in my birding trail books about the place. But the brochure does say "and nature center" so I've decided to take a chance.

My GPS sends me to the main entrance, but I discover that the visitor parking lot is across the street at the edge of a subdivision with neatly kept lawns around the houses. This is not looking very natural or wild, but I park anyway and head into the gardens on foot to search for the admissions office. I find it, pay the discounted senior fee, and pick up a map. Noticing a small group of schoolchildren toward the left, I choose the shady path to the right and begin studying the map as I walk along. A woman in a volunteer vest comes up the path towards me and asks, "Are you looking for the boat ride?"

What? The handwritten sign at the admission office said "boat ride at 3:00pm"—and it's only 10:30 in the morning. The volunteer gets busy with her walkie-talkie and determines that I have plenty of time to board the morning cruise, even though the cut-off time was several minutes ago. She walks back to the office with me, I pay the additional fee for what's called the Outpost Tour, then go back down the path with her. So far this morning has been two steps forward, two steps back, over and over. I eventually catch up with half a dozen other folks on the boardwalk on the way to the boathouse—good travel karma.

We each choose life jackets that sort of fit from the nearby rack, and after a staff member checks that we've fastened them correctly, we board the pontoon boat piloted by Captain Gary to explore Adams Bayou. In between tidbits about the personal life of H. J. Lutcher Stark, of Texas Longhorn fame, our tour guide Carol points out features of the habitats we're cruising through. Once again I'm in a real, watery swamp. A Red-tailed Hawk soars above us as we check the tree trunks for an unusual pinkish growth called Christmas lichen. We also enjoy looking at Spanish moss, a plant that's related to pineapples, something Danny mentioned yesterday in Louisiana.

I'm about one hundred twenty miles farther west from the swamp at Lake Martin that Danny and I explored, and this bayou and the adjoining swampland is slightly different in character. This area is a remnant of the original cypress-tupelo swamp forest ecosystem of Texas and includes two kinds of cypress trees—the bald cypress and the pond cypress. We stop to look at a pond cypress that is believed to be more than twelve hundred years old, based on a recent core sample. It's still alive and thriving.

As we motor quietly along, I hear a Northern Cardinal, then a Blue Jay. A bit farther on I hear a Carolina Wren trilling, yet another bird I know from the Ohio River Valley. Like so many North American birds, its common name comes not from a geographic preference for a particular state's habitat but is based on where the first specimen was found and described by the earliest bird naturalists. This cheerful, perky little bird, with a surprisingly loud voice for its size, is common in woodsy areas, wet or dry, from the Great Lakes to the Gulf Coast, from the Carolinas on the Atlantic Ocean all the way to the edge of the Rocky Mountains.

Carol and Gary tell us stories about the alligators that live here and how they choose basking spots in different sections of the bayou depending on the fluctuating water levels. From time to time we notice basking turtles, too.

Carol then describes some of the damage that Hurricane Rita caused in September 2005. That Category 3 hurricane's eye made landfall on the Gulf Coast over in Louisiana roughly one hundred fifty miles east of the Sabine River—and the winds over here were also fierce and mightily destructive. Since I've never been here before, I cannot pick out the areas damaged by the hurricane until she points them out to us.

But I'm not surprised at my inability to read the landscape for clues to its history. If Carol were to visit my farm back in Kentucky, I don't think she would be able to easily see the lingering effects of the extensive damage caused by the great ice storm of 2009. I'd have to point them out to her in specific areas of my woods and down by my farm pond. Hurricane Rita struck here twelve years ago, and this ecosystem in Texas is still recovering. New plants are growing up where old ones were destroyed, and it looks like it's thriving now. Of course, many of the trees and other plants made it through the storm without being killed. They managed to heal and keep growing. She shows us where to look for these survivors.

As we move slowly along on the muddy brown water, a Double-crested Cormorant flies over. We also see a Great Egret and hear a Fish Crow. I'm especially delighted to get a nice look at a Red-headed Woodpecker. This bird's velvety, solidly red head is quite distinctive, and since it prefers deeper woods instead of woodland edges, it is often difficult for me to find one in the places where I go walking the most frequently at home. We also get a good look at a pretty green anole lizard, too, as a Northern Mockingbird flashes past us.

Gary and Carol have figured out that the schoolchildren on a field trip here today are far away in a different area, so we can stop at the dock by one of the educational centers without interfering with their activities. He brings the boat gently into the pier, and we get out to go up on the land. As we walk around for a brief tour, we have to watch our steps very carefully to avoid the poison ivy. Good thing I recognize that plant!

The structures here have been designed to withstand fluctuating water levels in the bayou, and to be as energy efficient as possible. The screened-in classroom building features a nice collection of natural objects that children can touch as they learn about the ecosystems here, and there are plenty of living animals they can observe up close in small aquariums and terrariums.

§

Back aboard the pontoon boat, we pause to take a long look at an alligator basking in the sunshine. After the cruise, as we return our life jackets to the rack, I tell Carol that I'd really like to see more birds. She recommends that I go into the formal garden area and then take the path to the bird blind. That sounds good, even though I have no idea what to expect. I buy a miniature Moon Pie at the visitor's center cafe for a late-morning snack, study the map, and set off on foot down a different path.

As I get closer to the bird blind area, I catch up with the schoolchildren and their chaperones. I'll just lag back for a few minutes to give them plenty of time to finish what they're doing. Along the dirt path I find some breaks in the bushes on my right and catch glimpses of large birds flying back and forth. But I spend more time watching the dragonflies and listening to bullfrogs croaking. I see more turtles sunning themselves, and butterflies basking and nectaring on flowers as I wait for the children to come up the path.

When I finally walk inside the shady wooden bird blind, I am completely unprepared for the scenes visible through the open slats. Peering through the various openings, which are positioned at assorted heights to accommodate visitors of all sizes, I look out onto Ruby Lake at dozens of dead cypress trees filled with large stick nests, with many of the trees having multiple nests. The nests are big, some two feet or more across and at least a foot deep. And there are birds everywhere.

I have never seen a Great Egret's nest in person before—or visited any other kind of rookery—and here in front of me are dozens of Great Blue Heron nests and plenty of Double-crested Cormorant nests, too. I watch in fascination as these huge birds carefully land at their messy stick nests, tottering to keep their balance on the rims or nearby branches, with food in their long bills for their hungry, begging youngsters. The young egrets, known as aigrettes, are especially odd-looking. They seem to be all gaping bill surrounded by wildly sprouting feathers poking up in complete disarray. The word "gawky" only hints at their out-of-proportion appearance. They're covered with soft downy feathers, and their larger body and flight feathers are just beginning to develop and protrude from the down, giving them a spiky appearance.

Some of the nests are so close to the wooden structure I'm standing in that I don't need to use my binoculars to look at them. Watching the adult birds come and go, I think about yesterday's rookery that was off-limits to people, with the signs posted so far from the action Danny and I couldn't see anything of the nests at all. I'm so glad I made the decision to come here today, where humans are welcome as long as they're quiet and remain out of sight inside the bird blind.

As I look at more of the nests and watch the adults, this time with my binoculars, I realize that there is something different about one of the cormorants. The more closely I look, the more obvious it is—this adult bird has a thin white chevron going sideways where its bill meets the darker feathers of the head, the key field mark for the Neotropic Cormorant. I write the name in my pocket notebook and add an asterisk because it's a lifer, then continue to study the activities of the birds in front of me. They come and go, come and go, bearing freshly caught food for their squawking nestlings. I realize that I'm hungry, too.

§

Back at my car I sip some water and snack on M &Ms while studying my maps and books. I need to make a plan for the afternoon on my way to the hotel room I have reserved in Winnie. I program my GPS for Sea Rim State Park and get on the road. After about half an hour, quite desperate for lunch, I stop at a national fast food chain, grab a burger to go, and drive south around Sabine Lake. I nibble my lunch as I drive west to reach Sea Rim State Park on the Gulf of Mexico. The sandwich isn't very good, but it fills up the empty spot, and that's all I need right now.

In midafternoon, I reach the park, find a place for my car, and step out onto a boardwalk with handrails on both sides. The first section of the boardwalk crosses grassy, marshy ground with large, shallow ponds reflecting the blue sky. Here and there low sand dunes vary the flat landscape. I'm at sea level now, for the first time on this trip. As I walk slowly along, I hear the familiar cry of a Killdeer, whose voice sounds, with a bit of imagining, like those two words, then the distinctive "onk-la-ree" songs of Red-winged Blackbirds dashing back and forth over the bright green grasses.

One of the ponds has a little group of six slate-y black American Coots paddling at the far edge, and a pair of Blue-winged Teal drifting along at the other side. American Coots swim in a way that's almost like ducks, but their feet are shaped differently, not that I can see their feet as they drift around on the water. This is excellent habitat for waterfowl. They're not actively feeding just now, simply paddling about, trying to keep on the right side of the breeze so their feathers don't ruffle up backwards. A large contingent of Great-tailed Grackles fly around noisily. I walk a few steps forward and spend quite a long time watching a pair of Black-necked Stilts pacing back and forth in the next very shallow pond, looking for food. These birds always get my attention. I like the pattern of the feathers on their head and neck because the black-and-white design reminds me of a yin-yang symbol.

Now I'm ready to walk toward the sandy beach and the Gulf of Mexico. The boardwalk leads through the dunes and there, there it is, blue water as far as I can see, with long lines of white-capped waves rolling toward me. I don't know whether to stand still or speed up, so I do both, take a few steps forward, then pause to savor the view again. When I finally reach the end of the boardwalk I lean on the handrail to slip off my sandals, roll up my pants legs, then carry the sandals in my hand to walk across the wet sand littered with shells and seaweed. Oh, this is so nice! It's been more than a year since I last walked on sand, and the wet, gritty little particles feel just great between my toes. This is what I've been dreaming about for weeks. I stop to listen to the sound of the water as more little waves glide up onto the shore. And I take a deep breath of the salty sea air. This is well worth driving more than a thousand miles to enjoy. I spy a small seashell and stoop over to pick it up for a closer look. Lovely.

I see some Sanderlings at the edge of the waves, dashing about in their usual daredevil style, always managing at the last possible second to not get doused by the water. I'm not so quick, and when the water washes over my toes and up past my ankles it's a bit cold for my taste, not shivery, run-the-other-way cold, just a bit of a surprise. Cold water is not a problem for birds' feet. Their blood vessels and capillaries are arranged quite differently from those in my human feet. In a bird's foot, whether it's a species with individual toes or webbing or some combination, there's a constant heat exchange going on underneath the skin that keeps them comfortable.

I'm okay with the water temperature now that I'm used to it, and keep on walking on the wet sand amid the waves. I've been paying close attention to all the interpretive signs along the boardwalk, and now it's beginning to pay off. As I look out along the beach, I can identify another lifer, a Semipalmated Plover, based on the single black necklace, not the double necklace of the Killdeer, that's strutting along nearby and whose shape and size is so similar to a Killdeer. The solid black heads of the Laughing Gulls and their raucous shrieks make them easy to remember from Florida birding trips.

So far, so good, and I'm feeling much more confident with shore birds—but I still cannot distinguish the terns, and even though I know swallows, I have no idea what kind are zipping around here because they are moving too fast for me to get a clear look. And I can't identify the birds with long bills poking in the sand ahead, so I won't even make a guess. I've made progress, but I still have a lot of things to learn.

I turn back to walk along the sand in the other direction, retracing my steps toward the boardwalk. There I brush as much sand off my feet as I can, slip my sandals back on, and walk across the wooden boards to my car. I drive past a few RVs parked on the camping loop and on to another parking lot to explore the different habitats on the Gambusia Nature Trail. The trail marker notes that a gambusia is a fish, and a very helpful one at that—it likes to eat mosquitoes.

This boardwalk goes across open water in a marshy area and has no handrails. Instead, at foot level there is a small border of wood about an inch high nailed along the edges, a tiny little curb-like addition that isn't much of a barrier in case of a misstep.

Although the path is wide enough for two people to walk abreast, and would also be suitable for many different kinds of wheeled mobility devices, the planks are, as usual, not quite flush with each other. I think it would be smart to change from my slip-on sandals to lug-soled wellies for safer footing on this uneven surface, so I go back to my car, roll my pants legs back down, and put on my boots.

Back out on the boardwalk, the water swirls and laps against the supporting timbers just a couple of inches below the planks. I'm careful to keep my camera and binoculars against the center of my chest. Signs warn against close encounters with alligators in this marshy territory, so I'm watching to the left and right ahead. One of my favorite bits on an alligator etiquette sign says, "If an alligator goes after a fish you have caught, cut the line and let the alligator have the fish." Well, duh!

I walk very slowly and carefully in the exact middle of the boardwalk, stopping to take photos with both my cell phone and digital camera, occasionally using my binoculars, whatever works best to observe the many birds in this seaside habitat. I recognize the willows, but the rest of the vegetation is unfamiliar to me. I find a Neotropic Cormorant and more Great-tailed Grackles, then a noisy group of American Coots, squeaking and murmuring as they dabble for fish at the edge of some reeds.

At this time of day, so late in the afternoon, I've only encountered a few people at widely spaced intervals. As I often do, when I see other folks taking photos with their cell phones, I make them an offer. I'll take their photo with their phone if they will return the favor by taking a photo of me with my phone—works every time, and is so much better than a selfie, which I seldom get quite right. My plan works great with the couple who've recently retired to Texas and are exploring the boardwalk this afternoon. I take a photo of them, and they snap a nice picture of me. They're just beginning to get interested in birds and we chat for a few minutes about what we've each seen so far before going off in opposite directions.

As I amble along, I notice more Blue-winged Teal, more Red-winged Blackbirds, and more Black-necked Stilts. And then I get a very good look at a Common Gallinule, a bird that always looks to me as if it's on its way to a masquerade ball but can't afford much in the way of a disguise—just a piece of red paper stuck on half way down its nose.

The boardwalk makes a weirdly shaped zigzag loop out toward the Gulf and then returns me to my original starting point.

§

At my car, I take my boots off and slip my sandals back on, then re-program my GPS to take me to my hotel in Winnie. It should take about an hour to get there. For tonight and tomorrow night, the Hampton Inn in Winnie will be my base.

I check in and then, following the advice of the desk clerk, go next door to Al-T's, a local spot specializing in Cajun dishes, with some other standard bar fare and steaks on the menu, too. Sitting at the back bar is very relaxing and I enjoy chatting with Zack the bartender while I sip a glass of chardonnay. Zack's a brand-new, first-time dad, with a three-week-old son, and pretty soon we're looking at photos on his cell phone of his sweet little guy, already an enchanting delight. For dinner, the fried stuffed shrimp is delicious, even though the Cajun spices are a bit stronger than I would normally choose. The hush puppies and green beans are just exactly the right side dishes. Another glass of wine makes the perfect dessert.

After dinner I'm ready to unwind a bit more, so back at my hotel I stroll around the parking lot and into the one next to it, then loop back. There are plenty of streetlights here, so it's easy to find my way amid the many adjoining parking lots of the various hotels. On my next circuit I amble through a different parking lot and catch a glimpse of an orange tabby cat slinking away between a car and pickup truck.

After fifteen minutes of walking, I'm ready to go indoors, so I get my travel journal and field notebook out of the car and go up to my room. Flipping through the hastily written notes, I think about how different the three habitats I've visited today are, and the variety of birds each one attracts. A swamp that was dry with few birds within sight, a decidedly wet bayou with woodland and swamp birds and a small lake with active bird nests, and then the saltwater and brackish marshes along the Gulf with ducks and shorebirds galore. It's been a good day.

Tomorrow I plan to spend the day exploring other kinds of habitats, and I'll need to get up fairly early, so I'm going to turn the lights out now.

###

CHAPTER FOUR

Anahuac National Wildlife Refuge

Along the coast, confusing sparrows, and feathers

I wake up about an hour after sunrise and go downstairs to take a short morning walk around the hotel parking lot. I listen to yet another Northern Mockingbird sing through his repertoire of other birds' songs, quite musical, and then marvel again at the decidedly un-musical sounds coming from a little group of Great-tailed Grackles. Their calls are loud and insistent, a jumble of screeches and weird noises. The birds almost always tip their heads back so that their bills are pointing toward the sky, as if they were howling at the sun.

After breakfast in the hotel, I need to spend a few minutes neatening up the interior of my car to get ready for a full day of birding. Back home, when I was planning the outline of my trip, I chose to make Winnie my base in the Upper Gulf Coast region because it's the nearest town of any size to a premier birding spot, Anahuac National Wildlife Refuge. I plan to spend the day exploring as many sections of the refuge as possible, but I need to buy gas first, and figure out what to do about lunch.

I know from experience at other national wildlife refuges that services for people will be minimal, with no food available. One of my books notes that there isn't even any drinking water at Anahuac. That's not a problem for me, as I always carry water with me, but in the food department I don't have anything other than snacks. Fortunately the gas station across the road has a

Subway shop, so I pick up a turkey sandwich, and then program my GPS to take me to the main entrance of the refuge.

In just a few minutes I'm beyond the town and driving through sparsely populated farmland and ranches. It's a gorgeous morning and I'm cruising along on the flat roads, listening to an old favorite, Jack Jezzro's CD of Western swing music, an instrumental tribute to some of the songs made famous by Bob Wills and the Texas Playboys. The rhythms of the tunes make a good match to my cruising speed on these nice flat country roads. After an easy drive with no traffic, I arrive at the refuge at ten thirty. I have the rest of the day to explore almost thirty-five thousand acres of coastal marshes and prairieland and other habitats along the eastern edge of Galveston Bay.

At the visitor center I find a place to park by the sidewalk then stand by my car to look around as a warm breeze ruffles across my shirtsleeves. And the first bird I see is yet another Northern Mockingbird. Oh, well, that's fine with me. They are clever birds, and always fun to listen to, and each one has his own playlist of song samples. As I sling my camera and binoculars around my neck, I notice that the people over by a wooden gazebo are looking up at something inside. Walking toward them, I see various swallows swoop and jink overhead on their way to and from the inside of the pointed dome.

I walk past a support column and look up at the interior of the wooden roof. After spending the winter in South America, a colony of Cliff Swallows have returned to Texas to build their rounded nests, which resemble a jug or gourd turned on its side, against the eaves of the roof. This is where they'll raise their families, and they're busy at work getting everything ready, snatching up mud from the marshy areas of the refuge, then bringing one tiny beakful at a time to the underside of the roof, to stick the mud to the growing accumulation. Some of the mud is grayish brown, and other dabs are pale yellow, depending on the source. I take a photo of the pointillist pattern, then realize that Barn Swallows, with their longer tails and different color pattern, are also active in the area.

Their nests follow a different construction plan, with sticks included in the mud that holds them fast to ledges instead of the roof itself. Apparently the two species are willing to share the same general space for their nests and the same hunting grounds for their food.

Walking along the sidewalk toward the visitor information center, I look up at a bird that is similar in shape and general color scheme to a mockingbird, mostly gray and white. This bird sitting on a power line running parallel to the road is a bit stockier, with a hooked bill. Bringing my binoculars up for a better look, I discover my first lifer of the day, a Loggerhead Shrike, and one of the bird species I would have put on a target list—if I'd made one.

What's funny is that this species lives and nests back home in Kentucky, and is considered easy to find because of its hunting strategy of perching out in the open on utility wires and dead snags, then pouncing onto the short grasses in rural areas to catch insects and other prey. But I've never been in the right place at the right time (probably because I was zooming along too fast in a car) to see them—and now here's one right in front of me, almost eleven hundred miles away from home.

Inside the visitor center I chat with the volunteers who staff the gift shop about the best opportunities for the greatest variety of birds today. I make notes on the map they give me and pick up a bird checklist. Of course this is also a great shopping opportunity, and I've found a beautiful Caribbean blue zippered hoodie in my size with an embroidered Anahuac NWR patch on the left front as a practical souvenir. I make a special effort to spend some money in these kinds of gift shops because they're run by citizen volunteer groups, and the profits from the merchandise they sell go right back into projects that help the birds—and the birders who come to watch them.

I decide to do most of my birding from the car until I find a good place to eat my lunch. When I entered the refuge I turned off the music in my car, so I'm driving in silence. Well, almost. The road I've chosen to drive on first is paved and I idle along very slowly with the windows rolled down so I can listen for birds, as well as look. I hear Killdeer, then see a Turkey Vulture riding a thermal above the warm expanse of marshy ground.

§

I stop briefly at the tiny parking lot at The Willows, an area affected by Hurricane Ike in September 2008. That storm was so powerful that its remnants held together all the way up through the Mississippi River Valley into my home territory in Kentucky. Hurricanes are great natural engines of water distribution far inland, but that fresh water often comes with a price—in the case of Ike, sustained winds of fifty, sixty, even seventy-five miles per hour even as far north as where I live. By the time Ike got to my place there wasn't much rain left, but the winds still caused considerable damage, snapping off weakened tree limbs and toppling the occasional tree. Although there weren't any thunderstorms, the destruction caused by the wind alone was similar to severe thunderstorms but very patchy.

Tornadoes are the more widely destructive weather forces back home. When they touch the ground they can rip out trees and other vegetation across huge swaths of land, toppling giants and wrecking the undergrowth, too. But the path of destruction from a tornado varies greatly in width and length. One might travel on the ground for a few hundred feet across a short distance, but another one might be much, much larger and travel along a track continuing for many miles. But the typical debris field after a tornado is often very compact. Some trees and shrubs can sprout new shoots from the stumps, while other plants quickly take advantage of the fresh sunlight available at the base of fallen giants. The local plants are well adapted to the local weather patterns. After a tornado, the changes in the plant communities follow a predictable pattern, and continue for many years. As the habitat shifts and gradually returns to its former mix, the kinds of birds that use the area also change through the intervening years.

But already, as I travel along the Gulf Coast, I am learning that when hurricanes come ashore at the height of their power, the damage is much more widespread than after an ice storm or a tornado at home. Whole wildlife communities along the coast can be devastated by a single storm. As the eye of Hurricane Ike passed many miles farther west and on up through Galveston Bay, the extreme winds and the rains and especially the storm surges of seawater over normally dry land here at the area known as The Willows really tore up the habitat.

The animals and plants in coastal communities are just as well adapted to such local weather patterns and intermittent disastrous destruction as the different plant communities back in Kentucky are adapted to the occasional ice storm or tornado. But in both places the natural recovery period often takes many years. Since so much of the land along the Gulf Coast is now used for human concerns, most notably businesses related to the oil and gas industries, as well as shipping and other commercial pursuits, plus land that's managed differently for ranches and homes, when one natural community is damaged extensively by a hurricane there are fewer and fewer other natural communities nearby to take up the slack. So humans are intervening to help the recovery process in the wild areas through restoration projects like the one going on here.

It's good to know that nine years after Hurricane Ike this little cluster of willows and brushy understory plants is once again thriving and available for the use of the returning migrant songbirds who spend their winters in the Caribbean or South America. To return to North America, they fly nonstop for six hundred or so miles across the Gulf of Mexico, and when they reach land they are desperate to find a place to perch and rest their weary bodies. They need food, fresh water, and shelter, too. These willows and low bushes are just the right place for them to find insects to eat, water to drink and bathe in, plus hiding spots to rest safely out of sight from predators.

Unlike the small batch of Cliff Swallows who are building nests over at the gazebo, most of the migrating songbirds who come here this April and May will pause only long enough to quickly stock up on food. And then they will fly farther inland on their way to their breeding grounds farther north.

But right now all I can find is yet another resident Northern Mockingbird, so I get back in my car and head back out on the road. A Great Blue Heron flaps across in front of me. Great-tailed Grackles seem to be everywhere, and I hear, then see, a male Red-winged Blackbird.

As I drive along I think about the other role this refuge plays during the winter months. Before the lakes and rivers up north begin freezing over in autumn, hundreds of thousands of waterfowl and shorebirds fly south to their wintering grounds in various places in North America. Some will stop off in Indiana or Kentucky, but some will come all the way south to Texas and spend the winter months at Anahuac. That's what they did last fall, but it's already early April and most of them have already left on their journey northward. I've arrived too late to see most of them, but maybe I will see a few stragglers today.

Since I crossed the Sabine River into Texas, the places I'm exploring now are considered part of the Central Flyway instead of the Mississippi Flyway. Each species of bird, whether it's a songbird or a shorebird or one of the many kinds of waterfowl, uses a different path to migrate, and the flyways are a human division because there aren't barriers in the air. The birds do not see the Sabine River and say to themselves, "I must keep to the left side," or "I must only fly on the right side." The birds are free to move around as they see fit.

§

By the time I reach the turnoff for the Shoveler Pond Loop, another section of paved road, I'm thinking more about lunch than birds. I see a small raft of American Coots drifting along on the water next to the road, and hunt for a place to pull off and park. I find a wide spot, and look at the dark birds in the water—more

Common Gallinules with their funny red nose shields. I have a hard time with this bird because its common name used to be Common Moorhen, which is how it's listed in some of my older reference books, but the correct name now for *Gallinula galeata* is Common Gallinule. In my rough field notes in my little pocket notebook, sometimes I use one name, sometimes the other, and then I have to straighten it out later.

It's getting quite breezy and my contact lenses feel very sticky, so I take them out and switch to my no-line bifocals. Then I have to roll down the eye relief edges on my binoculars so I will have the proper distance to use them effectively against my glasses. And I'm getting hungrier by the minute. I'll nibble on M&Ms and keep looking for more birds until I can find a good place to take a lunch break.

As I roll slowly along in my car, driving almost at a walking pace, I notice two other birds I know from home and have already seen on this trip, the Double-crested Cormorant and some Mourning Doves. Then I see a tiny brown bird up ahead at the edge of the pavement. It's definitely a sparrow, and a very nervous one at that. The grass along the side of the paved road is mowed short in a swath just a few feet wide. This strip of short grass forms a border between the road and the edges of water-filled ditches that parallel the road in this section. Beyond the short grass are much taller marsh grasses, and other plants I do not know by name, waving in the breeze.

The sparrow darts down to the short grasses at the edge of the pavement to hunt for seeds and other edibles. But each time I get too close with my car it dashes back to hide in the shelter of the taller grasses. For this bird, the danger trigger seems to be about fifteen feet. I take some photos of the road ahead through the car windshield, but when I look at them on the camera's display screen they're no help—just another little brown job (LBJ in birder slang) hunting for food, and I am too hungry myself to try for better photos. For now, this will be the day's mystery bird.

As I drive along, the roadside vegetation changes, and between the clumps of plants I can see across big stretches of water connected to an even larger area of shallow, open water where Great Egrets and Little Blue Herons are finding their version of lunch.

When I'm in Florida I find it easy enough to identify a tallish bird with a downcurved bill as an ibis, but determining the exact species of whichever kind of ibis is in front of me takes me a while. I'm trying to study any ibises that I see here in Texas very carefully in an attempt to memorize key field marks. The dark one over there looks like a Glossy Ibis, so that's what I'll write in my notebook. On the other side of the road I see some Black-necked Stilts, which are impossible to mistake for anything else, with their distinctive black-and-white plumage, long, straight bills, and long legs.

I have no trouble identifying with complete certainty the small waterfowl over there as Pied-billed Grebes, and a pair of Northern Shovelers, for whom this loop road is named. Although grebes look like ducks, and paddle along on water and then dive for food in the same way that dabbling ducks do, they are in a completely different bird family, the Podicipedidae, so named for their unusual lobed toes. They're not webbed, but they're not bare, either. Not that I ever expect to see their feet—they seldom venture onto land and are reported to be very clumsy at walking due to the placement of their legs in relation to the center of gravity of their bodies. The swallows I was watching earlier cannot walk on land either, but their feet are just perfect for perching on twigs or clinging to the sides of their nests. Neither the grebes nor the swallows need to venture onto dry land—they can find all they need either on water, at muddy edges, or in the air.

The Northern Shovelers are easy to distinguish from any other kind of waterfowl due to the shape of their long bills that flare down in a sort of wavy fashion on the sides towards the front. And I always smile when I do see one, because that is the first kind of duck I identified all by myself, without anyone having shown me one before. I learned to recognize this duck at Muscatatuck National Wildlife Refuge in south central Indiana near Seymour many years ago. Back then, I did not know very much about the national wildlife refuge system, or its importance, not just for birds, but for other animals and plants, too. But years of birding have taught me the value of these places, and I often go out of my way to visit them. I plan to visit several more while I'm in Texas.

Many of the roads in refuges are laid out in a grid pattern, following the artificial dikes that make it easy for humans to adjust the water depth in the various impoundments to suit the needs of birds when nature doesn't quite cooperate. Here at Anahuac the roads are a mix of straight lines along human dams and curvy bits following natural boundaries, with something new to look at with each turn of the wheel.

Just up ahead I see a white edging at the end of the tail of a migrant who's recently returned to North America from its wintering grounds in South America, the Eastern Kingbird. It's perched about ten feet off the ground, and ready to dash out to capture a flying insect. This is one bird whose Latin name I memorized a long time ago because it's so easy and fun to say, *Tyrannus tyrannus*. The double name emphasizes that it's a feisty member of the Tyrant Flycatchers, a huge group of birds that often dash out from a perch to snatch up insects in mid-air then return to the same perch to make sortie after sortie.

I slow down and pull as close to the edge of the pavement as possible, but take care not to let a wheel go off into the grass. There are often warning signs throughout wildlife refuges that the shoulders are unstable, and motorists are asked to be extremely cautious to avoid damaging fragile turf. I get a good view of some Blue-winged Teal drifting slowly on the water near more marsh grasses that I cannot name. They are quite a contrast to the rich pink feathers of a small group of Roseate Spoonbills gathered on slightly higher ground on the other side of the road.

I think there's a pull-off area ahead on the left, so I slow down and check the mirrors for any other traffic. None. Then I see the telltale black wing tips of a White Ibis flying over the road. Hah! I just realized that it's like a negative image of a Black Vulture, the black bird that has white wing tips. I wonder what kind of advantage having contrasting wing tips gives either of these species?

I have no answer, and I'm going to eat lunch. I don't have any particular fondness for deli-style sandwiches and seldom eat them when I'm at home. But on the road they have the advantage of keeping fresh for several hours. I dig out a bottle of cranberry juice from the cooler and set up my birder's lunch on the hood of the car.

It doesn't take long to eat such a simple meal, and when I'm finished I decide to explore the nearby boardwalk. It's a short one, but the blustery winds make it difficult to see anything in the waving greenery, so I head back to my car.

As I drive slowly along, I spot an alligator in one of the side canals. I have the windows rolled down to listen as the American Coots and Common Gallinules keep up a steady stream of noisy calling back and forth.

§

While I was eating my lunch, I thought about how each kind of bird is different, with a bill shape and leg length and the position of the eyes and the shape of its wings all matched perfectly to the kind of flying it does and the kind of food it hunts, giving it exactly the right combination of tools to succeed in life. And then there are the decorative bits. Not just fancy feathers, but facial markings and other distinctive features.

A bit farther on, I stop along the side of the road to take a closer look at a marshy area. I'm looking across a large expanse of shallow water with a profusion of plants crowned with a huge single leaf and directly at what is clearly an ibis. But which one? I look at the bird, I look at a field guide. I look at the bird, I look at another field guide. Hmmm... magenta or rusty red feathers on the neck and shoulders. Sorta shiny green feathers on the wings. I look at the bird, I think. I look at the bird, I read.

I take a few photos, and then zoom the display on the back of the camera to see if it confirms what I thought I could see with my binoculars. Yes, a brilliant red eye, surrounded by reddish bare skin, which is in turn bordered by lemony-yellow, almost white skin. That clinches it—I'm looking at a White-faced Ibis, another lifer. I cannot think of any good reason for the color pattern around the eye—I don't believe it would influence hunting success. I think it's simply a decoration, a distinctive design that sets it apart from any another species in the same genus.

The more carefully I watch the White-faced Ibis, the more other kinds of birds I see in this lagoon, including a Purple Gallinule. Its face is even more extravagantly colorful than the Common Gallinule's, having an additional pale bluish shield above the red on its nose. The bill and forehead area, with yellow at the tip, orangey-red in the center, then topped off with the pale bluish purple shield makes me think of a piece of candy corn.

As I finish this driving loop I notice several Laughing Gulls and some other birds I know from the other side of the Gulf of Mexico in Florida, a little group of Boat-tailed Grackles flitting among the reedy greenery. The boat-tailed ones are smaller than the great-tailed ones, and it's easy to tell them apart. I slow down to admire the wash of golden orange feathers on the heads and shoulders of some Cattle Egrets in breeding plumage. They're shorter than Great Egrets, perhaps half the size, much stockier, but also very pretty to look at.

I think it's time to go back to the visitor center area to take a break, and then I'll pick another section of the refuge to explore.

§

Refreshed, I take the paved road that angles off to the west then south. Once again, little brown, streaky sparrows with a lot of gray on them dart into the grasses along the side of the road as I drive forward. I take photo after photo, but none reveal anything that helps me identify them. This is so frustrating because at home I can easily separate five kinds of sparrows from each other with only the quickest glimpse. I know where to look on the body or the head or the legs for the most important detail. And I know their distinctive songs. But here I have no experience, these little guys are not singing, and it's going to take a lot of fresh effort to figure out who they are. They dart around so quickly I can't get a good view of the bill or face, and I suspect that is where the key details will be.

The paved road stops, and to continue toward a boat ramp with access to the East Bay I must drive on hard-packed, gray gravel. As I drive very, very slowly to keep the plume of dust I'm stirring up down as much as possible, I see a medium-size, long-legged shorebird ahead on the gravel. It has a whitish belly, gray top, and long, straight bill—yes, it's a Willet. I take a lot of photos through the car windshield (these photos often turn out pretty good, despite the bug splats and dust streaks), and lag back so I don't accidentally frighten it. Eventually it moves off to the side and into the grasses.

Cars make excellent moveable bird blinds, and I'm content to sit inside mine to watch the road ahead and along both sides. My shiny red SUV would seem to be an unlikely place to "hide" from birds, but I discovered a long time ago that it isn't the color of the vehicle or its size that alarms birds—it's the noise. The best way to use a car as a bird blind is to stop and turn off the engine, then just wait for the birds to resume their usual activities. That's what I'm going to do now.

Sure enough, in just a short while the Willet comes back out from the grasses and, much to my surprise, sits down on the dusty road directly in front of my silent car. Turning off the engine has the added advantage of cutting down on vibration while using binoculars, and since I'm still inside my car, this bird has figured out that there is no immediate danger. It turns its head around and nestles its long bill into its back feathers, apparently getting ready to settle in for a nap. And then a second Willet appears. I suspect these two are mates, or at least trying to pair up. I don't want to disturb them, but my options are rather limited. I certainly can't drive forward, so I turn to look out the side window at the murky water in the ditch along the side of the gravel.

Another one of those streaky brown-and-gray sparrows is foraging in the short grass boundary zone between the gravel of the road and the taller vegetation near the water. I watch through the open driver's side window with binoculars and take photos. Finally, I get a good look at the bird's head. There's a tiny yellow patch between the base of the bill and the eyes, an area known as the lores. And I can just make out a bit of a white chin or paler throat—hard to get a distinct impression because it hops around so much. But that one glimpse of yellow is enough to clinch the identification as a Seaside Sparrow, a lifer for me.

When I look around to the front again the Willets have disappeared, so I turn the car engine on, make a sort of back-and-forth multi-point turn, avoiding putting my wheels onto the grassy shoulder, and drive back the way I came. Eventually I take a third loop of paved road out to Frozen Point. I see a Ring-billed Gull, one of the easiest gulls to identify, and a species that is widespread across all of North America. They're even easy to find along the Ohio River back home. Adults really do have a ring of black about half an inch from the tip of their yellow bills.

I can't find anything especially interesting to look at when I get to the end of this road, and I'm not quite in the mood for a walk, so I turn around to drive back to the visitor center. This section of road is on the western edge of a deep marsh. The vegetation nearest the road is mostly tall, green grasses with the occasional short shrub. I do not know any of the botany of this habitat and have to just enjoy it for what it is—a nice expanse of green plants.

Driving very slowly, I catch a glimpse of something quite large sticking up above the grasses. What a surprise! It's an American Bittern, with its striped neck stretched straight up and bill pointing skyward. It's standing stock still, completely motionless.

That posture is a good disguise amid reeds and cattails, but here the grasses are so short the bird stands out in vivid contrast to its surroundings. In fact, it's the best look I've ever had at this usually secretive bird, and I take many photos.

§

It's almost five o'clock, with several hours of daylight left to continue exploring. At the visitor center area, I figure it's a good idea to take advantage one more time of the restrooms, since I don't know where the next ones might be, then study the notes I made on my map when I talked with the volunteers in the gift shop. I have plenty of time to drive over to a different access point to a section of the refuge known as the Skillern Tract.

As I drive along I'm moving north and farther inland, away from the marshes, then I need to turn east a bit. It's only about seven miles across flat rangeland, wide acres of open country with short vegetation, kinda weedy-looking to me. I pass the little clump of parked RVs that I was told to use as a landmark, and turn onto the entrance road to the Skillern Tract, heading south again.

I'm already driving very slowly when an unusually long-tailed bird flies directly in front of me from the left and into the open field on my right. Following its flight path I watch until it finds a place to perch on a bit of weed sticking up higher than the rest of the vegetation. I pull over to the side of the paved road, turn off the engine, roll all the windows down, and grab my binoculars to get a closer look. The bird balances near the top of the stiff plant then swoops out across the field chasing an insect, then returns to the same perch. It does this several times, then moves to a different perch, and repeats the same hunting strategy.

The bird's body is about the same size as an Eastern Kingbird, but the outer tail feathers are extremely long, easily as long if not longer than the bird's body. I'm watching my very first Scissor-tailed Flycatcher, and it's a wonderful treat. So far, the other lifers

I've found on this trip have been variations on birds I know from the Ohio River Valley or coastal Florida, so similar to other species I'm familiar with that the main way to distinguish them is by subtle color differences. But this bird's extremely long tail feathers give it a distinctive shape, quite different from anything I know.

As I study it flying out and back from various perches, I realize that its hunting technique is almost identical to its relative the Eastern Kingbird, and in fact they are in the same genus, Tyrannus, but this is *Tyrannus forficatus*, a distinctly different species. This bird's tail feathers are different lengths, with the longest ones being the outermost ones, and the center ones short, so it does give an overall impression like the blades of a pair of scissors. Indeed, the second part of its Latin binomial, *forficatus*, means deeply forked like a pair of shears.

The Scissor-tailed Flycatcher has a much smaller range than the Eastern Kingbird, occurring most regularly in Texas, Oklahoma, and northward into parts of Kansas, and sometimes venturing into Florida. As I take photos with the zoom lens on the Nikon, hoping for something to turn out well enough to be recognizable, then shift back to binoculars, I catch glimpses of the apricot pink wash on the feathers on the bird's breast just below the wings. Oh, this bird's a real beauty, and I feel like all the miles I've driven are finally taking me into a new realm of birding.

When the Scissor-tailed Flycatcher flies out of good range for my binoculars, I start the car up again and drive farther into the Skillern Tract. I stop at a small parking lot with a boardwalk area that leads into a small clump of trees on the eastern border of the open field where I saw the flycatcher. There are only two other cars in the lot. I don't know where the people are, but I don't care. I'm used to going birding in places where the chances of running into other people are rather slim.

I get out of my car and walk along the tree-lined boardwalk slowly, but it is so late in the afternoon I cannot find any songbirds. Maybe another spot would be better? I turn around. A trail at the other end of the small parking lot looks interesting, so I stop by my car to sip some water and then head off in that direction.

This area is along the East Bay Bayou, a sluggish stream that feeds into the East Bay of Galveston Bay. The path here begins as paved asphalt, and the brushy, shrubby, weedy stuff along the sides of the path is densely leafed out, creating dappled shade. Someone has mowed the area recently, leaving bits of drying grass trimmings scattered across the path. Dragonflies shimmer and land near my feet—if I were at home I'd be able to identify some of them, but here I'm puzzled. I can only say that some appear to be darners. I wish I had time to examine them more carefully, but this is meant to be a birding excursion and I reluctantly walk on.

§

I hear someone approaching from behind me and move aside to the right of the trail. The woman says "hi," as she approaches, then sees my binoculars and asks if I'm hunting for a certain bird species that she names. She mentions that it was reported in this area an hour or so ago on a bird alert service, and she wants to find it. I haven't been checking social media or e-mail much today, so I'm unaware of the report. And I've said to myself that I would not chase after particular birds, so although I don't have anything useful to say in the way of guidance, I wish her well in her search and continue to amble along at my own pace. Maybe I'll find that bird, maybe I won't. I'm not going to make a special effort.

Eventually I reach a wooden platform with a view of a small pond that's a segment of the bayou. The borders of standing water areas are not well-defined here, and they blend in very subtle ways into drier ground—and it varies according to recent rainfall. I'm at distinct disadvantage when I look at places like this because I do not know the composition of the plant communities that surround salt water versus the ones that prefer fresh water. I lean against the rail and look out into the distance. Yes, there are birds here, so I bring up my binoculars for a closer look. It's easy for me to name off the ones I can see: Glossy Ibis, American Coot, Great Egret, Roseate Spoonbill, Blue-winged Teal. All familiar, all beautiful, all charming in their own individual ways.

As I continue to scan to the left, straight ahead, and to the right, I hear a man's voice, and then a woman's voice. They arrive with a spotting scope, cameras, binoculars, ready for anything and everything. We say hello and spend a few minutes talking about the birds we've seen in the area. I tell them a bit about my home in Kentucky and my plan to go birding all along the coast down to the Rio Grande. They're from Oxford, England, and they're here to explore many different areas of Texas. While they continue to take photographs, I'm beginning to think about dinner. As I turn away to leave, we wish each other safe travels and good luck birding.

Back at my car, I look through my books and study my maps—yes, I will have enough time and daylight to make a preliminary visit to the area I plan to concentrate on tomorrow, and then I will look for a place to have dinner. I drive east, then south, out to a small community called High Island. It isn't a real island, but it is a famous birding spot because it's a woodsy area a few feet above sea level, just a bit inland from the beaches along the Gulf of Mexico. It's the first place many migrant songbirds will stop to perch, rest, and eat after their long flight across the open water. Some might arrive tonight. I stay on the main highway through the human settlement and drive out toward the Gulf. The surf is pounding on the shore as a long string of Brown Pelicans fly over the waves. Their body shape always makes me wonder how they can stay in the air with so little apparent effort.

As I watch them I realize that I'm birded out for the day and so I find a place to turn around to head back to Winnie for dinner. As I drive past the houses in the town, I get quite a surprise—a peacock with its enormous tail spread out majestically is strutting around in a front yard. Clearly this is somebody's pet, and I can't put it on my list of wild birds, but it sure is fun to look at it.

The only place I know of in Winnie with bar service is the same restaurant where I ate last night, so I pull into Al-T's parking lot, which is much more crowded than yesterday. Zach is tending bar again—so nice to see a familiar face!—and he's chatting with the Saturday night regulars who are singing along to the songs on the jukebox from time to time.

I sip a beer and join in the conversation about Texas Red Dirt music, a style I'm not familiar with, and the other folks at the bar tell me about their favorite bands. One of the guys takes a cocktail napkin and begins writing on it—not his phone number, but a list of the names of bands I should try listening to. The guy on my left, Rodney, is a biologist doing some habitat survey work in the area, and has a particular fondness for eagles, so we have plenty to talk about, too. This is my kind of happy hour.

A short while later I look up from my dinner, a nice, juicy steak, to pay a little more attention to the folks on my right as they begin talking to a couple who've just walked up to the other end of the bar. The guy's tall, the woman has dark hair, and they're smiling in a sort of shy yet delightedly happy way. Turns out that although they'd been living together for quite a while, this week they decided to make it official and get married. Nothing fancy, just at the courthouse apparently, and all arranged rather simply. This is their first appearance as husband and wife. The guy tells Zack about where they found affordable wedding rings, and the woman keeps glancing at her left hand and smiling. When someone asks, "Where's the honeymoon?" the guy doesn't miss a beat when he answers, "Houston—we have tickets to an Astros game!"

Cheers all around, and I can't think of a better way to unwind after such a wonderful day of birding. After a second beer I go on "home" to my hotel room.

Tonight I decide that I should go through my rough field notes to begin a list of lifers for the trip. Before I left home I printed out my life list to date. It's actually a list of all the birds of North America, with the two hundred twenty-five species I've seen over the years highlighted in yellow—and a whole lot of blank spaces. I spend quite a while at the desk in my hotel room putting arrows pointing to the new lifers on the appropriate pages, plus the date I discovered each one, and check to make sure that I've added asterisks to my field notes as a cross-reference. Five lifers today! This has been a wonderful day, a big adventure, with thirty different kinds of birds to look at and enjoy.

Now it's time for lights out.

###

CHAPTER FIVE

At the shore and among the trees

Group birding, Bolivar Flats, riding a ferry

Half a dozen or so Great-tailed Grackles are making a racket while I walk around the hotel parking lot this morning. I'm going to make this a very short walk because I need to eat breakfast promptly and pack up to leave. It's breezy and warm, with a few white clouds in the blue sky, and I'm eager to go exploring in the High Island area. Now that it's the second week of April, my chances of seeing returning migrant songbirds are getting better and better.

I know from reading in my books that the Houston Audubon Society maintains several different bird sanctuaries on this part of the Gulf Coast, but I'm not sure how to get to them once I reach the town. When I was over there late yesterday afternoon, I didn't see anything but houses along the main road.

Today there are temporary signs pointing to a parking area for visiting birders, so I turn down a side street lined with neatly kept houses. I pull into the gravel space surrounded by trees and begin walking past the houses, following the signs to the Boy Scout Woods. While here among the houses, I hear yet another Northern Mockingbird and a Northern Cardinal. Some Common Grackles are nearby and I get a good look at an Eastern Kingbird. Some Chimney Swifts have already returned to North America from their wintering grounds in the Amazon Basin, and they chitter overhead as they fly about looking for insects to catch on the wing. Most people recognize them by their shape, which is usually described as being like a flying cigar, and I find that useful, too. They have rather stubby tails, not forked or notched like the swallows.

When I get to the entrance of the woods, the area next to the road is quite small, only about the size of two typical house lots, and doesn't seem very likely as a birding spot. But among the shady trees, I discover an information booth, a small gift shop, and restrooms tucked into the small space—and there are plenty of birders already here. From this small area streetside, the woods extend for several acres, with permanent boardwalks and viewing platforms.

At the visitors' center I pay a small fee that entitles me to an orange wristband, which is a day pass for all events today, and pick up a small map and assorted brochures. I also like a small refrigerator magnet featuring full-color paintings of ten shorebirds and decide to buy it as a souvenir. The Audubon Society volunteer is having some trouble getting her electronics to process all these transactions, so we talk about birds while waiting for signals to go back and forth from her tablet computer. When I tell her that I'm in no hurry, she thanks me over and over again for my patience. Apparently her previous customers were not so understanding.

When she hands me my wristband she says that at noon, which is only about twenty minutes from now, two professional bird guides from an international tour company will be leading a caravan out to Bolivar Flats to check out the shore birds. Participation in this event is included with my wristband at no extra charge. I'm in the right place at the right time today—good travel karma.

I walk back to my car, listening to noisy Blue Jays and Great-tailed Grackles along the way, then drive two blocks to the meeting spot and pull into position among the other vehicles to wait for this new adventure to begin. The tour guides gather us together on foot and explain the general direction of travel. We'll be driving our own cars and trucks and vans over to a two-lane highway heading southwest. The guys mention some landmarks to watch for, and then tell us where to park on the beach if we get separated while driving there, and off we go.

About half an hour later the various cars and trucks in our little group drive onto the hard-packed sand at the beach. We are on the Bolivar Peninsula, a thin strip of land that separates Galveston Bay from the Gulf of Mexico. The Bolivar Flats Shorebird Sanctuary out here is owned and managed by the Houston Audubon Society. This area is used year-round by some bird species, as a wintering ground for others, and merely a stopover for those birds on their way farther north or south, depending on the season. We park, and as some stragglers continue to arrive I change into boots, then gather up my camera and binoculars and pocket notebook. The tour guides have spotting scopes on tripods for everyone to use, and some of the other folks have brought theirs along, too, to share.

§

The pace the guides set to walk out to the best spot to see the most birds is a bit brisk for my taste. I have a long, steady stride, and I've walked up and down through hills and valleys for six hours straight with no place to sit down, but stamina is different from speed. Today these guides are eager to get to the most birdy section of the shore and fast, but I'm interested in looking around at the surroundings because this is new to me. Tidal flats are not something I encounter very often. I end up at the far end of the line of about two dozen walkers and try to keep the gap between me and the main group to something reasonable. A line of Brown Pelicans fly over in the distance in the opposite direction from us, intent on a different destination.

After about ten minutes the guides stop walking and we gather around to listen to their explanations of some important field marks for the birds they expect us to find. Our first area to examine is not towards the surf, but inland. We turn with our backs to the Gulf of Mexico and focus our attention, plus binoculars, cameras, and spotting scopes, on a space marked off with narrow poles with orange twine strung between them, and sporting flapping bits of yellow caution tape knotted on at widely spaced intervals.

There are two birds at the edge of the tide wrack on the sand where some green stuff grows at the edge of the poles and twine. I see them and the guides explain to us that they are Wilson's Plover, a lifer for me. I look carefully at their dark, muddy, brown backs, all-black bills, and the single, dark necklace. Well, this presents something of a problem for me. Yesterday I was so sure that a single necklace indicated a Semipalmated Plover, and now today I find out that a Wilson's Plover also only has a single necklace, so I can't use that feature to make a definite identification.

Several of us talk among ourselves about how the general body shape is like that of a Killdeer (and indeed, they are in the same genus), but these birds have a thicker bill. As it turns out, the bill is what I should pay attention to, instead of the number of necklaces. A Semipalmated Plover has a very short bill that's black at the tip, and orange towards the face. These birds in front of us have much longer, all-black bills. How long will I be able to remember this?

The low dunes nearby are good foraging ground for this species, and people are supposed to keep away from this area to avoid interfering with their nests above the high tide mark. That's what all the posts and twine are for. Wilson's Plover is a saltwater shorebird that lives only along warm coastlines, a bird that probably would never venture inland to the freshwater areas in the Ohio River Valley. Indeed, I'm here at just the right time to see them as some begin to move north along the coast of Texas from their year-round habitats along the coast of Mexico and in the Caribbean.

It's quite breezy today, and turning towards the water I see row after row of Sanderlings hunkered down with their bellies touching the wet sand, the breeze ruffling their feathers so that they look like fluffy cotton balls. The wind is gusty—I have to keep adjusting my ball cap so it stays firmly on my head.

The tour guides walk on, and we follow them at our own speeds. I keep looking in all directions, out towards the Gulf then back to the wet sand and the mud flats and the dunes, to the left, to the right, then sweep my eyes all over it again, trying to understand this flat, treeless habitat and the forces of wind and water that shape it. To my eyes there are few landmarks—it's just an ever-shifting, glimmering, wet, sandy expanse, with waves lapping up to one level at one time of day, a different level later, according to the action of the tides.

Out in the water at a slight distance from the beach we are standing on, I notice a thin line of rocks that appears to be some sort of man-made barrier that separates this sandy shore from the shipping traffic out on the Gulf. As I look at the various birds on the sand near me, a huge oil tanker out on the open water glides across from the left, then an enormous container ship approaches from the right.

In the meantime, the tour guides point out some Western Sandpipers, the grayish birds sitting down on the sand. They've spent the winter here and will soon fly northwest all the way to their breeding grounds in Alaska, so I'm lucky to see them before they leave. The birds with the sort of rusty, speckled backs and ever-so-slightly down-curved black bills are Dunlin. They've spent the winter here, too, and will soon leave to fly all the way up through the United States and across Canada to breed and raise chicks in the Arctic regions.

As I try to keep the field marks of each of these variously colored brown, gray, white, and black shorebirds straight in my mind, and take photos to remind myself of the key features, I'm also thinking about what I need to study tonight. There's a chart of shorebirds in silhouette in one of the field guides I brought with me. It's arranged from largest to smallest, and although I've looked at it casually in the past, I did not do so carefully enough for it to be ingrained in my brain. I have some birding homework to do.

§

I sidle around the crowd of folks listening to the tour guide to get to a spot so I can hear him better as he explains something about a migrant that's spent the winter months along the coasts of the Caribbean Islands and South America, and that stops here in

Texas on its way to breeding grounds in the high Arctic regions. I look at the bird he's discussing, and get the part about black bill and black legs, but beyond that, I'm lost. To my eyes, this newest lifer, the Semipalmated Sandpiper, is just about the same in appearance as the Western Sandpiper, so I need to look again. Okay, okay, now I do see that the Semipalmated's bill is just a teensy bit shorter, and quite straight, with no hint of a droop at the end. But it's going to take more than one look on one afternoon for me to get this right so that I can differentiate between the two very similar sandpipers the next time I see either one.

And what's with the "semipalmated" in the names of two different kinds of shorebirds, one a sandpiper, the other one a plover? I ask the woman in an olive green ball cap and blue shirt standing next to me if she knows what it means. "Yes, it has to do with their feet," she says as she adjusts her binoculars. "They have some webbing between their toes but it only goes partway. Somebody had to explain it to me, too. I've only been watching birds for about a year." She's from the Houston area and likes to come out here as often as she can.

Someone using one of the spotting scopes calls out a plump duck straight ahead, and much discussion follows about what it is. The identification is difficult because the duck is facing away from the shore, giving us only a view from the tail end instead of the side or head-on.

When it's my turn to look through one of the spotting scopes, I have my usual trouble. The view in a spotting scope is so narrow and it's only for one eye—essentially an old-time sailor's telescope on a tripod. And in any sort of breeze stirring up waves or during the ebb and flow of the tide that causes the water level to shift, the image of a bird on water bounces up and down in the eyepiece in a most unsettling manner. I blink and try to keep the image steady.

This duck is squatting on the sand, quite stationary, and I get a good enough look through the spotting scope to agree with the other birders: yes, it is a female Greater Scaup, another lifer for me. I've seen the other kind of scaup, in a spotting scope and through my own binoculars as they moved through the Ohio River Valley, and the differences between those birds and this one are quite subtle, mostly about head shape and overall impression of feather colors. I do not think I would have been able to make this identification if the other birders who are more familiar with them had not discussed what to look for before I put my eye to the spotting scope, and I really appreciate their help. This female Greater Scaup and others of her kind will soon fly north, so again I am lucky to be here at the right time—and among the right birders, too.

Nearby a Royal Tern flies over. It's one of the larger terns, and the key is the pale orange, rather thin bill. Some Willets walk back and forth on the sand, then we encounter a Piping Plover. They're very pale gray, with a stubby little beak and an incomplete necklace. I would like to say that I know this bird, but I could not have given it a name without the help of the experts here. I put a star by its name in my pocket notebook as a lifer, although it's entirely possible that I've seen them in Florida—but back then I had no idea what I was looking at, just another peep. Birders often call sandpipers and plovers "peeps" because most of the time we can't think of what their real names are. They dash around so fast, they all have similar feather colors, and they're really hard to identify without a lot of practice. And some of them do make little peeping noises as they rush around on the sand.

And of course, none of these birds occur in isolation. There are often three or more species clustered around the same big puddle of water, or dashing along at the edge of the waves at different speeds. They're often all mixed up, jumbled together. What I'm trying to learn to do is notice the most significant field marks of each kind at a glance, but I have so little experience it takes me much longer to do this than most of the other folks in today's group. Listening to their conversations, I've figured out that almost all of them are local folks, and many are members of the Houston Audubon Society. This is a familiar beach to them, and their eyes are well attuned to the features of these birds.

I've also noticed that many of them are well-acquainted with each other, and today's excursion isn't just about enjoying today's shore birds. It's also about catching up on news from friends who've been traveling to all sorts of exotic places. Over drinks and dinner, I'm sure I'd enjoy hearing about those kinds of trips, but this afternoon this Texas mudflat is exotic enough for an inland birder like me, and I want to pay attention to what's in front of me right now.

I wander off to the left, away from distracting conversations, past some nearby Dunlin, and stop at yet another puddle on the sand to take a photo of a Short-billed Dowitcher. The part about a short bill is completely misleading because the other kind of dowitcher's bill is often the same length, and without a direct, side-by-side comparison, that's not a good field mark. What's better, as I've learned today, is that there are subtle differences in body color. The most distinctive feature, a patch of feathers making a white streak up from the tail onto the back, can only be observed when they fly. Of course, the ones here are studiously probing the muddy sand with their bills, moving them up-down-up-down like sewing machine needles, and they seldom fly up to a new feeding patch. But when they do, that white patch of feathers sure helps confirm their identity. They've spent the winter here and will be flying up to the tundra in northern Canada soon.

As we encounter and study the many kinds of shorebirds, I find myself silently asking myself, is that the same as the bird I saw before, or is it different? Same or different, same or different, becomes a steady refrain in my mind as I look at individual birds within each group on the sand. Sometimes it's obviously different, sometimes I have to puzzle—and I have to admit that sometimes I give up and look at something else that's easier to decipher.

Another winter visitor who will soon head to the far north, a Ruddy Turnstone, is poking around and flipping little pebbles on the beach. Its back and wing feathers are a sort of reddish orange, but for me the easiest and most obvious thing to notice is the semicircular black bib on its upper breast. That's how it's different from the other birds we've seen so far. And bib is the right word—the black feathers on this bird do extend down onto the breast in a semicircular patch, just like a child's bib, very different from the single-line black necklace of the Wilson's Plover, or the double black line of necklaces of a Killdeer. This is exactly the kind of field mark expertise I'm trying to develop while on this trip, and I'm smiling again.

When we turn back to look at the dunes again, we are just in time to see a Northern Harrier, formerly known as the Marsh Hawk, sweep across the grasses quite low, looking for unwary shorebirds to snatch up. It cruises back and forth two times but finds no prey and glides off to hunt another section of the beach. I know this slim hunter from home, where it will cruise in just the same style over farm fields as well as cattail marshes.

Here and there we see a few overwintering Lesser Yellowlegs, so called because they are shorter than the other kind, and their legs are somewhat thinner but of course still yellow. At a glance, the Lesser Yellowlegs looks a lot like a Willet, but it's smaller, with a more speckled feather pattern and a shorter bill. Now that I've seen both today, I hope I will remember these differences.

In the distance, on the open water, several American White Pelicans glide around together. It's nice to see a bird I know well and that cannot be confused with anything else! They're one of the largest birds at the shore, and that long bill with the pouch of loose skin is unmistakable. They're bigger than Brown Pelicans, and the feather colors also make them easy to tell apart from their cousins.

Another distinctive bird, a White Ibis, its black wing tips easily seen, flies over.

A short while later a Forster's Tern appears. For this species, the best way I can remember it is by using two field marks together, the black tip on the orange bill and the fact that its wings are almost entirely the same whitish gray with no darkness at the tips. Conveniently enough, a much larger tern flies past next, the huge Caspian Tern, which, along with its enormous size, is easy to remember because its thick bill is completely orange. Both of these tern species spend the winter here on the Gulf Coast then fly inland on their way to breeding grounds up north. Yet another tern zooms past, the aptly named Least Tern, the smallest of the terns I'm likely to encounter anywhere in North America, and one I also already know from Florida. It's like a miniature version of Forster's Tern, but with a white forehead when seen from the proper angle.

§

The birds along the shore are constantly in motion, walking or running along the sand, then flying up for short distances, then settling on a fresh patch of sand to look for food again. One with black armpits (I guess wingpits would be a better word) flies over—that's the Black-bellied Plover. It's easier for me to identify it by the wingpit field mark than the belly, because the black feathers appear on the belly only during breeding season. And there are other bird species that have black bellies. These plovers have a long journey ahead up to their breeding territories in the Arctic tundra regions.

Someone much more familiar with the subtle differences among shorebirds, which would be just about everybody here but me, points out a Red Knot to the right of two much taller Willets. When I hear the word "red" in a bird's name I tend to think of the scarlet or crimson feathers of songbirds like cardinals and tanagers, or the bright red head markings on woodpeckers. But the reds on shorebirds are more in the rusty or brick red range of hawk feathers. Indeed, the Red Knot's breast feathers are russet. The Red Knot is sort of stocky looking, and yet another lifer for me. Like so many of the birds I'm encountering on this trip, being able to look at them here on the gulf coast of Texas is probably the only practical way to see them, since they, too, spend the summer in the Arctic regions far north in Canada.

The small, grayish birds on the sand are actually Black Terns who've recently arrived on the Texas Coast from their wintering grounds somewhere in South America. With their gray wings folded down onto their bodies, it's hard to see any black on their breasts from this angle. Although it is easy for me to distinguish the body shape of a tern from a gull, figuring out which tern is what, other than the really big ones like Caspian or the little guys like the Least, is much harder. And to make it more complicated, there are some Sandwich Terns mixed in with the Black Terns. The Sandwich Terns are bigger, lighter colored, and the tip of the bill is slightly yellow, instead of the more typical black or orange. To remember this one I've had to resort to a trick—if the bill looks like the bird's been tasting mayonnaise, then it's a Sandwich Tern. Silly, but it works. When the terns fly up from the sand to go elsewhere, their wings create the illusion of a shower of confetti, only this shower begins at ground level, bursts upward instead of floating down, and then flies away to the next stretch of beach.

The terns squeal as they move around, and the various gulls make a lot of noise, too, but the only bird sound that I recognize belongs to the Laughing Gulls that are swirling around and kiting above me in the breeze. In fields, marshes, swamps, and well-treed areas I know the sounds of a lot of songbirds, but here at the shore my ears are not much help to me. Part of that is because I'm focusing on the visual clues and have not studied the vocalizations of shorebirds. They don't sing long melodies, but rely on short calls to communicate with each other. I suspect that even if I did study their calls, there might not be enough of a difference among them for that to be useful, and it's also hard to pick up individual sounds above the background noise of the surf. I haven't learned yet to tune out the ambient noises at the shore, so I have to rely on my eyes instead of my ears.

We've been out on the sand for about two hours and the guides are ready to leave to go back to High Island, so we turn to walk toward the cars. As we get closer to the parking area we pass near some dune grasses. A small, streaky brown bird flits back and forth, and we stop for a closer look. With binoculars I can see a whitish—or is it yellow?—eye stripe, and the really tall guy standing next to me identifies it for me. It's a Savannah Sparrow, another lifer. It's spent the winter here and will soon go north to nest in grassy fields, anywhere from northern Kentucky all the way up throughout Canada.

More noisy Laughing Gulls fly over, then I spot a Ring-billed Gull just as I get to my car. Gulls are notoriously difficult to tell apart because they change their plumage so many times as they mature over three to four years. That's not the case with songbirds, who reach adult status in roughly a single year. Generally speaking, songbirds have a short period of juvenile plumage during the summer and fall of their hatch year. Then as adults they alternate between breeding plumage each spring and non-breeding plumage each fall, although many look the same year-round. The biggest trick with songbirds is to be able to memorize the difference between adult males and females, who are often drabber versions of the more showy males.

But with gulls, things can get very complicated. Gulls take a much longer time to reach adulthood, and there are subtle differences in the colors of the feathers on the body and the head and the wings between first-, second-, and third-year plumage, then final adult plumage—and sometimes a third-year gull of one species can look almost like a second-year gull of a different species. And to my eye, there doesn't seem to be much difference between the males and the females in the various species.

Among the few adult gull species I know, if the bill has a black band towards the end but not actually at the tip, and if that band goes all the way around, and if there are no red marks on the bill, then it's a Ring-billed Gull. It takes longer to think through that string of details that than it does to see it—I can pick out all I need to know about that gull's bill in a microsecond and know for sure if I am looking at a Ring-billed Gull. They're a very widespread species, often wintering in the Ohio River Valley, and I've learned to recognize the adults quickly and easily.

As I get closer to my car, I'm looking down at the sand for pretty shells. Instead I find a gull feather, so I pick it up to study. It's solid white. When I want to measure things when I'm outdoors, I have my own system that relies on what I know about parts of my own body. When I spread my fingers out as if to play an octave on a piano keyboard, I know that the distance from my thumb tip to my little fingertip is eight inches. When I hold this feather across my hand, it reaches a bit beyond, so it's about nine inches long. The stiff center part of a feather has two names. The tubular section at the base is the quill, and the tapering, stiff section supporting the vanes is called the shaft. The vanes on this feather are not of equal length on each side of the shaft. The ones on the right side are short, maybe half an inch, and the vanes on the left are more than an inch long, so that the overall shape is asymmetrical. Other details about the way the vane curves slightly instead of being perfectly flat are clues to its function. This is a gull's tail feather, and because it's rather long I think it belonged to a Ring-billed Gull.

It's been here on the wet sand for a while because some of the vanes have separated from each other. But I can fix that easily by running my fingers across the vanes, sort of the way a bird would use its bill when grooming itself. Each vane has tiny little structures called barbs, barbicels, and barbules that overlap and interlock in a gridlike pattern. There. I've zipped it back together so all is smooth again.

I've been considering getting one of my folding chairs out to go sit on the sand and watch the shorebirds quietly just by myself. It would be a good test to see how much of what I've learned today I can remember, and if it will help me identify more shorebirds than I knew how to recognize when I got here. But it's been a very long time since breakfast, and there's another guided tour back in the woods at High Island later this afternoon. Lunch wins.

I stop in at a local place along the highway, the Fanta Sea BBQ and Grill restaurant, for a quick meal at the bar and to relax a bit out of the wind. The wooden bar stools are each painted a different color, some deep pink, others blue, yellow, or green, very tropical looking. The slatted wood seats have no back supports. I choose a blue one and settle in to wait for my chopped barbecued beef brisket sandwich.

I take a few minutes to check social media and see alluring photos of handsome Texas birds, birds that I hope to see soon. But will I know them when I see them for real? I don't know how I'm going to sort out all the different field marks I learned today at the shore. Well, "learned" may not be the right word. They were pointed out to me, but whether I actually know them in the sense of being able to remember them and recall that information to use in the field from now on is a question that remains to be answered.

After lunch I drive the rest of the way back to the High Island area and confuse the daylights out of my GPS trying to get to the Smith Oaks Bird Sanctuary area. Eventually I find it, but the gravel parking lot is very crowded already. I finally find a spot big enough for my SUV and once again load up my neck with the straps for my camera and my binoculars, rub on a few squirts of Avon Skin-So-Soft as insect repellent, adjust my ball cap again, put pen and notebook in my pocket, and look around for the meeting spot.

I walk over to a small collection of birders, easy to identify because most of them have binoculars or cameras or both, and ask them about the guided hike. Yes, that's what they're here for, too, but nobody seems to know where the guide is. It's getting hot standing in the sun, but all of us have on hats of some sort, some fresh looking, others quite well worn and shabby at the edges. Several people have enamel pins depicting favorite birds or favorite birding sites decorating their hats.

A few minutes later one of the same guys who led the caravan to the beach turns up and says we will enter the woods on foot from the other end of the parking lot. He's been here all week, checking the woods several times a day and trading notes with other birders about what they've spotted. He thinks we'll have the most opportunities to see songbirds if we walk a certain path in a certain direction, even this late in the afternoon. I'm trying to shift my brain into search-greenery mode, which is what I do at home, from the search-sand-and-mudflats mode of a few hours ago.

§

We walk single file to get around a sawhorse trail barrier and onto a brown dirt path just as a Turkey Vulture soars above us. This is the kind of birding I'm accustomed to, walking through dappled shade, scanning the tree limbs, and leaning this way and that to look into dimly lit clumps of leaves, with ears on alert for familiar songs and calls.

As we walk along, I stop and say, "There's a red bird over there that is not a Northern Cardinal," and as we peer through the green leaves, we get a good view of a male Summer Tanager. That's the kind of red I know so well. These woodland birds spend the winter on Caribbean islands and in Central America. Perhaps this one just flew over the Gulf of Mexico last night. That's why this tract of mature live oaks and the brushy undergrowth is so important here, not just because it's a place to perch after that long flight, but because it's full of food. Caterpillars, bugs, spiders, all sorts of protein-rich insect and arachnid food is available here for the migrants, and they search greedily among the leaves and on the bark for tasty morsels.

Someone else spots a Blue-headed Vireo a bit farther down the trail. I get a glimpse of the white spectacles and a head that looks more gray than blue to me, but by the time I get my camera focused, all I capture is a swaying green branch where the bird was—but is not now. Oh, yes, this, too, is a familiar part of birding, a photo of the Nothing Bird. I hear a Northern Cardinal calling, then some squawks from a Blue Jay.

The trail leads into an area with large openings in the tree canopy, and the guide looks skyward, alerted by a shadow on the trail ahead, just in time to announce a raptor overhead. It's a new one for me, a Swainson's Hawk. My overall impression is of a bird that's light on the underside with a dark, hooded look to its neck and head. The other hawks I know are either found throughout North America, or just in the east, but Swainson's Hawk is a bird of the western United States, so it's no wonder I haven't seen one before. This is the far eastern edge of its summer range.

Since we're not seeing or hearing many songbirds, we talk quietly about hawks for a while, and the tour guide mentions that hawks do not like to fly over open water. This bird has been making its way north from South America through Central America over land, preferring to hug the coast or stay well inland, hunting for rodents and grasshoppers and other small prey over farm fields and other open grassy spots.

As we walk along, a keen-eyed birder spots a bonus, a pretty green frog hopping across the leaf litter in the path. If it doesn't find a place to hide soon, it might be a bird's dinner later.

Somewhere nearby I hear the familiar song of a White-throated Sparrow, a species that often spends the winter at my place in Kentucky. I did not know that they also come this far south. As we walk along, we come to a mulberry tree and find a beautiful red-and-black male Scarlet Tanager, newly arrived from South America, and then a handsome, rich blue male Indigo Bunting, one of my favorite songbirds, busily eating the berries. I've been thinking about these woods as a nice place for insect food, but they do offer fruit as well. The Indigo Bunting may have spent the winter in Texas, or could have just flown in from the Caribbean.

The next part of the trail skirts a more open area, and we see a Black Vulture soaring above us. We've been walking for at least an hour with few birds spotted, but our guide is not yet ready to give up on finding more migrant songbirds.

He recommends that we take a fork in the trail that will lead us to something called Don's Drip. I have no idea what he is talking about until we get to a spot in lightly cleared brush where I see a contraption with fresh water dripping out of it. Bird baths in the shape of elevated puddles I know, and many of my friends put up artificial feeders to attract birds, everything from sugar water "nectar" for hummingbirds, to seed dispenser tubes, suet cakes, orange slices, even saucers of grape jelly, but a watering device like this is news to me. Apparently birds hear the water as each droplet falls and will come to drink and to splash around.

Sure enough, we see a Hooded Warbler skulking around in the brushy undergrowth by the dripping water, yet another lifer for me. This one, a male, is easy to recognize because his head does appear to be covered by a black hood, but one with an exceptionally large oblong opening that extends from ear to ear, if one could see the ears beneath the feathers. The area not covered with black feathers is bright yellow, as are his belly feathers, but his wings are a sort of olive green. Perhaps he's just flown across the Gulf of Mexico nonstop from the Yucatán Peninsula of Mexico last night, and fresh water to drink this afternoon is exactly what he needs.

As we walk back to the parking lot I hear the soft cooing of a Mourning Dove, then the rattling call of a Belted Kingfisher. We talk about the weather and how it influences the flight behavior of the migrants. Just now the weather's been too good—no big lines of thunderstorms to keep the birds here along the coast for an extra day or two before they continue northward, so there are no big concentrations of migrants. And it's still a bit early in the season for many species. But I have enjoyed the afternoon very much.

Back at my car, which is quite hot from sitting closed up and tightly locked in the sunshine, I open the windows and look through the folder with all my travel confirmations. I find the one for the hotel in Galveston where I have a room reserved for tonight and enter the address into my GPS system. While it plans the route, I also take a look at one of my paper maps. The hotel is only about thirty-five miles away, but the journey will take extra time because I will have to take a ferry to cross over the waters at the entrance to Galveston Bay from Bolivar Flats to get onto Galveston Island.

§

The first part of my drive is backtracking, going south along the road I just traveled when going to look at the shorebirds on Bolivar Flats from High Island and back again to the woods. As I cruise along this time I take a closer look at all the houses on stilts—even the air conditioner compressors are on stilts—and think about the differences between how birds cope with life along the Gulf Coast and what people do. The shore birds that live here year-round at the side of the water build simple nests of twigs and such, or just scrape together some rocks on the sand in the spring, well before hurricane season. Their children have fledged and begun independent lives by the end of summer, and they don't need permanent bases. The larger birds such as the heron and egrets and cormorants build bigger stick nests in trees, but their young are also able to fly and fend for themselves before hurricane season starts. When the winds and rains and tidal storm surges come with hurricanes, birds of all sizes can just fly away inland, and return when things get back to normal.

I don't get much farther with that train of thought because I'm starting to see highway signs about the ferry, and my GPS keeps adjusting my expected arrival time at my hotel. The free ferry service is very busy this time of day, and there will be a delay.

Near the water I pull into the holding lanes filled with cars and trucks and look around. Dozens of Laughing Gulls scream as they fly over the vehicles waiting in line, some in daredevil fashion, others obviously begging for food. Some folks do toss out tidbits for them, so apparently it's a worthwhile feeding strategy. When it's finally my turn to drive onto the ferry, I notice a Rock Pigeon perched on the superstructure of the ferry. Apparently it, too, wants a free ride over to the island.

The crossing is easy, and one of the ferrymen soon waves my lane of vehicles off onto land. I've arrived at the northeast end of Galveston Island. This is the first real island, surrounded completely by water, that I've visited on this trip. It's a skinny barrier island, roughly twenty-seven miles long and only three miles across at its widest. Right now all I know of its history is that there was a tremendous hurricane in 1900 with a storm surge and winds and rain that killed at least eight thousand people and utterly destroyed many homes and business. I think Ike made a big mess here, too.

It takes only a few minutes to get my hotel on Pier 21. As I drive along the street, I realize that I've come far enough south to be in another vegetation zone—there are palm trees here! My GPS has done a good job getting me here, except it doesn't know where the entrance to the parking lot is. I figure that out for myself and check in to the hotel a little before sunset.

The Harbor House is a local independent hotel, affiliated with an international hotel group that I seldom use. It's not a chain in the usual sense because each hotel is a unique property with a unique design. This one is rather small, with only forty-two rooms. It also has a style of hurricane shutters I've not seen before. On one side of each window, a big flat square that resembles a barn door lies flat against the building's exterior. When needed, these swing over to cover the windows, like a closing a book's cover.

Inside there's no large, formal lobby, just a small registration desk on the ground floor—the rest of the building at sidewalk level is taken up by restaurants and bars that are separate businesses from the hotel. I take the one elevator up to my room, unlock the door, and am amazed. It's even nicer than the photos! It's big, with modern furniture and classily elegant seaside decor. I chose it using the internet, and it's living up to my expectations. I look out the window across the parking lot and into the distance at the piers and ships on the water. This is going to be my base for a while, and I like it.

After washing my face and freshening up a bit, I go downstairs to explore the pier. I find a fun statue of a boy feeding gulls and listen as the real Laughing Gulls flying about call to each other before sunset. This is a working pier, with bollards for large ships to make fast to, and a small marina for pleasure craft. Hotel guests sometimes do arrive by their own yachts and dock here.

For dinner I choose a restaurant in my hotel's building that faces the water. The Olympia is a grill and bar with a Greek theme to the menu. Instead of my usual indoor dinner request, a seat at the bar, I ask for an outdoor table and the hostess finds one for me slightly around the corner of the patio, a bit out of the breeze. Other than standing by the hood of my car, this is my first nice outdoor meal of the trip. And I'm glad I thought to bring my windbreaker along, because now that the sun's set, the breeze feels cool. I choose a glass of chardonnay from Becker Vineyards, a Texas winery. When my waiter Marvin brings it he kindly takes a photo of me with my cell phone so I'll have something to share with my friends back home.

While enjoying a small plate of fresh blue crab cakes with a superb remoulade sauce for dinner, I think about today's birding adventures. My field notebook is out in the car, so I can't refer to it for details, but my overall impression is one of great pleasure and satisfaction. I saw birds I know from Florida and birds I know from the Ohio River Valley, and learned the field marks of at least seven new birds. No, eight. I must look kind of silly sitting here with a wine glass and counting on my fingers, but I don't care. I go over their names again. Ah, yes, it's really nine new birds in one day, some at the shore, some in the woods.

After dinner I walk out onto the concrete pier for a while and find a very pretty black cat with white paws and a white nose. It seems very comfortable and familiar with the area but doesn't want me to get too close. It wanders off toward the end of the pier and I go upstairs to my room. I had the best intentions of studying some of my bird books tonight to help remember what I learned today, but that second glass of wine with dinner has made me ready for sleep instead.

###

CHAPTER SIX

Galveston
and Goose Island State Park

History tidbits, puddle birding, camping

When I walk outside this morning, Laughing Gulls soar and flap above me. It's sunny, and the air is warmer than last night.

After a light breakfast in a smallish room on the hotel's second floor, I've decided to explore some of the human history in Galveston today from the point of view of the water. When I walk up to the sidewalk sales booth for the harbor and dolphin cruise, I find out that there is room for me on the first cruise of the day—which will leave in five minutes. Good travel karma once again. I buy a ticket and as the ever-present Laughing Gulls wheel overhead, I step aboard the small boat. It's a jet-drive boat with no propellers, so it's safe to maneuver around any dolphins we may encounter this morning. I'm the last passenger to board, and as soon I settle into a seat, the captain steers the boat out into the shipping channel that runs between Galveston Island and Pelican Island.

This is the local Pelican Island of Texas, a mostly commercially developed area, not at all like the Pelican Island I know in the Indian River Lagoon on the Atlantic coast of Florida. The island in Florida is strictly for wild things, with no human structures, and is the centerpiece of more than five thousand acres of land and water that are protected within the Pelican Island National Wildlife Refuge, established in 1903, the first of its kind. I visited the mainland section of that refuge during a trip to a friend's wedding several years ago, but the boat ride I'd scheduled to cruise around the island that day was cancelled due to bad weather. My visit did spark my interest in learning more about the other places within the refuge system. From its simple beginnings, it's grown to include more than five hundred sixty refuges and other protected areas, with more than one hundred fifty million acres of land and water in all.

As we motor along here in Texas, the captain keeps up a steady stream of informative talk, pointing out where oil rigs have been brought in from the Gulf for repairs or dry dock on this Pelican Island. Then he shows us where the banana boats from Central and South America deliver their cargo at a pier on the Galveston Island side of the bay, and the place where cruise ships moor, although none are in port today.

For a few minutes we idle in front of an area where huge emergency response vessels stand ready to go out at a moment's notice in case of an oil spill or other disaster on the coast or out in the Gulf. As the captain talks about the fleet of six ferries that operate around the clock between Bolivar Peninsula and Galveston Island, weather permitting, he maneuvers our boat cautiously so we can get a good look at a dolphin swimming nearby. The captain also tells us about the Galveston-Texas City Pilots group that provides skilled navigators throughout the Galveston County area to guide ships to and from their berths. Their services are necessary for the safety of humans and their property—and to protect wildlife, too.

On solid ground again after the hour-long cruise, I walk over to the next pier to visit the Texas Seaport Museum. I enjoy maritime history, especially the age of sail, and this is the home of the restored Elissa, a cargo ship built in 1877. She docked here in Galveston during the 1880s to load Texas cotton and sail across the Atlantic Ocean to deliver the cotton to mills in England. The short movie inside the museum tells about the ship's history and how she was restored to her present beauty. I'm outside now to go aboard her. She's a tall ship, and does sail out onto open water at least once a year, but right now her cloth sails are tightly furled while she's moored in port.

As I explore belowdecks to look at the living quarters of the captain and crewmembers, I think about the early naturalists who traveled the world making observations and discoveries in ships like this one. Their notes about birds at sea and along the coastlines of islands and continents provided the first accurate information about bird migration—and they did it with quill pens trimmed from bird feathers, dipped in ink of often indifferent quality, written on paper—no keyboards, no computers, no flat screens, no cell phones. Often their carefully prepared and preserved bird skins and detailed natural history notes and drawings made it back to private collections or museums on land—and sometimes they sank without a trace during a storm or battle at sea. I marvel again at what they managed to accomplish in spite of hardships and disasters.

Returning to dry land again, I notice some Brown Pelicans in the harbor area. Generally speaking, Brown Pelicans prefer salt water and hunt as individuals. Small groups of them may hunt in the same area, but I have never seen them engage in any kind of cooperative hunting behavior. One bird sees one fish and plunges in, that's it. American White Pelicans, however, will bunch up together and form a circle around a school of fish, closing in tighter and tighter, and then feed together as a group on the fish trapped in the center. I've seen both species hunting in their own styles in Florida, but these Brown Pelicans are not actively hunting, just loafing around this morning.

I'm beginning to get hungry so I walk a few blocks inland to Galveston's historic district, where Great-tailed Grackles are calling and strutting around on the sidewalks. Some European Starlings flit past, too. At the local candy shop, La King's Confectionery, I buy a small sampling of chocolates shaped like lobsters, crabs, and seashells, to snack on later, then start looking for a place to eat a real lunch.

I find a nice table in an inner courtyard at the Stuttgarden Tavern on The Strand and enjoy a cold Texas beer, a crisp pilsner from the Alamo Beer Company over in San Antonio, and a big, lopsided, loopy pretzel with their version of beer cheese. Unlike the spicy cheddar version invented in Kentucky and usually served cold, this local Texas delight is more like a fondue, a warm blend of smoked gouda cheese and beer, a deliciously creamy concoction. I tear off small pieces of the soft pretzel and dip them into the cheese—perfection!

After lunch I look in some shops, buy a sarong-type batik cotton scarf with a palm tree design, then retrace my steps to my hotel. I can drive out of and back into the hotel parking lot as many times as I want to for one daily fee, so I'm going to go exploring some World War II history out on Pelican Island. I've cued up some big band jazz to listen to on my way, with some classic swing tunes by Benny Goodman and Tommy Dorsey from the early 1940s.

To get to the other island I will have to drive all the way to the end of Harborside Drive on this island, go across the huge Galveston Causeway and then on to the west side of Pelican Island. Along the way there are bits of marshy ground off to the sides of the road, and as I drive along in the light afternoon traffic I duck my head this way and that way trying to follow the flight of a Roseate Spoonbill. It's not really the best technique for driving a car, but I can't resist such a pretty bird.

Driving down from the causeway's steeply pitched bridge, I discover that this end of Pelican Island is home to the Mitchell Campus of Texas A & M University, the Sea Aggies, which offers undergraduate and graduate students classroom and practical instruction for a variety of maritime careers. Right next door to the campus is what I've come to see, the ships on display at Seawolf Park. Here I can tour two historic World War II–era ships, the USS Stewart, hull number DE-238, a destroyer escort that saw service in the North Atlantic, and the USS Cavalla, hull number SS-244, a submarine that was built in a Houston shipyard and served in the Pacific Ocean.

I walk up some steps and across a short gangway to board the USS Stewart. This oceangoing vessel is much bigger than any ship I've been on lately. On the upward-sloping deck at the prow, an instructor from the university explains the intricacies of the various thick ropes coiled on the deck to half a dozen students in blue Sea Aggie jumpsuits. She tells them about the proper sequence for casting off mooring lines and stowing them—apparently this will be on the quiz tomorrow. I move aside and watch terns swooping over the bay, and hear gulls screaming nearby. Only a few parts of the lower decks are open to tourists, so it doesn't take long to walk through the various compartments.

The odd thing about the submarine is that it isn't in the water like the destroyer escort, which is still afloat in Galveston Bay. Instead, the sub is perched on a grassy strip of dry land. But as I climb farther and farther down into the USS Cavella's lowest quarters, I realize that I wouldn't last even one full day on a submerged cruise. It isn't just the careful movements required in the confinement of such small spaces that distresses me—the thought of not being able to look up freely at the sky is truly oppressive.

Back at my car, I'm ready for some different music, so I cue up my "Victory at Sea" CD from the award-winning television documentary series aired in the 1950s. I'm also ready for some more birdwatching but don't know what I'll be able to find so late in the afternoon on such a breezy day. I make a very quick check of my books and ask my GPS to take me to a local municipal park that's supposed to be a good birdwatching site. Re-crossing the causeway to return to Galveston Island, I get a good look at a Great Blue Heron flying over, then a Great Egret.

§

This is odd. When I get to the small local park it is deserted—no people in sight at a time of day when working folks should be home and out walking their dogs or playing with their children. There are plenty of houses nearby. At the very least there ought to be some folks exercising, taking walks, something. But the small parking lot is completely empty of cars, and I do not see anyone on foot or on bicycles. There are mature trees that might host some birds, but the complete lack of people in a park in daylight is not a good sign from the safety standpoint. I stay in my car to make a quick study of my maps and decide to drive out toward the Gulf.

My route takes me through a very old residential area of Galveston with wooden houses painted a variety of colors, some pastel, some bright, and then I reach Seawall Boulevard. This is the modern, tourist-oriented section of Galveston, with big hotels, condominiums, and apartment complexes on the landward side and fishing piers and beaches on the Gulf side. The surf is pounding on the beach, with big waves throwing spray every which way. Gulls dash about and I pull off into a parking lot to look at one of the small local maps I have. The only place with a binocular icon, the common symbol for birdwatching and wildlife viewing areas, is Galveston Island State Park, several miles farther to the southwest. I don't take the time to look at my birdwatching books because the sun will be setting soon and I need to make a quick choice.

My travel karma is shifting. When I arrive at the park, the visitor center is closed, and there are only a few RVs parked in the camping areas nearest the Gulf. I don't see anywhere in the immediate area that looks like a good place to find birds, and it's getting late and I'm getting hungry after such a light lunch so long ago. My maps show that there is another section of the park on the bayou side, but I'm ready to drive back to my hotel and call this day done.

Back at the hotel pier, I walk to a nearby restaurant I'd noticed in the morning, but only indoor tables are available and the wait time is too long. Instead, I return to the Olympia to dine outdoors on shrimp with asparagus and a Greek variation of potatoes au gratin, with grilled triangles of pita bread. As I leave my table, I catch a glimpse of a tortoiseshell cat who apparently has a good relationship with some of the restaurant's servers regarding leftover food tidbits. I take a nice, long look at the full moon rising between two palm trees before going up to my room.

Since I didn't see any new birds today, and very few species of any kind, I'm going to take a few minutes to review my notes and bring my rough life list for the trip up to date. I also need to reorganize my duffle bag and make notes to myself about what to do in the morning. I'll be checking out and heading farther south, and I want to get on the road as early as possible without rushing.

§

After a quick walk on the pier and breakfast upstairs in the hotel, I check out and spend a few minutes studying maps in my car. I can drive along the coast going south for a while, but not very far. Generally speaking, the barrier islands are not suitable for roads, and huge sections are set aside for wildlife. So to get to today's destination I will need to go inland to the west before I can drive south. I drive back through the old residential section of Galveston where I was late yesterday, stop to buy gas on Seawall Boulevard, and clean not just my windshield but also my side mirrors. Driving along the coast presents new challenges. Yesterday I saw a road sign that said, "watch for debris on road," which is a good reminder for me to be on the lookout for seaweed and driftwood and such. Today's highway sign says, "watch for sand in road" —but I knew that already. Sand blows everywhere and it's all over my car!

Business signs here are interesting, too. I just passed one that said, "Don't let your boat house become a bird house — we sell anti-bird netting." Apparently not everybody thinks that swallow nests are desirable.

But my favorite road sign this morning is a simple yellow triangle that says, "Drive friendly." I like it.

The wind is really blustery today. At the toll booth on the bridge over San Luis Pass, the toll keeper's made a hand-written sign on a piece of cardboard and taped it to the inside of the glass window: "Put money under rock so it doesn't blow away. Thanks." I follow his instructions with my two dollars and drive on south and west.

In mid-morning I pull off the side of the road to get a better view of waterfowl at one of the many roadside puddles. Traffic here on this section of road is extremely sparse, with just an occasional car or truck zooming past very infrequently. Often ten minutes or more pass with nothing to obstruct my view of the water on the other side of the road from where I'm parked.

I'm feeling quite satisfied with my birding skills today—I can immediately see that the pretty ducks with day-glo pinkish-orange bills at the far side of the water are Black-bellied Whistling-Ducks, a species I just saw for the first time last week in Louisiana. Identifying the Ring-billed Gulls and American Coots is also easy, as I've known these two species for several years at home and in Florida. I take a few photos and keep scanning the area with my binoculars. Some Brown Pelicans fly over in their stately yet somewhat lumbering fashion, and Great-tailed Grackles keep up a steady stream of crazy chatter. The Blue-winged Teal bathing and preening are easy for me to recognize, too.

But I get my comeuppance when a tern shows up. Black bill, black eye, white wings with a grayish wash. What is it? Could it be a Forster's Tern? That seems logical, but when I write the name in my field notes I add a question mark. I really need to work on terns whenever I get the time to study my books. Maybe later I can make my own chart of key field marks to use as a guide.

I'm ready now to get back on the road, so I check my GPS info and start the engine. The commercial activity on this section of the coast is mostly part of the oil and gas industry, but exactly what the various companies do is something I do not know. I see lots of complicated structures with huge pipes that form interesting geometric tangles, but their purpose is not obvious to me. While gawking at the structures on the side of the road I manage to miss a turn and end up going in a lopsided circle that puts me on a single lane of crumbling, dirt-covered asphalt underneath an overpass, with signs saying "road closed ahead."

I don't want to say that I'm lost, but for sure I am not where I should be.

I back up, turn around, and start over, driving very slowly, waiting for my GPS to catch up with my mistakes. Back on track, I continue to drive northwest to go inland to the better roads that will take me further south. Sometimes it's necessary to jog around the compass, rather like a sailing ship tacking, to get to the roads that have bridges over the various rivers and creeks between me and where I need to be later today.

After another hour of driving, I find a place to pull off the road and catch up with some of my travel notes for this section of Texas State Highway 35, and take another look at my paper maps. I'm in Bay City, the county seat of Matagorda County, near the courthouse, a very modern, boxy-looking building. Looking carefully at my maps I see that yes, I really am making progress toward my goal and should arrive in midafternoon.

Back on the road, I enter Calhoun County, where a huge billboard asks, "Hungry yet?" and provides some advice: "Turn left at the light after the causeway." It only takes me a split second to determine that I am indeed ready for lunch, so after driving over the very long causeway across Lavaca Bay I slow down to look for the Texas Traditions restaurant in Port Lavaca. I find it near the heart of the town's old center and enjoy an ample lunch of home-style cooking—meatloaf, green beans, mashed potatoes, a roll with butter, then fresh banana pudding for dessert. After lunch, the case of homemade pies at the cash register requires careful study before I settle on a slice of apple crumb pie as takeout for breakfast tomorrow.

I drive almost straight south on Texas 35 for about an hour to reach my base for the next few days, Goose Island State Park, which is not really an island. It's just the name of the park on the Lamar Peninsula that juts down from the mainland between Aransas Bay and St. Charles Bay. Unlike many other parks, my advance reservation here did not include a specific site, so I'm delighted to find out that the one I want in the wooded area is available for tonight, tomorrow night, and the next night.

As I settle all the details with the very friendly park ranger, I mention my interest in birds. She gives me a little piece of salmon-colored paper with a drawing of shorebirds at the top and the schedule for this month's bird walks neatly typed below. The first one this week is tomorrow morning, so I've timed this visit very well. I also pick up a beautifully illustrated visitor guide map to the nearby towns of Fulton and Rockport.

§

I find my campsite number, pull in, open the liftgate of my SUV, and set to work to make my home away from home appear. It's sunny, warm, and humid as I work at my own pace, and I'm glad to stop for a phone chat with my daughter when she calls on her way home from work back in Ohio.

My notion of camping is definitely not roughing it, no indeed, none of that crawling around on hands and knees, sleeping on dirt stuff for me. Nope. My campsite is more like the general's headquarters, deluxe in every way I can make it so. I spread out my blue ground tarp, peg it, then begin setting up my tent. It's sold as a six-person tent—which means it's perfect for just me! The base is eleven feet by nine feet with a center interior height of six feet. That's enough headroom so I can stand up inside it with ease, plus have a place for my air mattress, a folding chair, and my duffle bag, and there's extra floor space for whatever else I might want to add. It's just like a real bedroom.

I know from experience that I can do everything by myself while I'm setting up camp, except for one detail. I need someone else to hold the opposite end of each of the two tension poles that form the dome of the tent. This is easy when I'm traveling with friends, but when I'm traveling solo I have to improvise. I look across the way and see that a couple with a gray Ford Ranger pickup truck and a pull-behind teardrop camper have already settled in. I walk over and ask if one of them could spare a minute or two to hold something for me. While Marcy introduces me to her little dog, her husband John says he'd be glad to help me.

At my campsite John tells me he had a similar tent years ago. When he sees that I already have the tension poles threaded through the tent's sleeves in the proper positions, he knows exactly what to do to get the hollow tip over the support and secured at the grommet on the base tab at his corners while I work on my corners. When we finish that, he very kindly offers to help me slide the rain fly over the tent, too. I've been checking the local weather forecast off and on all day, and getting the rain fly positioned correctly is a crucial detail. When we finish, I thank him, and we agree to visit back and forth later.

Now that I have everything pegged down securely, I can set up the interior just the way I like it. The blue-and-white striped quilt goes on the tent floor as an extra puncture preventative for my air mattress. This is one of the more expensive ones, but well worth it. I don't need to pump the air in. All I have to do is flip a switch for the self-contained, battery-powered fan to suck air in to fill up the mattress. Later, I can turn the switch the opposite way and use the fan to move air the other way to deflate the mattress when I'm ready to pack up and go.

I think I'd better take another look at the weather forecast. Although I brought my kitchen-in-a-box with me and my screen house with the shade canopy to put over the picnic table if I need to prepare real meals from scratch, I don't know if I'm going to use it. Rain is likely very soon. I'll just put off making any decisions about cooking until later and leave all that stuff in the car for now.

Looking at my new maps, I see that Fulton and Rockport, each with plenty of stores and restaurants, are only about a twenty-minute drive away. I check over the position of the rain fly on my tent one more time, look around to make sure I haven't left anything loose at my campsite, and get ready to drive to town to check out the food situation.

§

A line of intense thunderstorms with jagged lightning bolts and blasts of gusty winds rolls in just as I reach the main road. Severe thunderstorms with torrential rain and crazy winds are quite common in the Ohio River Valley, and I have plenty of experience driving in such conditions. I already have my headlights on and the fog lamps, too. The trick to driving in these kinds of storms is to keep both hands on the wheel and slow down—and keep a greater gap between my car and the next. I'll just keep going.

Some sort of roadwork is in progress here, and as I drive toward yet another causeway, this one connecting Lamar Peninsula to the mainland over Copana Bay, huge winds skid some of the orange barrels along the edge of the work zone right out onto the roadway in my lane of travel. I stop and put my hazard flashers on. A fellow in a pickup truck driving towards me from the opposite direction stops, and puts on his flashers and light bar (probably a member of the local fire department) to stop traffic on both sides. He walks out into the roadway and tosses the barrels out of the line of traffic back to where they belong. I cross the causeway with my windshield wipers on at top speed in the torrential rain, and begin looking for the turn to the restaurant that I have in mind for dinner.

By the time I arrive at Moondog Seaside Eatery, at Fulton Harbor, outdoor dining is out of the question, so I've found a seat at the bar inside. I chat with the bartender while sipping a beer, then order the fish tacos. Some other folks come in, and we talk up and down the bar while listening to the rain pounding on the roof.

The big fella at the far end of the bar works for a construction company that gets a lot of contracts from the state highway department. That suddenly makes his conversation much more interesting to the bearded guy sitting on my left who has oil rig and trucking experience but isn't all that happy with his current job. Big guy says, "Yes, we often have work available for someone with a CDL. Can you drive a straight line?" Bearded guy looks insulted, but big guy isn't being smart-alecky about the requirements to get a CDL. Big guy's quick to explain that his company paints the stripes on the sides and center of roads, and even with onboard computers and GPS systems, being able to physically keep the truck moving in a perfectly straight line is the key job skill to have. We all have a good laugh at that, and then I order a second beer when my fish tacos arrive.

After dinner on my way back to camp I stop at the convenience store at the corner gas station near the entrance to the park to buy milk and fresh ice to put in my coolers. I've got that slice of pie from the restaurant where I had lunch today, so I'm good for breakfast tomorrow. I can keep putting off making a decision about cooking in camp until lunchtime.

Rain is still dripping down steadily when I get back to my campsite. I'll just sit in my car for a while and check the weather radar again. The charge on my phone has run down a bit lower than I like, probably due to all the navigation today and that long phone call with my daughter. But when I plug my phone into the car charger nothing happens. The LED cord doesn't light up, and the battery-charging icon doesn't appear on my phone's screen, either. I jiggle things, I re-plug things, I try every electronics trick I know, until it is obvious that the charger is kaput and I'll have to buy a replacement somewhere in Rockport tomorrow.

As travel glitches go, this one is just a small annoyance, and I do have a backup solution. I can get my heavy-duty, all-weather extension cord out of my kitchen-in-a-box camping bin and plug it into the electric outlet at my campsite. Then I can add the power strip I carry with me for my electric skillet and burner coil, and use the wall charger device for hotel rooms to charge up my phone here in camp.

But I can't do any of that yet. It's still raining way too hard. I will have to wait until the rain stops and I can safely open the campsite electric box and flip the breaker switch to open the circuit. This is the first substantial rain of the trip, so I don't really mind the inconvenience. And a stormy night often means good birding the next day!

§

While I'm waiting for the rain to stop, I'd like to read through my field notes and look up a few things in my birding books. When I get inside my tent and sit down in my folding chair, I realize that I don't have good enough light. No matter how I hold what I want to read in my lap, the light from the LED lantern suspended by a carabiner clip in the center of the tent is not strong enough for eye comfort. Hmm. This is an unexpected problem. I only discovered the fun of camping two years ago, and on each trip I was always so busy doing things outdoors that when I finally got in my tent the only thing I wanted to do was go straight to sleep. I've never had time for reading. When I'm in town tomorrow to buy a new phone charger, I'll take a careful look around for possible solutions to this new lighting dilemma.

Ah, the rain has finally stopped. Now I can add the finishing touch to my campsite. My daughter gave me a string of battery-powered LED lights that I can attach to the rain fly support over my tent flap for a cool porch decoration. This is my first opportunity to use it, and I like the way the tiny lights gleam. It makes my tent look festive in a holiday sort of way.

Next, I plug in my extension cord to the electric service outlet at my site, then connect the phone charger, then the phone to let it recharge for a while. I stand by my car watching the latest camp arrivals maneuver into their site about four spaces to my right. The man is driving the pickup truck with an enormous camper on the hitch. The woman stands between the trees and holds a powerful light. Ever so slowly she guides him backwards between the huge live oak trees. It's obvious that they've done this many times before, no swearing, no frantic gestures, all very calm, very smooth, and no trees were harmed.

While watching the man angle and re-angle the truck to back into the campsite, I think a little bit about today's birds. I didn't make many birding notes during two hundred or so miles of driving, but that's okay. Tomorrow there will be new birds, new habitats to explore, lots of notes to make about whatever turns up.

When my phone's recharged past fifty percent I unplug it, switch off my decorative tent light string, set my alarm for early, and go into my tent to settle in for the night.

###

CHAPTER SEVEN

In and around Fulton and Rockport

Bayside birds, warblers, neighborhood parks

I set my phone alarm last night to be certain I'd have enough time this morning to eat breakfast and drive to the other side of the park for the guided bird walk that will begin at eight, but as it turns out, I really didn't need it. The fabric of my tent is designed to block out rain but not much daylight, so I wake up as the sky brightens before sunrise and am just sort of dozing when the alarm chimes. I get up and get dressed for the day, then go for a short walk past the shower house toward an open, weedy field beyond the campground. A brilliant red male Northern Cardinal is singing his cheerful song from a high tree branch, then a Northern Mockingbird begins a string of imitations. I listen for a while to these familiar birds, then go back to my campsite for breakfast.

This morning I'm having a birder's breakfast, tailgate style, standing by my now clean and shiny car. Last night's rainstorms provided a free car wash to rinse away the sand. The apple pie I bought yesterday is almost too sweet, but still very welcome with a cup of cold milk from my cooler.

Earlier this week some friends in a Texas bird group recommended the walks at this park but didn't give me any details. I finally figured out last night that the people they named in their post must be the same people who are going to guide the birding walk this morning.

It's an easy drive over to the opposite side of the park to the meeting spot at the fishing pier at Aransas Bay. I find a spot to park, then gather up my binoculars, camera, and notebook and look around for other birders. They're always easy enough to find—just look for more binoculars. Sure enough, I see half a dozen folks standing near the water's edge.

It's cool this morning, so most people are wearing windbreakers and ball caps. It's windy, too, so I also have a headband on over my ball cap to keep my ears comfy. Jane and Dave introduce themselves as our guides and give us a quick run-through of the plan for the morning. On many organized bird walks I've taken part in, the leader keeps up a fast pace and names off birds as he or she spots them. For those who don't see it right away, the leader gives some directional clues, such as "perched on the limb that would be at three on a clock face" or "in front of the closest cattail clump," and then it's rush on to the next thing. See bird, walk. See bird, walk. All very fast—and sometimes I don't see the bird.

When I lead bird walks or nature rambles back home in the Ohio River Valley, I go at a slow pace and ask as many questions as I answer because I like to get the people who've joined my group actively involved. I want them to have fun, whatever their level of experience. I like to provide context for why we're seeing what's in front of us at that particular time of year.

Dave and Jane are like that, too, and they don't plan to rush. Instead of simply marching along, pointing and naming as the leaders, they encourage us to make this a team effort, with all of us walking slowly and looking carefully, helping each other learn. Anyone can simply say the word "bird" to alert the group to something to look at. It could be one of us or it could be Dave or Jane. Whoever gets the first look should also give the usual directional clues such as "to left of the fishing pier" or "next to the biggest rock" so the others can find it. Then the spotter should begin describing whatever field marks are noticeable. This way everyone will be taking careful looks in order to notice something about each bird that will help us identify—and remember—whatever's in front of us or flying overhead. We're standing still, and I like this bird walk already! The name of the bird will not always be the first thing mentioned, especially if the bird is not common. We'll focus on the field marks first, then get around to a name a bit later.

Their system sounds good to me and all the other birders. We begin introducing ourselves briefly, then walk closer to the water's edge. I'm the only birder from Kentucky, although some folks have visited my state. Some of the other people have brought along their spotting scopes, so if something is really far away across the water, we can take turns looking.

Many of the folks here this morning are experienced birders, familiar with most of the larger coastal birds. I know a lot of the big, unique birds from Florida, and the ones that live in the Ohio River Valley, too. All of us recognize a Green Heron and a Great Blue Heron right away, and the wild chortling of some Laughing Gulls.

Then Jane sees a mostly gray bird approaching and as it flies over the other birders more familiar with its shape start telling me what to look at, the thick bill and the rather large feet trailing behind, and soon I know that it is a Common Loon. I've only seen one loon floating around on a freshwater lake in Kentucky one time, and that was just a few days before I began this trip, so I had no idea what its flight silhouette looks like. I'm learning something already!

The plump, mostly gray bird with a straight black bill walking along on the grassy edge between the gravel and the water is a Willet, and close enough for me to get an excellent photo.

My first lifer of the day is another shorebird, one that's a bit taller than a Willet and with a distinctly down-curved bill, a Whimbrel. The shape of the bill is the most easily noticeable feature, but looking closer, there are other differences, especially the dark brown and white stripes on the bird's head. And instead of gray, this new bird's body is a beige-y brown. The sky is covered with gray clouds, so the light is rather flat, but I actually like it because there isn't any glare. That makes it easier for me to see some of the finer details of the various birds on or near the water.

Some chunky Brown Pelicans fly over in a line, then I spot a Black Vulture flapping and gliding in the distance. Great Egrets like to hunt in the marshy grasses here, and I get a good photo of one stalking along, only its head and neck showing above the vegetation.

Jane helps us identify the tern flying past by telling us to focus our binoculars on the solid orange bill and listen to its two-note call. The bill color is something I can see easily, but the call is difficult for me to recognize. It just sounds screechy to me and I seriously doubt that I would recognize the call again, even if I heard it again within the next ten minutes. The bill and general size of the bird are enough for me to write it down in my notebook as a Royal Tern.

As we walk along I have no trouble recognizing a Black-crowned Night-Heron, or the Black-necked Stilt that flies over us. I'm more familiar with stilts standing in water, so to see it flying is a bit of a treat. The salt marshes here are the preferred habitat of another bird I know from Florida, the Tricolored Heron. The one stalking through the grasses is turned towards us, face-on, so we can see the white underparts on its breast, and that helps with the identification since there are other heron species of a similar size. When I first started learning the herons in Florida, this particular species' common name was Louisiana Heron, but somewhere along the line that was changed to Tricolored Heron, which I have to admit makes a lot more sense.

Turning towards the open water again, someone notices a shape out on the waves and calls out "bird on the water." We point our binoculars in the general direction but can't find it at first. We need help. Jane says, "See where the fishing pier stops? Now look towards us about thirty feet." We try, and try again. "See where there's an extra set of ripples on the waves? Now look to the left of that," she says, trying to think of features on the choppy water that will serve as clues to where to look.

Finally I get something bobbing up and down in view, and just as I sharpen my focus, it dives below the surface. Wait. Wait some more. Ah, it's back on the surface, and it's a Red-breasted Merganser. And now I see three others floating nearby. I often see this pointy-billed, ragged-crested species in the Ohio River Valley in autumn, resting and feeding on any available open water before flying on down to the Gulf Coast for the winter. I figure this little group will soon leave the coast to begin their journey back to their breeding grounds, and it's likely that they'll stop over briefly somewhere in my home area on their way north.

Jane and Dave live up near the Canadian border during the warmer months but have been spending the winter months along the Texas Coast for many years. They know the birds in both places extremely well, not just their field marks and songs, but also their migration patterns and the sequence in which they appear. As we walk along to a new section of the shore, Dave tells us that yesterday's wind patterns pushed many of the migrants to landfalls west of our location right now. Then he talks about the wind direction today, what the weather forecasts predict for the next day and a half, and how this is likely to affect the birds' movements and landfalls.

Just now a small group of grayish-brown birds flies past, showing us the patch of white feathers on their rumps. Those feathers and the time of the month—this is the second week of April—are the best clues to identify these migrants returning from South America. It's a little flock of White-rumped Sandpipers, an obvious name, and a lifer for me and two other birders in our group this morning.

As we walk along we talk about other birds with white patches of feathers, and how sometimes the best field marks show only when a bird is flying. Jane's carrying a field guide with her this morning that I haven't seen before (which is odd, considering the shelves full of bird books I have at home), and she turns to an especially useful section with a two-page spread of shorebirds in flight. We look at the illustration of a White-rumped Sandpiper and compare it to the other birds on the two pages. I like the way they are shown in correct relative size, with brief comments about the key field marks next to each species. Looking at the color paintings, I see exactly why the White-rumped Sandpiper is different from other similar species. I take a cell phone photo of that page and then ask Jane to close the book so I can get a photo of the cover, too. When I get home I can order a copy of the National Geographic's *Field Guide to the Birds of North America* to add to my collection.

Some Forster's Terns (the one with a pale orange bill tipped with black) fly over, then a White Ibis (the white bird with black wing tips and a very noticeably down-curved bill). I'm quickly gaining confidence in my ability to pick out key features of more shore birds this morning. That's important because so many of them don't sit still the way songbirds often do. I may only get a good view for a split second before the bird is out of easy visual range.

Cattle Egrets are plentiful in the marshy areas. The accents of orangeish breeding plumage on their white bodies make me think of marshmallows just beginning to toast over a campfire. A band of Barn Swallows swoops over, each bird dashing and jinking and veering up or down or left or right to snatch up insects rising from the grasses, tilting this way and that to reveal their handsome colors and deeply forked tails. A Snowy Egret flies over next, with its golden slippers (a bit of an exaggeration, as the feet are yellow, not gold) dangling below its white body.

Now we've come to a sandy area of shoreline and, sure enough, some Sanderlings dash back and forth at the edge of the waves. I recognize the Sanderling mostly by its behavior, skittering along at the edge of the waves. Something about its motions makes me think of a wind-up toy, a field mark that even guidebooks point out as a characteristic. There's something distinctive about its stride, too, that makes it ever so slightly different from other birds on the beach. It's as though it were stretching its legs to the limit with each hurried step, perhaps like a ballerina performing a grand jeté, although the bird doesn't actually leap up into the air. But its legs certainly are fully extended as it dashes along the sand.

A bit farther on, a Ruddy Turnstone lives up to its name, poking and flipping tiny rocks and turning over the stones at the water's edge as it looks for something good to eat beneath them. The next bird we see prompts some discussion about the size of leg joints, the thickness of legs, and other tiny little clues that help us determine that it's a Lesser Yellowlegs. Above us some Chimney Swifts tilt and flutter, their chittering calls so familiar to my ears, something I can easily pick out amid the other sounds at the shore.

Dave and Jane believe we'll have a good chance of seeing more birds if we walk over to an area with some bushes, so we change directions. Great-tailed Grackles make a commotion near a guardrail at the side of the road as we amble along. Some of the plants in this area have flowers open and we catch a glimpse of a Ruby-throated Hummingbird searching for nectar among the blossoms. No matter where I see one of these flying gems, I always admire their incredible energy and determination, and all of it packed into such a tiny body.

As we continue our walk to a new observation point, we pass a Little Blue Heron, hunting. We talk as we walk along about the key difference between this bird and the Tricolored Heron we saw earlier. The Little Blue Heron has a slatey blue belly, not white, and its neck feathers are sort of a purplish plum color. We notice a perched Double-crested Cormorant sunning itself with its wings spread out from its body, and more Sanderlings dashing across the wet sand.

§

As the songbirds who've spent the winter in the Caribbean or South America fly across the Gulf of Mexico, the first land they come to in this section of the Texas coast is Matagorda Island, a mostly sandy barrier island that we cannot see from here because it's way far away on the other side of this bay. Apparently there isn't much vegetation on that island, and the returning songbird migrants keep right on flying until they see the green brushy patches and live oak trees here on the mainland on this side of the bay.

Dave shows us where some bushes and short trees form a shady clump around the back of the concrete block shower house that the RV campers use. "Back" is what we say because the entry doors for people are on the other side, but to the birds flying northward, the little clump of greenery is front and center on their flight path. They'll see it after flying across many hundreds of miles of water and come in to find a perch and something to eat.

We walk carefully around the side of the clump, which includes some prickly pear cactus at the edge, and find a way in among the overhanging branches so that we can stand quietly on sandy dirt, with our backs to the building's wall. We let our eyes get accustomed to the shade, and wait. I recognize one of the trees—it's a hackberry, just like the dozens that grow on my land more than one thousand miles north of here.

As we peer into the shadows we notice a movement. It's one of my favorite little birds, a Black-and-white Warbler, with such an elegant pattern of black and white streaks on its feathers. Instead of moving around upright, hopping from branch to branch in typical warbler fashion, it creeps along with its breast parallel to the small branches as it walks, going up and down the bark on the main trunk, too, moving in and out of the foliage, searching for tiny insects to eat.

The more carefully we examine every inch of the trees and shrubs, the more movements we notice amid the leaves. But it takes quite a bit of patience to get a definite look at anything, and we murmur directional clues to each other before we know what we're really looking at. The trouble with warblers is that they're so small, many only half the size of a Blue Jay. Finally, what was at first just a tiny blur of motion turns into a little bird with a black head and a yellow mask—it's a Hooded Warbler, the handsome little fellow I just learned to recognize on Sunday in a similar brushy environment at High Island, farther north along the Gulf Coast.

I keep peering into the thicket, shifting my feet a bit to the right, a bit to the left, trying to get a clear view of a dull yellowish-beige, maybe slightly olive green, bird. Now I can see the head. I whisper directions, and say, "It has yellowish-beige and black stripes on its head, kind of like a wren, but I can't think of what it is." The pattern of buff and dark head stripes is quite distinctive and very pretty to look at, and I know I've seen that particular combination somewhere. I manage to keep it in focus for several minutes. Finally someone else who knows this bird calls it by name, a Worm-eating Warbler.

This is an exciting find for me, another lifer. Until now I've only known about this bird by pictures in books—that's why I thought the head pattern looked familiar—and its slightly inaccurate name. The "worm-eating" part of its name makes it sound as though the place to look for this bird would be on the ground, foraging for earthworms like an American Robin. But it doesn't actually eat worms in the way we understand that word today. In the late 1700s, when early naturalists were describing new bird species, the word "worm," which in Latin is rendered as "vermi," could be used for any thin wiggly thing, from earthworms to caterpillars—even pasta! It's why the delicious food that's thinner than spaghetti is called vermicelli, literally "little worms." When those early naturalists found this bird eating caterpillars, they called those wiggly things worms, and that's why we're stuck with this species name today, the Worm-eating Warbler. What the bird really likes to eat is moth caterpillars, not worms, and it often finds them along tree branches amid clumps of dead leaves. I like the way the bird looks, and I hope it's finding plenty of thin wiggly things to eat today as it hunts in these trees.

We watch a little while longer and, just about the time I'm getting ready to ask if the bird I have in focus is another Black-and-white Warbler, I see that its back and wings have a bluish cast to them. Then it turns slightly to show a bright yellow throat. Oh, dear. There are so many warblers—and a vireo—with yellow under their bills, and so many with the word "yellow" in their names, I don't have any quick idea about what this one is.

I see white wing bars. And what's the black mark around its eye? One of the other birders says it is definitely a Yellow-throated Warbler, and I have to accept that as correct—and then try to think of a way to make the name and the bird's features stick together in my mind. I have a sort of fuzzy memory of someone pointing this species out to me several years ago on one of those dash-along-at-top-speed bird walks somewhere in the Louisville area, but apparently I didn't do a very good job of actually learning it. I consider this a second chance, and hope this time I'll be able to retain the image in my mind and keep it connected to the name.

Dave and Jane lead us out of the thicket and we pause on the sidewalk next to another small group of brushy trees. A bird flits from these trees to some on the other side of the parking lot, then back again. Its overall coloring is quite similar to an American Goldfinch, but something is different. Its flight style is not the bounding-up-and-down-on-invisible-curves of a goldfinch, and its breast isn't bright yellow, but rather a lemony color near the shoulders and white on the belly. Great details, but it's really no help. Then I notice that it has white eyes. Aha! Another lifer, the aptly-named White-eyed Vireo. Dave is standing nearby and we review the chief differences between this vireo and other birds with similar feather colors and patterns. I sure hope I can remember this later.

Dave and Jane's next idea is to take a look around the other campground area on the bay side for more shore birds. Some people decide to walk over, but some of us opt to move our cars and then we'll get back together as a group.

§

At the new location our little group re-gathers and we walk past the big motor homes at this treeless campsite to a place where we have a good view of the water. The first bird I see is an old familiar friend, a Pied-billed Grebe. Bird names are so fascinating. The "pied" part doesn't refer to anything at all like the apple pastry I ate for breakfast, but means having two or more colors. During the breeding season this particular kind of grebe's bill is light at the tip with a dark band in the center, then light colored again nearest the face. It's the first bird I ever tried to make a sketch of many years ago, not knowing its identity as I drew, but carefully marking the two-toned bill in case that detail would be useful later. It was, and I still think about that early success every time I see this kind of grebe.

Nearer the shore a Black Skimmer and its companions come racing along, flying low over the water looking for food. This is a bird that is impossible to mistake for any other. It, too, has a two-toned bill, but in a different way, with orange near the face, black at the end. But that isn't the most distinctive feature. It is the only bird I can think of whose bill is two sizes—the lower bill, known as the mandible, is noticeably longer than the upper mandible, which makes it just perfect for skimming along the surface of the water like a narrow soup spoon as it flies, plowing a furrow through the water to sweep up tiny morsels to eat.

We turn from the water and walk across to the edge of the asphalt where we can look at some short grasses and the salt marsh. There's another Great Egret here, its head just visible above the tall marsh plants, but what catches my attention is a small brown bird on the short grasses closer to me. I can tell it's a sparrow by its size and shape, plus its quick little hopping steps. I bring my binoculars up to study its plumage, and get a surprise. The head looks like a mosaic of rusty brown patches, white streaks, plus black streaks, each with clearly defined borders like a paint-by-number picture. It's very handsome and we discuss among ourselves how these markings differ from the other sparrows each of us knows. This one is a Lark Sparrow, one I do not know from any previous encounter, so it's another lifer for me today, and one that I'm confident I will remember—and I have a nice photo, too.

Oh, wait, there's a different sparrow on another section of short grass. I study it with my binoculars and name off the first field mark I notice, a yellow streak above the eye. Um, yellow eye stripe. Near dunes. This is a significant combination, I think. Or is it? Near dunes. Yellow eye stripe. I'm casting around in my memory for those field marks, and then I have it. This is a Savannah Sparrow, the one I just learned to identify on Sunday in a similar habitat on Bolivar Flats near Galveston. This is just the sort of thing I hoped would happen when I planned this trip, that by spending several weeks along the coast I would see new birds more than once and be able to recognize them at each sighting.

As we walk slowly along, a large bird comes flying toward us. My overall impression is that it's a hawk, but the color scheme is all wrong for any of the hawks I know at home. It veers to the left and I see a dark head, white neck, dark wings with white towards the tips, white tail, dark band at the bottom. Basically a black-and-white bird. This color scheme makes it obvious to everybody else what it is, but I have to ask for help. The others tell me it's a Crested Caracara, another life bird for me. Although it looked like a raptor to me, they tell me that it has a lifestyle similar to a vulture, eating mostly carrion, although it will hunt small live prey from time to time.

We amble along, looking toward the water side again, and find a Western Sandpiper out by some large boulders. Someone sets up a spotting scope to reveal the slightly down-curved bill, but I have a good enough view with binoculars and take a photo of the bird that I can zoom and crop later for reference.

A Least Tern flies over the water fast, and from the marshy side we hear Red-winged Blackbirds claiming their territories with songs that sound like "onk-la-ree." The Osprey that flies past us has nothing in its talons, so apparently it is heading off to go plunge fishing somewhere else. From the wooden fishing pier built for humans, we can look across to a pond and see a Yellow-crowned Night-Heron standing at the water's edge on the left, then a Great Blue Heron a little farther to the right. For patient stalkers like these two birds there are plenty of fish to go around. Instead of plunging feet first into the water like the Osprey does, these birds stand still and use their long, sharp bills to capture prey. They can utilize shallow water that doesn't suit the Osprey's diving hunting technique.

A House Sparrow is the surprise find in this area. Apparently the campers' picnic tables offer plenty of tasty scraps.

Jane and Dave live here at the state park in their RV for many weeks, sometimes months, each winter and spring, and serve as volunteer bird hosts during their temporary residence. They invite everyone to come over to their campsite to look at whatever woodland birds and migrants might show up at the feeding and watering station they've established there. I get directions and head to my car for water and a snack of M & Ms and pretzels to nibble as I drive back to the other side of the park.

A few minutes later I find the gravel parking lot tucked in among the trees near Jane and Dave's campsite. When I get out of my car, the first sounds I hear are more Red-winged Blackbirds, then a Northern Cardinal. I walk across the shady road toward their huge RV, not knowing what to expect. They have a small sandwich board at the road's edge announcing bird viewing hours from 8:00 to 5:00 daily—that's part of their deal as volunteer bird hosts in exchange for using this campsite. Leading bird hikes several mornings a week is also part of their agreement with the park's paid staff.

I walk around to the other side of the RV and find an assortment of half a dozen or so mismatched lawn chairs lined up with good views into a small clearing with various feeders and seed platforms, and beyond into the live oak trees. I choose a chair and settle in to relax and watch. This is a style of birding I enjoy at home, often taking a folding chair out by my pond or near one of the fencelines to sit still and enjoy whatever birds turn up. After all the wandering around we did this morning, this feels very good.

I catch a glimpse of a Ruby-throated Hummingbird as a few other birders drift in and choose chairs. Then, in front of me, a different sort of movement at ground level catches my eye. From the body shape it's obviously a dove, but I have to study it with my binoculars to figure out which kind. It's rather small. The body feathers are sort of scallop-shaped, with a slightly contrasting color along the edges. It reminds me of the feathers on a heritage chicken breed that one of my friends in Indiana raises, but that's not much help here.

I whisper a question to the guy sitting next to me and discover that it is an Inca Dove, a bird I know I've seen only once before. Then I have to think a few minutes to recall where—ah, yes, somewhere in Arizona many years ago, when I knew very little about birds and was just getting into studying them carefully. I knew what it was then because a convenient signboard on a walking trail had a painting with the name on it, so when I saw the bird I could put its name in my travel journal, but that's all I can remember. It's nice to have the leisure time today to take good long looks and get a few photos of the feathers. The bird is quite handsome.

I scan back and forth close to the ground, then several feet out in the distance, across the dirt and scattered dry leaves, and notice a sparrow. It has a broad gray head stripe, and I know instantly that it is a Lincoln's Sparrow, even though I've only known this sparrow since last spring. That bird was also on leaf-covered ground, in a shady bit of woods along the boardwalk at Magee Marsh on the shores of Lake Erie, pausing on its way north to Canada. It won't be long before this bird takes off from its wintering grounds here in Texas to head north.

Four Brown-headed Cowbirds show up to perch in the trees. I recognize them by their appearance and their weird, gurgling, gulping call. They might stay here for the breeding season or move further north. I often find them at home in Kentucky. Wherever they go, the females will lay their eggs in some other bird species' nest and let someone else raise the youngsters. It's the only example of brood parasitism that I know of in North America, and all part of the natural world's system.

The next movement I notice is a gray shape in the shadows, a familiar slim bird with a streak of black on top of its head, a Gray Catbird. As it hops from branch to branch just slightly above us, we get a glimpse of the rusty red feathers under its tail, always nice to see. And every time I do, I wonder what good it does to have something pretty in such an odd location. I suppose only another catbird could explain that. From time to time I hear a slightly down-slurred "mew" call, which is how the bird got its name.

Much to my surprise, the next creature I notice is an obviously pregnant Virginia white-tailed deer picking her way carefully though the underbrush. If the Texas deer follow the same seasonal patterns as the ones who live on my farm in Kentucky, she'll drop a fawn, or possibly twins, about four or five weeks from now.

The tree canopy is not very dense here, and through an opening on the left we see a Turkey Vulture riding a thermal higher and higher, then taking a few broad wing strokes to travel on in a northerly direction. I turn my attention back to the clearing amid the brushy undergrowth just in time to see a White-throated Sparrow hunting for seeds to eat. The precise pattern of black and white head markings, although of similar colors to many other sparrows, makes it impossible to mistake this bird for any other species.

Dave arrives and chats quietly with us for a few minutes, then goes inside his RV for minute. He returns with something I would never have thought of to use to watch birds with—a swivel office chair. Out in my own fields I do like a lawn chair with arms to use as an elbow rest when I'll be using binoculars for a long time, but what he finds most useful on an office chair is the swivel part. He can sit in one spot but pivot to look at birds in any direction without making any noise or standing up to re-position the chair. Of course, this only works on flat ground, but there's plenty of that here, so close to sea level along the Gulf.

§

For several minutes I've been watching a different dove. It's rather plump, and the overall color is lighter than a Mourning Dove or an Inca Dove. It's bigger than either one of those species, too. But the key field mark is a black mark on the nape of its neck that gives the bird its name, the Eurasian Collared-Dove, another lifer for me.

I'm beginning to think about lunch, but I'm still scanning the area for more birds. I see something bright yellow. The bird is yellow all over, with some thin reddish streaks on its breast like a striped shirt. This one's easy—a male Yellow Warbler. Although there are plenty of warblers that are yellow, or mostly yellow, this is the only one with such a distinctive feather pattern of rusty red streaks on its breast. It's returned from wintering far to the south, perhaps in Cuba. He won't stay here long and will soon fly north, perhaps to the Ohio River Valley, to sing his rich, chirruping warble of "sweet, sweet, sweet, I'm so sweet" that I know so well, making the spring days at home sweet indeed.

Thoughts of lunch are now beginning to interfere with my ability to concentrate, but I see another bird with yellow feathers. This one has white bars on dark wings. But I don't think it's a warbler because the bill shape is wrong. The more I look at it, the more details I discover, including an interesting facial pattern of yellow feathers that make it look like it's wearing wrap-around glasses over its dark, black eyes. That gets me to the right family, vireos, but it's been a long time since I've seen a Yellow-throated Vireo, and I've had to work hard at matching what I see in front of me today with a memory and a name.

I really need to take a break for lunch, so I get up quietly from my borrowed chair, whisper "thank you" and "goodbye," then walk back to my car. I'm so hungry I don't give much thought to the call of a titmouse nearby as I open my car door.

§

I stop by my campsite to freshen up a bit, splash water on my face at the shower house, and get back in my car to drive into the towns of Fulton and Rockport to look for a place to eat lunch. The main road has four lanes and I'm keeping my eye on the right side where there are shopping centers and freestanding businesses and, I hope, a good restaurant. Ah, I'll give K-Bob's Steakhouse a try.

I've hit the jackpot here, with a four-course lunch. A cold Corona Extra, a plate of fresh veggies from the salad wagon, a cup of spicy potato soup with tiny bits of chicken in the thick broth, and chocolate pudding with a crumbled Oreo cookie garnish for dessert. Birding requires ample nutrition, and this is just what I need after an active morning.

The town is bigger than I realized last night, and I make an executive decision that I will not set up my camp kitchen. Wherever I go birding, I like to spend some money at local businesses, even if it's just something as simple as buying gas. This is especially important in places with community parks that don't charge an admission fee. The upkeep for these parks comes from tax revenues, and anything I can do to help local businesses make a profit means more tax dollars for the park systems. While I'm here in the Rockport and Fulton area, buying lunches and dinners in restaurants will help the local economy stay strong so the town leaders can keep the parks in good shape. The money I spend buying milk and sweets for breakfast at the local grocery will help, too.

Up ahead I see a nice big H E B grocery and pull into the parking lot. In the bakery department I ask one of the workers to recommend something for breakfast. He suggests the empanadas. I've never heard of breakfast empanadas before. Empanadas with meat and cheese for lunch or dinner, sure, but not filled with something sweet. It sounds good, so I'll buy some. He also suggests that I try a concha, a sort of round, puffy thing. Into the basket it goes.

My next stop is Wal-mart to figure out how to solve my reading-light problem. Instead of looking for an expensive table from the garden furniture department, I roam around in other departments looking for ideas. Aha, this will work—a four-dollar, white plastic wastebasket that I can turn upside down so I can use the flat bottom as a tabletop. Over in the camping department I find a cute little adjustable LED lantern that should cast a nice glow for reading inside my tent. I pick up a new charger cable for my phone and get in line to check out.

Back at my car, I study the colorful map of the Rockport-Fulton area. The map is not just a grid of the streets but includes photos and paintings of businesses and parks, plus wildlife scenes. The businesses in these two communities rely on tourists year-round, and they've devoted a lot of time, effort, and space to making things bird- and birder-friendly. I'm not sure where the boundary between Fulton and Rockport is, but I don't think it matters very much because the two towns work together on projects. I check one of my bird tour books to choose some places to go birding, look at the pretty map again, and figure out what to enter into my GPS system to get me to the first place I want to explore.

Back on the main road I pass the grocery and arrive at a park at Tule Creek, which includes an attractive wood gazebo and a short boardwalk. The excellent graphics and illustrations on the signboards in the gazebo here help me understand these Gulf Coast habitats and introduce me to some local birdwatching history. Long before anyone dreamed of internet technology or sharing data with a mouse click, Connie Hagar was a superb citizen scientist. From 1935 on, she became a self-taught authority on Texas birds, carefully recording her daily observations. By hand. No computer databases, no smartphone technology. Her expertise was sought by professional and amateur ornithologists from around the world. Her notes about bird behavior and flight movements helped make this place—Aransas County, Texas—a birding hot spot. I'm so glad to be here today to look for birds.

While I'm strolling along the boardwalk, a Great Blue Heron flies over, then I hear the harsh, croaking "squark" of a Green Heron. This is a wetland area, and these are exactly the birds I would expect to find in this habitat. Walking a short way on the paved, shared-use path meant for both bicyclers and walkers, I hear a titmouse while I'm looking at a black swallowtail butterfly. I also see an American Snout butterfly, and spot two Virginia white-tailed deer. This all seems so familiar, yet I'm fifteen hundred miles away from home. And then some noisy Laughing Gulls fly over to bring me back to the geographic present.

After about forty-five minutes here, I'm ready to see something else, so I drive back up the street a short distance to a different area, the Rockport Demo Bird Garden and Wetlands Pond. There's a nice, shady parking lot, almost empty of other cars, and this looks like a good place to go for a late afternoon stroll.

The first section is a groomed path, pleasantly shady in spots on this now-warm day. This section of Tule Marsh is right next to a major highway where cars and trucks are zooming past at high speeds, and across the street from the huge retail shopping center and acres of asphalt parking lots where I was shopping earlier, but within a few steps that's not important. The noises of the bustling town fade away and I can focus on listening to and watching birds.

I spy a Northern Cardinal, then hear the mewing voice of a Gray Catbird in the leafy vegetation. Around another curve in the path, first I hear one Indigo Bunting singing, then see a second male and hear his answer—a slightly different version of paired phrases that sounds like "sweet, sweet, chew, chew, sweet, sweet, chee-oo, chee-oo"—that makes me think of spring back home. Some of these migrants will likely reach my place about the same time I get home and be there to greet me with their charming songs. Scientists have done some very sophisticated experiments with captive Indigo Buntings in planetariums, proving that these night-time migrants navigate using the patterns of stars to guide them, a behavior and sensibility that continues to astonish me.

Different species of birds use different combinations of skills when they migrate. Some birds, especially geese and cranes, travel in large flocks, with the older, more experienced birds showing the first-year birds the way to go. But other birds, especially songbirds, do not gather in flocks to migrate as a group, but travel independently. Many individuals do cover the same ground at the same time, but they are not acting as a coherent flock. Ingenious experiments have also shown that some birds have a special sensitivity to the earth's magnetic fields and can orient their flight using that as a guidance system. And of course they use sight to figure out where to land for stopovers. It's quite fascinating, and many mysteries of bird migration still remain to be explained.

This path leads to a wooden boardwalk that zigs and zags through swampy sections, and I find several groups of Black-bellied Whistling-Ducks loafing around on the water and amid the green plants on the squishy margins. As I watch them, a White Ibis with its distinctive dark wing tips flaps overhead. Then a much larger Great Egret flies across a distant patch of tall reeds and drops down to stalk slowly along the edge of some open water. A small group of Blue-winged Teal fly over. About forty feet away from me a pair of Northern Shovelers dabble in the water, searching for their dinner. As I near the end of the boardwalk, a Double-crested Cormorant flies over.

I've been here about an hour, walking at a very slow pace, pausing to look and listen, then taking a few more steps, enjoying the variety of birds here in the late afternoon sunlight. As I near the trees by the parking lot I hear the insistent trill of a Carolina Wren, that familiar "teakettle-teakettle-teakettle" song, but I cannot find where the singer is perched. I do see a Northern Flicker perched on a snag. It is probably the yellow-shafted form of this ant-loving woodpecker, but since it's perched, not flying, I cannot see the color of the underside of the wing feathers.

Now that I'm back at my car I'll take a few minutes to quickly number the bird species I've written in my pocket notebook today since breakfast—rough count seems to be fifty-five distinct species, with seven lifers. This calls for a celebration, and since I'm already in town and only a few blocks from the bay, I think dinner at a restaurant next to the marina would be fun.

§

Tonight this area of Fulton looks a lot better in the sunshine than it did in yesterday's pouring rain. I see Charlotte Plumer's Seafare Restaurant and there's an open place in the parking lot, so this will be tonight's dinner spot. Up on the second floor, the first table I choose on the covered deck has fine views of boats of various sizes and shapes in the marina below, but the stiff breeze is blowing the palm tree fronds all crazy—and it's making it difficult for me to find a comfortable way to sit. I move back to a different table in a sheltered corner, and the people at the next table laugh. "We had to move, too, because that wind is too rough."

I enjoy a glass of wine while making a selection from the menu. When the bacon-wrapped shrimp served over a bed of rice arrives, it looks good and tastes even better. Although the strong wind blowing in from the Gulf is annoying to me and the folks at the next table, for the birds it may be a distinct advantage, giving them an extra push for the final stretch of their long-distance flight across the open water. This could be a real plus for birding tomorrow.

When I get back to my campsite, I set up my new "table" and put the little LED lantern on the upturned wastebasket. It will not turn on. Hmm. Ah, that would be because the batteries are not included. Why did I not notice that when I was shopping? I search through my camping essentials box and discover that, among all the kinds of spare batteries I carry with me, I do not have any of the right size for the new lantern. I put that on tomorrow's shopping list and decide to go visit with John and Marcy for a few minutes.

We stand around at their campsite in the dark, chatting about our day's adventures, and then I hear a loud rustling in the fallen leaves just beyond the glow of their camp lights. Suddenly, two armadillos come scuttling past the picnic table, so intent on their own travel plans they pay no attention to us and are out of sight in seconds. Whether they were rivals or mates, I cannot say. But they certainly can move fast!

I head back to my tent to get ready for sleep. Once again I set my phone's alarm for early. Tomorrow Jane and Dave will lead a songbird walk, and I want to get there on time.

###

CHAPTER EIGHT

Habitats around Aransas Bay

Sound puzzles, hummers, new migrants

I wake up, kinda, a little before daybreak, because I hear something strange. A lot of people come to Goose Island State Park to fish, and at first I think I am hearing someone test a small boat motor. The sound's an insistent ter-ter-ZEEE-eer, repeated, maybe more like pur-pur-WHEE-oh—like someone pulling the start cord on a lawnmower? That can't be right. I fall back to sleep, fitfully, not sure if I've been dreaming.

A while later, my alarm chimes, and I get up for the day, hungry as usual and still thinking about whatever that weird noise was earlier. I walk over to the shower house, and later, on the way back, I'm still puzzling over what I heard. Do I hear it again while I'm walking? Of course not.

I rush through breakfast (I like the sweet empanada better than the concha), and get in my car to go meet Dave and Jane at the Turk's Cap Trail parking lot for this morning's guided songbird walk. I just learned to recognize the turk's cap plant yesterday near the brushy spot by the other shower house where we watched migrant songbirds. It has an attractive red flower, and it is native to Texas.

When I arrive at the meeting spot, many of the same people who were on the shorebird walk yesterday are here this morning, plus some newcomers. The big topic for conversation is what to use to repel insects, always a favorite discussion among birders.

I'm a firm believer in Avon's Skin-So-Soft and used some when I was getting dressed back at camp, so I'm all set to go exploring. The trail here is a dirt path through dense live-oak thickets skirting the campground, and the folks who are familiar with the area expect to encounter plenty of bugs.

It's already hot this morning, so the shade will be nice later. As Jane and Dave go over the plan for this morning's walk, which is the same as yesterday's guidelines, I hear a Northern Cardinal, and then some Royal Terns fly over. Many Barn Swallows are already swooping over the short grasses near the parking lot to catch insects in the air. The more they catch, the fewer there will be to annoy us, so we think they're great birds. A pair of Red-breasted Mergansers fly over, perhaps the same ones we saw yesterday.

I hear the familiar "whick-whicka-whicka" of a Northern Flicker somewhere nearby. Some Rock Pigeons zoom over, and then we stop to listen to insistent whistles that have the same rhythm as the phrases "look at me," then "here I am," then "in the tree," with a brief pause between each series of notes, which are crisp and clear in the morning air. No doubt about this one, it's a Red-eyed Vireo singing. We would look at him, if we could find him, but he stays hidden among the leaves.

Red-winged Blackbirds call back and forth and we see several males, their red epaulettes flashing as they defend their territories. Laughing Gulls make plenty of noise, too, and that sparks a conversation about bird sounds. Dave knows which ones of us are camping and asks if anybody heard the Common Pauraque carrying on before dawn. "The what?" I'm getting ready to ask, when he says, "You know, the bird that sounds like a lawn mower." So I wasn't dreaming; it's a real bird, and another lifer for me. Such a distinctive sound counts, even though I haven't yet seen the bird. It's a species that is active at dusk, dawn, and through the night, so I might not see one. But I'll sure remember the whirring, buzzing sounds it makes. It goes in my notebook with an asterisk as a lifer, and with the mark (h) because so far I've only heard it.

We walk slowly along the leaf-covered path until we reach a special spot. Behind a low border of upright wood shakes at the edge of a trailside clearing, half a dozen or more assorted bird feeders hang from metal poles. Stone cairns support some additional feeding stations, and a squirrel scampers along the twisted tree limbs looking for something to raid. Dave mentions that the full name of the tree species is Virginia coastal live oak, with a range that obviously extends far beyond that state. The names of plants in North America have the same quirkiness as the names of birds, often referencing the place where they were first encountered and described, without any knowledge then of how wide their growing ranges really are.

This little alcove also includes a water drip to entice migrants into view, and we catch a glimpse of a White-eyed Vireo lurking nearby in the shadows. As volunteers, Dave and Jane work with the park staff to set up areas like this and keep them replenished for the birds. I hear the chittering calls of some Chimney Swifts high above us, scooping up more insects, and look up briefly, but try to stay focused on the birds among the feeders.

I see a dove-shaped gray bird on a tree limb and use my binoculars for a closer look. A second dove flies in and stands a few inches away from the first one. The field mark is easy to see, a line of white feathers on the edge of the wing—yet another lifer for me, the White-winged Dove. This dove is a southwestern species, not one I would not expect to see back in Kentucky.

Dave thinks we'll see more birds in a different section of this woodsy area, so we retrace our steps and set off for new places to explore. I mention that I've been hearing a titmouse, and he explains it's not the same as the bird I know from farther north. The call sounds the same to my ears, and I am reluctant to enter a different name in my notes until I can see one. Dave takes that as a friendly, good-natured challenge and will be on the lookout for one for me. "We'll find you one this morning," he promises, and I have no doubt that if there's one to be seen, he'll point it out, not just to me but for the whole group to enjoy.

As we stroll along we notice some Yellow-rumped Warblers. The sun is shining exactly right to highlight the red feathers of a male Ruby-throated Hummingbird. Two Great Blue Herons fly over, separated from each other by about fifty feet, then a string of about half a dozen Brown Pelicans fly over toward the bay.

We can hear a "peter-peter-peter" call in the treetops, and I start scanning the limbs and branches. Dave begins giving directional clues to all who are curious. And there it is, at last, a Black-crested Titmouse, centered in my binoculars. Sure enough, it has the same basic shape as the bold, friendly little titmouse I know at home, but instead of a smudge of black on its forehead and a gray tuft for a crest, this bird has a white forehead and a big patch of black feathers all the way up to the tip of its crest—quite handsome and perky looking. While we're all watching, Dave explains that we are south and west of the Guadalupe River and that is a natural dividing line between titmouse ranges. In suitable habitat like this, the Black-crested Titmouse is the local species.

My ears perk up when I hear the familiar burble of a Carolina Wren, and then we find it singing from a nearby perch. A bit farther on I discover a Black-and-white Warbler prospecting for insects along a branch.

As we cross a more open area on our way back to the parking lot we have a clearer view of the blue sky. A Crested Caracara flies over, then we see some Purple Martins hunting insects in the morning air. Their glossy feathers gleam a sort of bluish purple in the morning sunlight. A few Black Vultures are riding thermals, then we spot a Turkey Vulture gliding along much higher in the clear sky. Just as we reach the parking lot a Northern Mockingbird flies out from the edge of the trees, flashing the white feathers on its wings and tail.

§

Once again Jane and Dave invite everyone over to their campsite to watch birds at their feeding and watering station. Some folks have other plans for the day, but I am eager to give their spot another try.

A short while later, as I settle into one of the lawn chairs in the shade by their RV, I see a pretty, rust-colored bird I know so well, a Brown Thrasher. It's foraging among the fallen leaves beneath one of the oaks, scratching and kicking to stir up tasty insects. When I was first learning about birds, the patterns on the feathers on its breast had me fooled into thinking it was a thrush of some kind. Only later did I realize that, instead of spots, the dark areas are stripes, and this bird belongs in the same group as the other mimics we've seen this morning, the Northern Mockingbird and the Gray Catbird. This Brown Thrasher is silent just now, though, concentrating on finding something to eat.

I don't have much experience watching birds at artificial feeders because I don't have any at home. Instead, I provide a variety of habitats at my farm, with naturally occurring foods such as insects and berries and seeds available in each season. So my attention keeps drifting away from the feeders and into the trees behind them. I'm the first person to see the Brown-headed Cowbirds fly in to a perch on a bare branch about twenty-five feet away. It may be a pair—certainly one is a female and one is a male because their feathers are different—but this might just be an accidental assembly.

Dave's brought his swivel office chair out on the dirt again, and while we're looking straight ahead, he's looking to our right at the water drip that's just behind the end of the RV. He begins speaking in a very soft, even voice, describing a bird there with a very noticeable eyeline, and we twist ever so carefully around in our lawn chairs, not waving our arms or raising our hands to point, being very quiet and conserving motion so as not to startle the bird. Eventually I can get the bird in view with my camera and snap a nice photo of a Tennessee Warbler. He may have arrived here just last night, as this second week of April is when the first birds of this species begin returning from their wintering grounds in Central America and the northern parts of South America.

That's one of the complications of birdwatching during migration. Each species follows its own timetable. All of the birds that spend the winter months on Caribbean Islands or in Central or South America do not leave on the same day. Their departures are spread out over many weeks, so that one species will arrive on the North American mainland in late March, others in early April, some not until weeks after that. Then, as they fly farther northward, it's a case of a few birds in one spot one day, a few more—or a few less—the next day, all raggedy, not a solid line of advancement. I have not memorized these timetables for the Ohio River Valley, and I sure don't know them for coastal Texas. But Dave and Jane do, and that's helping all of us today.

A short while later I am able to identify a Lincoln's Sparrow and get what I hope will be a good photo. As usual, the wide gray patch, sort of an eyebrow streak, is the main field mark that I use to recognize this little bird, combined with its feeding behavior of scratching around in leaf litter. I keep my fingers crossed that the image turns out well.

§

I have it in mind to drive around to some other locations outside the state park today to visit other birding spots in this area, so I slip away quietly and return to my campsite to make a list of potential sites. I also need to make a short shopping list. While I'm at my campsite I see that John and Marcy are at their place and I walk over to chat. We discover that tonight will be the last night of camping for all of us, and we decide as a treat to meet for dinner in Fulton. We settle on a time and place and trade cell phone numbers.

I've driven by a little bar and grill on the road leading to the state park several times now, and today I stop in at Pop's Tavern and Cafe for lunch. When I sit down at the small bar counter I am puzzled why there are beer bottle caps in plastic cups along the edge of the bar. The bartender explains that they save them for the team of artists who make the murals on the walls. I turn around to look at the main dining area and discover the most unusual and beautiful mosaic pictures of fish. Instead of tile or glass, the mosaic chips are bottle caps of different colors. The pictures are at least fifteen feet wide and six feet tall, and stunningly artistic. I marvel at the amount of planning it must take to create them, and take photos to share with my friends back home.

After a juicy cheeseburger I'm ready to go exploring. I head inland, driving on a good road through ranchlands, and stop to buy gas in the county seat of Refugio on my way to Lion's-Shelley Park on the Mission River. At the park I discover that there's some sort of family reunion picnic going on in one area, but not much else. It's the wrong time of day during a school week for many children to be using the playground, and it looks like I will have the trails to myself. I gather up my binoculars, camera, and notebook, take a big gulp of water, and walk out onto the asphalt path that leads into the woods.

This is a forest remnant amid land that's now mostly devoted to farming and ranching, a little island of wild greenery. Signs warn that this is also alligator and snake habitat, so while I'm here I'll be looking down as much as up. The sun is high in the sky, just past noon, and it's hot and humid, with scarcely any air stirring. I hear the distinctive "picky-tuck" song of a Summer Tanager up ahead, and eventually locate the scarlet male high in the tree canopy. His song is being answered by another bird on my left, but I can't find that one. They seem to be rivals, and if they can work out who gets which section of the park, both of them may settle here for the nesting season instead of moving farther north.

Walking along the paths I am careful not to stray over into the grass because I can see plenty of poison ivy amid the weedy brush at the sides. Butterflies and dragonflies dart along the edges of the path. While near an open, weedy field I look up just in time to notice a Turkey Vulture soaring high overhead. I hear the shriek of a hawk but I can't find it. A Northern Cardinal hops in and out of the brush, then I catch a glimpse of a Black Vulture cruising in the rising thermals. Each time the path is near the river I see several turtles sunning themselves on half-submerged logs, but no alligators.

I've spent almost an hour here but found very few birds, so it's time to move on. I get settled in my car and ask my GPS to navigate me to Aransas National Wildlife Refuge. Driving back over the road I used to get here, I encounter a large flock of Barn Swallows flying through a swarm of tiny insects. There's a wide shoulder on this flat road, and I pull off to take some cell phone photos of pretty yellow flowers and a big Texas longhorn bull in a pasture.

When I cross Highway 35, the land-use patterns change. Instead of slightly hilly rangeland for cattle, I'm now driving amid flat agricultural fields. The roads here are flat, too, so close to sea level, and there are more right-angle doglegs, probably based on long-ago farm boundaries. I see a hawk-shaped bird with black and white markings and immediately know that I'm looking at yet another Crested Caracara.

§

At the visitor center at Aransas National Wildlife Refuge, I discover that I have arrived twenty minutes too late—the center closed at four o'clock. The doors are locked, but I can see people inside in the office part, so I knock. Eventually a woman comes out and we chat for a few minutes about my interest in birds. Turns out I'm a bit late for the cranes, too—they left to fly north last week. Oh, well, I am determined to see as much as possible wherever I am, and I'm sure I will find other interesting birds to look at here. The roads will be open until sunset, so I pay my three-dollar fee to the little honor system box on the wall and pick up a map and a bird checklist.

If I'm not careful, I will also end up being late for dinner with John and Marcy, so I study the map of the auto route, look at the car clock, and try to figure out where I can also get out and walk. This is going to be a challenge in time management, finding a way to explore several different kinds of habitat here without rushing too much.

The main road is paved and wide enough for traffic going in either direction, and it follows the shoreline of San Antonio Bay, sometimes close enough to see the water, sometimes not. I'm driving with the windows only partially down because the wind has kicked up a notch this afternoon. There's a distinctly fishy smell to the air coming in off the water. Some Virginia white-tailed deer cross the road in front of me as I arrive at a fishing pier area. I pull off in the little parking area and get out to look around.

Above me a Turkey Vulture tilts in the stiff breeze. Out on the water a large raft of American Coots are bobbing up and down on the choppy waves. The wind is making it very hard for me to hold my binoculars steady. Three Brown Pelicans fly over in a straight line, but there isn't much else to look at here. I get back in the car and drive on to the end of the two-lane road.

There's a turnoff to the right onto the one-way auto tour loop that looks worth a try. This one hundred fifteen thousand–acre refuge on Blackjack peninsula includes many different kinds of habitats and plant communities in addition to the shore along the Gulf. This road will take me away from saltwater and brackish habitats into grasslands with freshwater ponds, but I do not know how much open water I will see. The woman at the visitor center said there's been a six-year drought and apparently water levels are low in many places. It's not that it hasn't rained at all, it's just that the rain has been sparse. Maybe sparse throughout an entire year, but Tuesday night's downpour was torrential at times, so I don't know what to expect. A Northern Cardinal darts into in a thicket of trees as I turn onto the driving loop.

A little farther on at a shallow pond I slow down for a good look at a Great Egret standing at the edge. Farther on, Barn Swallows criss-cross above a weedy field. Around a gentle curve, a larger body of open water appears in the distance. A flock of Roseate Spoonbills sort of shimmers in a pink haze. Bringing my binoculars up to scan more carefully, I presume the smaller, solitary hunter is a Little Blue Heron—the color and shape are right.

I move along slowly, driving at about my own walking pace, a proven strategy for locating birds. Some Mourning Doves flutter across just in front of me, and at the edges of another brushy area I see two more Virginia white-tailed deer grazing.

I've recently learned a new word, "motte," to describe a grove of trees. In this area the trees are usually oaks, and an oak motte is a common habitat here, a valuable, brushy island of sorts amid flat grasslands. I'm close enough to hear an Indigo Bunting just as I get to the end of the driving loop.

I look at the clock on the dashboard and figure I have just enough time to take a quick walk somewhere. Back on the main road I make a split-second decision to pull off by the alligator viewing area, where I see two other cars parked. I can see some trees soaring above the marshy ground. On days like this when the wind is strong, birds often hunker down in brushy areas instead of flying much, so this area could turn out to be birdy.

The grassy walkway nearest my car is called the Rail Trail, and it goes alongside reeds growing at the edge of Tomas Slough. I hear the deep "jug o' rum, jug o'rum" calls of a bullfrog and that makes me smile because it sounds like home. I'd like to see a rail, one of a rather secretive group of birds that like to skulk around in dense vegetation. The ground here seems like great habitat for that kind of bird but seems a bit squishy for me to walk on, as I don't think it drains all that well after storms like that the one that rolled through on Tuesday night. I'd rather be on a boardwalk, so I change directions and step onto the wood just as two other people are leaving the area. They're visiting from Oregon, and they tell me how excited they are to have seen an alligator, and then I walk on towards the water to look for birds.

And I see nothing. Nothing. No, really. Nothing. I'm getting tired, I'm getting hungry, and I don't want to be late for dinner, so I'm not concentrating well. I force myself to relax, to look, and look again, and still I see nothing. I'm getting discouraged. I've driven all this way from camp and the afternoon hasn't turned out very well. I walk on forward for twenty more steps and decide I've had it. I'm done. When I turn around to leave my steps are heavy.

Suddenly I hear something behind me. What was that? It's loud, it's not a frog, and it seems to be coming from my left. I'm on a stretch of boardwalk that is like a bridge over what I would think of as a creek, but there doesn't seem to be any current. It must be a long, skinny pond. I hear the call again, sort of a loud harsh note, more like a squawk, not at all song-like.

There, on a limb overhanging the water, is a bird about the size of a jay, but plumper, with a thick black stripe through its eye, a mostly white face, brown wings and back, and a yellow breast. I get several photos to use later to identify it—my mind right now is a complete blank as far as bird species go, and I can't even begin to guess at what I'm looking at. The bird seems completely unconcerned that I'm standing out in the open just forty feet away.

On the right, on a different limb, much lower and just at the water's edge, I see a very tall bird, at least two feet tall, with a longish, thick bill, gazing to the left, then turning its head to the right. I wonder, is this the bird that made the noise? That seems more likely than the jay-sized bird. Looking more carefully, I know this one is a night-heron, but it's not in adult plumage and I'm not sure of the species. I will have to study my photos later to solve this puzzle, too. Right now, I use the viewer on the back of my camera to zoom in on the smaller bird, and then take a photo of that image with my cell phone.

My digital camera is not equipped with the right software or anything else to allow me to make posts directly from it to social media. So a lot of birders out in the field use this tech go-around as a quick and sloppy way to get photos out into the world when we're away from our desktop computers. I want to let friends back home know that I'm finding birds this afternoon, even if I can't name them.

I really can't stay here any longer, so I go back to my car and discover that I am already going to be late for dinner. But when I try to call John and Marcy, I have no cell phone service because apparently I'm too far from any towers. They would be rather inappropriate in this wild place, and I really can't complain. I start my car, and just before I put it in gear a Scarlet Tanager dashes across to the trees on the other side of the road.

§

Twenty minutes later, back to the main highway, I pull off to see if I have enough signal to make a phone call. Yes, so I call to let John and Marcy know I'm on my way to meet them at Moondog. They live in Texas and are used to the distances so they don't mind a bit that I misjudged the amount of time it would take to drive back in to town.

Although it's clear this evening, we choose a booth inside because it's still so breezy. We have a good view right at dockside of all the boats in the marina. I especially like to look at the palm tree trunks wrapped in strings of tiny white LED lights—very tropical and festive.

As it turns out, we will have two servers tonight because one guy is training the other one. They seem to be college-age fellows, and I ask if they're local. When they both say "yes," I realize that they might be able to help me solve one of my bird puzzles. I figure that a bird as comfortable around people as the one with the black eye stripe was when I stood on the boardwalk would be familiar to local people, even if they don't study birds carefully. After I order a glass of chardonnay, I find the photo on my cell phone and have it ready when they return. Then I show it to them. "Kiskadee," they both say at once. Well, that was easy. John and Marcy and I spend the rest of the time talking about the places we've visited and where we want to travel to next.

On the way back to camp I have to stop for fresh ice for my coolers, and to pick up the right size batteries for my new lantern.

A very pretty tabby cat, a pale gray one, lurks in the shadows at the gas station. When I ask the clerk what its name is, he says, "doesn't have a name—yet" with a smile that makes me think that cat will certainly have a name by the end of the weekend.

I drive through the campground gates just minutes before they will be locked, and I'm glad I don't have to use the entry code the park ranger gave me when I arrived. Fumbling around in the dark to tap in numbers on an unfamiliar device is not at all what I want to do right now.

At my campsite I install the batteries in my new little LED lantern and set up my reading nook. It works great. I'm ready to settle in to study my photos with a field guide in my lap and to catch up on writing my notes for the day.

As it turns out, the full name for the bird the guys at the restaurant identified for me isn't just a kiskadee, it is a Great Kiskadee, rather like the way I say cardinal at home when I mean Northern Cardinal. The Great Kiskadee is a very welcome addition to my life list. As for the tall bird perched at the water's edge, the more I study my photo, the more I'm leaning toward an immature Yellow-crowned Night-Heron. And, as I think about, I'm sure it's the night-heron who made the noise, not the kiskadee.

When I go out to my car to put my field guides back in the laundry basket on the front seat, I enjoy how quiet this campground is, even though the campsites are very close together. I live out in the country at home, far from other people's houses, and when I'm camping I sometimes find it unsettling to have a lot of noise nearby. But here all is quiet.

Quiet, until I hear a scratching kind of sound. I look down just in time to see a single armadillo skittering along between my car and my tent. When it gets to the front of my tent it veers off to the side—I'm sure glad I always keep the entrance flap zippered closed—and out of sight into the deep shadows of the tree line. That seems like a good way to end this day, and I go into my tent to get settled for the night. There's another songbird walk in the morning, and I will have just enough time to do that before I need to strike camp. Now it's time for lights out.

§

In the morning, as usual, the birds around my campsite start singing before the sun is above the horizon. While waiting for my alarm to chime, I'm listening from inside my tent to a particularly insistent Northern Cardinal. His song is so familiar and cheerful, I might as well go ahead and get up. I turn off the alarm before its electronic tones can spoil his song, and step outside.

It's another clear day, just right for a tailgate breakfast with the other halves of the sweets I bought at the local grocery. As I drink my cup of milk, I now know that the bird singing "peter-peter-peter" in a nearby tree is a Black-crested Titmouse, cousin to the titmouse that sings at my place back in Kentucky. I also heard some airboats out on the bay, but no Common Pauraque this morning. A Northern Mockingbird keeps up a steady stream of borrowed songs.

While I'm enjoying my birder's breakfast I look at the gnarly branches of the live oaks. At home, the oaks I know have relatively straight branches that spread out in regular angles with plenty of space between them. The trees here have a completely different shape. The branches twist and turn and loop in the oddest ways. They seem to interlock in some spots, almost like a tangle of yarn after a kitten's been playing. I wonder about the reason for this growth pattern, and if it somehow is a strategy to cope with fierce coastal winds. I don't know, but I'd like to find out more.

After breakfast I drive over to the Turk's Cap trailhead again to meet Dave and Jane for today's songbird walk. I recognize several of the other birders from yesterday and Wednesday, but there are more newcomers, too. This is the biggest crowd yet, as more people have arrived to visit the park for the weekend. The days tend to lose their calendar meaning for me when I'm traveling, and I have to keep reminding myself that, for the rest of the world, this is a Friday.

A young woman has brought her three young daughters with her, and Dave and Jane are particularly attentive to them. The oldest girl, perhaps about seven years old, has her own pair of binoculars and already knows how to use them. Jane goes over the plan for the walk, which is the same as on previous mornings, and while she's explaining the details, someone who already knows the system says "ducks!" We look up to watch and listen as some Black-bellied Whistling-Ducks fly over.

Birding by ear is something Dave excels at, and he's good at explaining it, too. As we listen to a string of loud notes, repeated at regular intervals from a singer hidden amid the leaves, he helps everyone understand the pattern and the cadence of the White-eyed Vireo's song. This is the third day in a row that I've heard this bird, and I recognize it much more quickly today.

As we walk slowly along I hear another Black-crested Titmouse, then someone calls our attention to the large bird flying over—I know immediately from the pattern of dark against white that it is a Crested Caracara. This is the third day in a row that I've seen this species, too, and that's what's so valuable about using one place as a base for several days. I'm developing a deeper understanding and appreciation of the local birds here. Familiarity really does build confidence.

As we amble along we hear a different singer, a bird who seems to be talking to himself, asking a short question, then answering it, over and over again, quite tirelessly. I know it is a Red-eyed Vireo, as do several of the other experienced birders, and we spend some time chatting about how different this vireo's song is from the White-eyed Vireo's song that we heard just a few minutes ago.

Dave and Jane explore all areas of the park, even when they're not leading bird walks, so they know what to expect where. They think that, instead of concentrating only on the dirt path of Turk's Cap Trail, we'll see a greater variety of birds if we walk along one of the campground roads, the Lantana Loop. Edge habitats along roads can be very rewarding, and those of us with experience birding such places are eager to see what we can find.

All of us trek over to the paved road. We don't anticipate much traffic in this secluded spot, but we will still need to listen and watch for cars, and be prepared to step off into the grass.

A Northern Cardinal singing towards the end of a leafy branch is easy to spot, his red feathers gleaming in the morning sunshine, and some Red-winged Blackbird males flash their crimson epaulettes as they fly past us. The feathers of the next bird we notice are quite a contrast to those boldly patterned species. The body, head, and belly of the bird we have in view are bright yellow, with grayish wings—but that description fits a lot of migrating songbirds, so I have to look much more closely. Yes, it has very noticeable white wing bars, but I think the thin black eye stripe might be the key. The more I look at the wings, the more I think the color is slightly blue, and that, coupled with the black eye stripe, will clinch the identification, with some help from one of the other birders and Jane. This is a Blue-winged Warbler, my first lifer of the day.

We take note of a pair of Inca Doves sitting close to each other at the edge of the pavement, and watch as they flutter away when we walk closer, then I hear the familiar, insistent "dee-dee-dee" of a Carolina Chickadee in the oak trees. A Great Blue Heron flies over us, flapping its huge wings slowly, then I hear another familiar woodland bird, a Grey Catbird, mewing somewhat peevishly from the brushy undergrowth.

There's a tiny little bird jabbing at something at the end of a thin branch, and at first all I can make out is a yellow breast. Then I see that farther down the bird's feathers become white. The wings are grayish blue, with two white wing bars. I have to think and think about what this could be. In the meantime, others are pointing out what they observe—"broken eye ring," "kind of a rusty band across the top of chest," and we realize we have a Northern Parula in view. I have no idea how this bird got its name, or why. The word "parula" has nothing at all to do with the field marks, at least in any way that I can think of right now. I simply memorized the field marks and the name a few seasons ago, and that's the extent of my knowledge. I will put that on my list of things to research when I get home.

A snowy white Great Egret flies over at an angle. While I was watching it the group kept walking, and now I have to catch up to see what they're looking at in the trees. Following their directions I finally spot the burnt-orange breast of a very handsome bird, an Orchard Oriole. While I'm looking at him I hear something else. "Pee-a-wee, pee-oo," the bird sings, slurring the last part down. That's an Eastern Wood-Pewee, a bird I hear much more often than I actually see at home. I like it when a bird's name imitates its song because that makes it so easy to memorize.

Chimney Swifts flutter above us, seemingly with lopsided wing strokes, but that is an optical illusion. Or is it? I recall reading that this species has such a tiny tail that it must use its wings for steering, and it could be flexing the left wing to turn while keeping the right wing still. But I don't know if that movement, and the corresponding flexing of the right wing a split second later, would really be enough to cause the strobe-light effect of their jerky flight pattern. Maybe our human eyes perceive it this way by mistake.

A Turkey Vulture glides along high above us on almost motionless wings, then in sharp contrast a tiny speedball hurtles past us almost at eye level, its wings beating so fast they are a blur. Easily mistaken for a large insect, it's really a Ruby-throated Hummingbird. I haven't seen many flower blossoms on the plants here, so I don't know where it will find nectar, although the Turk's Cap are blooming. And hummers are attracted to red things and will investigate any flower of that color to see if it contains nectar. That's why artificial feeders for hummers have red on them.

The hidden mimic singing pairs of songs above us is a Brown Thrasher, and this one is singing with particular vigor, seldom pausing in his lively string of song after song after song.

§

I hear a series of squeak-toy call notes, a string of "pik-pik-pik" that sounds almost exactly like one of the small woodpeckers that lives at my place back in Kentucky, and that I've encountered in many kinds of woods throughout the eastern United States. But this bird's voice is a bit deeper, and something else seems a bit different. We continue to hear it calling up in the treetops. When I suggest the name of the woodpecker I know at home for this guy, Dave explains that here in this part of Texas the more likely bird is indeed in the same genus, Picoides, but is a different species, the Ladder-backed Woodpecker.

For several days Jane and Dave have been watching a pair of these little woodpeckers excavating a potential nest hole in an overhanging limb of a large tree along this road, and they take us to the exact spot just a few steps ahead. We look and look, but there is no activity while we are standing there. When I write down the name of this new woodpecker in my field notebook as a lifer, I am careful to also put (h) beside it, meaning that so far I've only heard it. I will certainly keep my eyes open from this point on for a small woodpecker with zig-zag barring on its back like the picture Jane showed me in her field guide. Apparently the range for the bird I know at home stops somewhere near here, and the Ladder-backed Woodpecker takes over in this part of Texas and down into Mexico. It's a similar situation to the different ranges of the Tufted Titmouse and the Black-crested Titmouse.

Some of the people in our group are ready to leave for other activities. Those of us who are still discussing the birds we've seen this morning welcome the invitation to walk over to Dave and Jane's campsite to watch for more birds at their feeders and water drip. We stroll over to their campsite and, as I settle into one of the lawn chairs, a hummingbird shows up almost immediately to hover at a sugar-water feeder, but dashes away before we can get a good look.

As we relax in the shade by the RV, Dave quietly begins an impromptu lesson about how to tell one hummingbird species from another. This is something I really need to learn, because the only kind I've ever seen at home is the Ruby-throated Hummingbird. I automatically wrote that name down in my notebook when that hummer barreled past us earlier while we were walking, without considering other possibilities. But now I realize that there is very good chance that it could have been something else. Until this morning I did not know that a similar species in the same genus is also common in this part of Texas. Dave mentions a difference in the feather colors of the males and a detail about bill shape, but I don't understand these subtleties yet.

As we watch for hummers, several squirrels frolic along the tree limbs and scamper across the dirt. A rich red Northern Cardinal poses briefly on a nearby branch, then we see both a male and female Red-winged Blackbird. Some Inca Doves peck at seeds on the ground.

Finally another hummingbird shows up to hover at another one of the sugar-water feeders. I look at the bill and discover that, instead of being perfectly straight, it has just the slightest downward curve from about the midpoint to the tip. I would never be able to see this difference while the bird is flying. Even while it is paused to hover in front of the feeder, I can only get a hint of the curve. For some reason I thought all hummers had completely straight bills. Not my first birding mistake, but one I have the chance to correct today. A bit of sunshine creates a pool of light around the feeder and, as the bird maneuvers to sip and moves this way and that in the light, I see that the throat feathers do not gleam red. Instead, I see some dark feathers under the bill and a hint of purple towards the breast where I would expect to see red. Aha! I am looking at a Black-chinned Hummingbird for the very first time!

This is a delightful conclusion to today's bird walk, and a very satisfying way to end my visit to Goose Island State Park. I whisper that I must leave to go strike my tent. I thank Jane and Dave for all that I've learned and tell them how much I've enjoyed these mornings. Our handshake goodbyes turn into quick hugs. They are my kind of birders and I'm so glad I met them.

§

When I'm striking camp I have a very efficient routine that I follow, but before I can begin that this morning I have to deal with the insect life on my tent. Ever since I set up camp here I've had to watch out for a particularly handsome and bristly critter, the white-marked tussock moth caterpillar. They are gorgeous and I've taken a lot of photos of them, but they're strictly a look-don't-touch animal, as the long bristly hairs decorating their plump bodies can be extremely irritating to human skin. The little whisk broom I carry in my camping essentials box is not working very well to shoo the caterpillars off the tent fabric, and I need something longer. I find a convenient stick on the ground nearby, pick it up and use it to set about knocking and sweeping more than a dozen caterpillars off the rain fly and tent, being careful not to knock any of them onto my sandals or bare toes. And I make a mental note to buy a cheap long-handled broom when I get home. I think that would be a very useful addition to my camping gear on future trips.

Once I've cleared all the critters away, I make good, steady progress dismantling everything inside my temporary bedroom and stowing the various pieces and parts into their proper stuff sacks and plastic bins. My new wastebasket table presents a challenge as I begin re-packing the car, but I soon figure out that all I have to do to conserve space is to nest my bedroll inside it.

When I pull up the pegs holding the tent guy wires in place so I can let my tent collapse flat, I make an interesting discovery about Wednesday night's rainstorm. Not all of the water ran down the sides of my tent and into the ground. Some of it flowed between the base of the tent and my ground cover—and some of the water is still there. This is not an uncommon occurrence. In fact, it almost always happens during a rainstorm, and when it does I use some old towels I carry with me to sop up the moisture. But I hadn't planned on quite so much water remaining. This is more than the old towels can handle. I'll have to move my car so that I have enough space to spread out the wet ground tarp on the gravelly asphalt in direct sunlight to finish drying. The outside of the bottom of my tent is also wet, so I'll turn the flattened tent upside down and drape it over the picnic table so it can dry it off, too. Mildew is the enemy of every camper, and taking the time to do this now is my only good option.

While I'm waiting for things to get dry, I take a break to study my maps and plan the next section of my trip. I have at least two hundred miles to cover today. If I were traveling by boat I could go straight down between the barrier islands and the mainland via the Gulf Intracoastal Waterway to get to my destination. But I have a car, and once again the roads do not follow the coast. I will have to drive west inland, skirt around Corpus Christi, then drive south to reach tonight's hotel on South Padre Island. I enter the address into my GPS and return to finish packing up my now-dry gear.

I'm finally ready to get on the road, about an hour later than I planned, but that's fine. I stop in at the ranger station to let them know my campsite is clear and tell them how much I've enjoyed my visit. As a souvenir I buy a small enameled pin depicting a Brown Pelican. On the way over here nothing squeaked or rattled inside the car, but I realize that I don't have the striped quilt that covers all my gear in the back positioned quite right—I can see a big, distracting lump in the center of my rearview mirror. I open the liftgate and smooth things out properly. Finally, I'm ready to head out to the main road.

###

CHAPTER NINE

South Padre Island and Laguna Madre

More new birds, local lore, horses on the beach

My route south leads from Aransas Bay to Corpus Christi Bay, then skirts around the center of that city. As I take the multilane highway around the edge, I'm getting really hungry for some lunch, but finding a place to eat proves challenging. Traffic is moving very fast on the highway and when I finally see a cluster of national chain restaurants in a suburban shopping district, I can't figure out how to get to them. I will just have to take the next available exit and trust to luck. I do not want to eat at a national chain, but it's a good bet that some regional or local places will be tucked in among the splashy places. But where? And what kind of food?

Pulling into the first available shopping center parking lot to get my bearings, I look around and up. Amid the thicket of tall signs advertising all sorts of restaurants bordering the main road, I spot one for barbeque and realize that is exactly what I want. But what is the pattern of access roads? How can I get from this particular parking lot, where I've been idling to make my decision, over to the place I want to be on the other side of the highway, with the fewest left turns?

Those are questions that temporarily stump my GPS, but ten minutes later I'm parked in a crowded lot and walking in the door of a very plain-looking place called Bill Miller Bar-B-Q. I look around and see that this is a no-frills family sort of restaurant with simple tables and chairs, just a big square dining room—and it's filled with lots of local people even so long past noon. I study the menu and place my order at the counter, pay, then wait for my meal to appear at the far end of the counter. I take the tray over to an empty table near the back windows and settle in to eat.

The beef brisket is absolutely amazing, tasty and tender. While I'm eating I check my phone, and at the restaurant's website I discover that this family business began in the San Antonio area in the 1950s. The meats are still prepared the old-fashioned way in brick pits with hill country live-oak wood, no natural gas flames, no electricity, just wood fires to provide the heat and just the right amount of smoke. Ah, totally good travel karma, because I found this place completely by accident. The side dishes are delicious, too, squishy green beans, hash brown potatoes with crispy edges, and the sweetest creamed corn I've had in years. This is hearty food for a Texas-sized appetite, and just what I need to refresh myself with after such a busy morning breaking camp.

Back on the road again, my GPS sends me due south on a four-lane divided highway, Texas 77. It's flat, it's straight, and the speed limit is seventy-five miles per hour, even though access is not controlled. There are little farm and ranch roads branching out perpendicular to the highway, and I have to keep looking far ahead for those intersections because pickup trucks and cars can and do turn directly into the fast-moving traffic or cross straight over to get to the other side. This is a major, multi-purpose, north-south transportation corridor, with high-voltage power transmission lines on my left and a railroad on my right. The miles glide by as I listen to Western swing music today and think about cattle ranches.

After about an hour of driving I reach an unusual place to go birding. Smack in the middle of the wide median strip, I've arrived at the Sarita Rest Area, stop number 205 in the Coastal Bend Loop of the Texas Gulf Coast Birding Trail. As a traveler's rest stop, it offers the usual amenities beyond the parking places. Amid wild olive and mesquite trees, trimmed up to provide headroom for humans walking around, I see a large, single-story building with restrooms, then some picnic tables, a dog walk area—and signs advising visitors to "watch for poisonous snakes." I laugh at that (it's the editor in me, I can't help it) but the correct word from the scientific, natural history standpoint would be "venomous," not "poisonous." Whatever, the sign gets the point across just as well. Look out where you or your dog are walking!

What this rest stop does not have is fences or guardrails to keep people confined to the center median and separated from the traffic. It is quite possible to walk across the highway to the far shoulder and along the grassy margins over there and explore the tree lines of the fields bordering the highway to look for birds. Traffic whooshing past at seventy-five miles per hour—oh, let's be honest, some of the vehicles are going eighty-five miles an hour—makes this seem like a very bad idea to me today. I'll just spend my time looking around in the center of the rest stop.

Above the noise of the speeding cars and trucks it's easy to hear the distinctive voices of Great-tailed Grackles, and there are some Common Grackles mixed in, too. I think those are Mourning Doves in the trees on my right. That's all I can see, and, considering that I have at least another one hundred miles to drive this afternoon, I'm going to get back on the road. Just as I'm pulling out of the rest stop I catch sight of the unmistakable shape of a Scissor-tailed Flycatcher flying over to one of the brushy fields.

When I have to slow down for a pickup truck pulling into the traffic ahead of me farther down the road, I catch sight of a large bird with white wing tips and a white tail with a black stripe at the bottom flying nearby, a Crested Caracara.

§

I continue driving south for a while, then turn east toward the coast. In Los Fresnos I buy some gas, then it's an easy drive over to the town of Port Isabel and across a long causeway over Laguna Madre, then out onto South Padre Island. This is the only way to reach the island, and once there I must turn north to find my hotel. It's up ahead on the right.

Most of the hotels in the Holiday Inn Express brand of the Intercontinental Hotel Group cater about half-and-half to business travelers and leisure travelers. I know from experience that the service will be friendly and efficient, with good options for relaxing after the workday. This spring weekend this four-story hotel at a fun destination is completely packed with folks eager to have a good time, no business travelers. The lobby, with a large see-through aquarium, is busy with kids, teenagers, parents, grandparents, young couples, every combination of friends and family, and I see a lot of folks in swimsuits coming and going to the outdoor pool and the beach.

I pick up some tourist brochures from the rack in the lobby and head over to the front desk. Checking in for my three-night stay here is easy, and I take my duffel and big suitcase to the elevators to go up to my room. For an unknown reason, only one elevator is working. The other one has a sign saying "sorry for the inconvenience, temporarily out of service." I'm almost the only person in street clothes waiting for the elevator—just about everyone else is wearing a swimsuit and dripping water onto the hallway floor mats. I brought a swimsuit with me, but I don't know if I'll have time for that this evening.

Once I'm in my room on the third floor, I have a nice view across the tops of apartment buildings and condominiums out to the Gulf of Mexico—I'm just two blocks from the beach. I've made a good choice, and I'm glad to be here at what will be my southernmost base for this trip. However, the long, hot, private shower I've been looking forward to after three days of camping is not exactly my dream. The water is barely warm, not steaming hot like I've been imagining for miles. Apparently all those folks coming back from the pool and the beach have exactly the same idea as I do, and the hotel's water heaters can't quite keep up with the demand. Oh, well, I'm refreshed and ready to go in search of dinner.

As twilight sets in, the roads here are chaos. There are cars, pickup trucks, topless Jeeps, people on bicycles, people on foot, and people driving street-legal, souped-up golf carts decorated with multicolor LED lights and blaring music as they zip past. It reminds me of Daytona Beach, only packed into a much smaller area. I drive to the area where the hotel desk clerk told me I'd find the most popular restaurants and discover that some of the streets are barricaded to provide more room for people wandering around from place to place, and that there's no space left to park. I successfully dodge pedestrians and more golf carts, then backtrack to the main road to see if I can find someplace to eat in a less crowded section of the town.

Close to my hotel I see an old building that's been divided up into several different styles of bars and restaurants, and right next to it I find a place to park on a side street. I sit upstairs at the open-air bar in the section called Kraken and sip a nice cold Corona while chatting with the bartender and watching baseball on one of the big-screen TVs. This place seems to be more of a local resident hangout than a tourist place, and I like the laid-back, low-key atmosphere.

As I unwind I study the menu and order a basket of catfish tumblers. I don't understand the name, but apparently it's the local version of fried catfish nuggets. When they arrive they're breaded in crispy cornmeal, the perfect bar food snack, juicy and flavorful on the inside. By the time I realize I could eat another portion, the bartender informs me they're sold out for the night. I guess the locals know a good thing, too. I order a second beer, and after that I head back to my hotel.

§

Before I get out of my car back at the hotel, I gather up the book about birding locations along the Gulf Coast, two field guides, my camera, my travel journal, and the bird lists I printed before I left home and take all of that up to my room. My room has a nice desk with a comfy chair and reading lamp, the perfect place to work on catching up with my notes, and I have plenty of time this evening to study.

My first project is to look through the travel brochures I just picked up and compare them to the birding sites described in my book to come up with a tentative plan for the next three days. I use my phone to check the weather forecasts and jot down some notes. I want to do some touristy things, too, and will need to build in time for those activities.

Now I can focus on birds. As I review the photos in my camera, look up descriptions of the lifers I've learned so far, and put different symbols and colored dots next to birds' names in my field notebook and on the printed list, I am glad that I brought more than one field guide. When I was home I chose to bring along Peterson's because it's the book I know the best, and the paintings accentuate field marks very clearly. But I also like to carry the National Wildlife Federation's *Field Guide to Birds of North America* with me because of two important features. First, the illustrations are color photographs of living birds in their habitat, which sometimes is more useful than a stylized painting against a plain white background. Second, the range maps are right next to the photographs instead of being at the back of the book as they are in my copy of Peterson's. Having the map on the same page as the photo is really convenient and saves a lot of flipping back and forth.

But now I realize there's another advantage to having the second book with me on this trip. Somewhere about midway down the Texas Gulf Coast, I drove out of the area covered by Peterson's guide to eastern birds, and now I'm actually in the region covered by western field guides. I don't have that book in the Peterson series, but the National Wildlife Federation book covers all of North America, east and west, so if I can't find a bird in Peterson's I can look in the other book.

I've not had the time, or even the desire, to keep a running list of all the bird species I've seen so far on this trip, and it seems too complicated a task to attempt tonight. That's something I'll sort out when I get back home. As I transcribe all my notes later I can double-check my cross-referencing system more carefully using my computer. But I am trying to keep up-to-date with the lifers I've seen and heard so far, and that's what I'll do tonight—continue to add hand-written notes to the printed list of lifers I brought with me.

Tonight's also a good opportunity to catch up with social media for information about the Texas birds that are active this week in this part of the state, plus the info and comments from my birding friends in other states. When one of my pals in Kentucky asks me to name my favorite bird so far, I have to think for a few minutes before answering.

Just going on looks alone, the Scissor-tailed Flycatcher is by far the most unusual new bird I've seen so far. It's immediately recognizable because the long white tail feathers tipped with black are so out of proportion to the body, and so deeply forked. Every time I see one—and I've seen them in three different places so far—I think, who did you steal those feathers from? They really look like they ought to be on a much larger bird. And yet the birds are not clumsy at all, but extremely graceful. So that's one favorite.

For shorebirds, I really like the looks of the Whimbrel. Although its plumage is similar to so many other birds that dash along at the water's edge, a mixture of browns and buffs, the long, down-curved bill is very interesting to see. I don't know why it's curved like that, what kind of advantage such a shape provides for catching food, but I like it.

Then again, I really enjoyed seeing my first Hooded Warbler. The brilliant yellow eye mask is such a vivid contrast to the bird's black hood—I hope I get to see another one soon.

I drift off into a reverie about all the many birds I've watched during this trip and realize that I'm getting really sleepy. It's time to turn the lights out and call this day done.

§

Before breakfast I take my field guides and bird lists back down to the car, then go for a short walk around the hotel parking lot, listening to the Great-tailed Grackles chatter. Back indoors, I have to wait in line for a few minutes at the breakfast buffet in the hotel gathering room because there are so many other guests here this weekend. I don't know when or where I'll eat lunch, so I load up my plate with everything I like. The bacon is delicious.

I'm outside again shortly before ten, ready to drive to this morning's birding site, which is only half a mile away. The South

Padre Island Birding and Nature Center is on the same road as my hotel, but on the opposite side.

This site has glossy advertising placards similar in style to the ones promoting commercial adventures such as boat rides and zip lines, but it's based on an ecotourism economic model that's not about making a profit. Even though I already knew about the center from a Louisville friend who grew up on a ranch in Texas and returns to this area often to visit, I picked up one of the ads from the rack in the hotel lobby yesterday. My overall impression is that this place is designed to appeal to people who don't know very much about birds or wildlife and want an easy way to give it a try. The ad does include beautiful close-up photos of especially alluring birds—and an alligator!

For casual visitors, the boardwalk's three thousand, three hundred–foot length offers a quick way to explore forty-three acres. And that's a clever choice of words to avoid saying something potentially daunting for casual explorers such as "more than half a mile of planking." The site also includes a five-story enclosed observation tower with an elevator to the top for views out across the wetlands and the bayside habitats of the Lower Laguna Madre. The photos are very attractive, and they appeal to me as an experienced birder, so I'm eager to visit.

This site is a bit different from the kinds of places where I often go birding. It's not a state or national park, or a federal wildlife refuge. It's not a slice of land owned and managed by an individual conservation group such as The Nature Conservancy or by a local Audubon Society. Instead, it's a partnership involving three groups—the Parks and Wildlife Division of Texas state government, the U.S. Fish and Wildlife Department, and the Town of South Padre Island's Economic Development Corporation—and it's so easy to get to, right here, amid hotels and restaurants at a popular vacation destination.

When I arrive, the parking lot is almost empty and I have no trouble at all finding a place for my car. Walking toward the building, I pass an artfully landscaped pond where a hen duck and her ducklings are enjoying a swim. For a moment I'm taken aback—

I've driven nineteen hundred miles now, and the ducks look just the same as the ones at home! Well, that's okay with me, because I've been seeing many of the same bird species I know from home during this trip, along with the new ones I'm discovering, and it's a beautiful sunny morning. Inside the building I pay the five-dollar entrance fee at a computer screen, sort of like a reverse ATM machine, and walk into an attractive lobby and gift shop.

The woman at the front desk mentions that one of the things that sets this area apart is the high salt concentration of the water in the bays and estuaries that make up the various habitats within the Laguna Madre. The water is actually saltier than the ocean, a condition known as hypersalinity. But even though it's extra salty, the plants and marine animals are well adapted to this and thrive under these conditions, and there's plenty of food for the birds. She then explains the layout of the boardwalk, which is in typical loop fashion, with several covered observation spots with benches scattered about, and I walk outside to begin exploring.

I'm dressed for a morning of intense birding—camera with zoom lens and binoculars hanging by their straps around my neck, water bottle in a convenient pocket—and wearing my favorite ball cap, the slightly faded, sweat-stained one with a birding event logo above the bill and four embroidered birds above that. I walk just a few steps and lean against the boardwalk railing to get out my pocket notebook and begin jotting down the birds I see. This is a deluxe boardwalk, with the decking and rails made not of wood but of a man-made composite material—no splinters, no knotholes, no uneven treads, quite civilized.

After noting the ducks I saw in the parking lot, I also write down the Great-tailed Grackles that were so noisy on that side of the visitor center. Swimming near the reeds below me are several Black-bellied Whistling-Ducks, with their bright pinkish-orange bills, and some Laughing Gulls begin making a racket nearby. So far so good, and so easy to identify. But I'm not so sure what that bird over there in the distance is, so I raise my binoculars for a better look.

§

Just as I write down "Willet" in my notebook, a guy about the same age as my daughter walks over and strikes up a conversation with me about the birds here. I mention that the Willet we're both looking at now is one of the shorebirds I saw a few days ago farther north, and tell him a little about my trip exploring the whole Texas Gulf Coast. As it turns out, he lives in one of the inland towns I drove through yesterday. He's an avid birder and enjoys coming over here to the bay and seashore as often as he can.

We begin strolling along together, looking from side to side at the different habitats, some reedy and marshy, some more open and sandy.

A little farther on I see a bird that I have trouble identifying. I can tell from the long and slightly upturned bill that it's a godwit, but I don't know which species. I've only seen such a bird once before, and that was more than a year ago on the Atlantic coast of Florida at Merritt Island National Wildlife Refuge. I tell the guy who's walking along with me a little bit about that trip, and then we talk about the field marks of this bird. I focus my binoculars on the bird's upturned bill. It's orange near the face, black near the tip. My overall impression of the body is beige on the underside, mottled black and beige on the top. This is where his local knowledge comes in handy. He says it's a Marbled Godwit, and as I review the field marks of this bird and think again about the one I saw in Florida, I agree. He mentions that it is the most likely godwit species to find here at this time of year.

Many male Red-winged Blackbirds are flitting back and forth among the reeds and cattails on our right, epaulets flashing to show all the yellow feathers and all the red feathers, too. Some of the streaky brown-and-beige females are darting around, too, and I think they will soon form pairs or threesomes and start building nests. Red-winged Blackbird males often attract two or more females to their territories, and that apparently suits the females just fine. This looks like ideal habitat for them, and they seem eager to get things settled so they can begin raising broods.

We continue to walk along together, watching for birds and chatting from time to time. A bit farther on we have a nice view of a patch of sandy soil where we discover a Ruddy Turnstone flipping small pebbles aside to find something to eat. Farther from the shore we see a Black Skimmer flying along in a straight line just above the surface, dipping its long, lower bill into the water, but we cannot tell if it's found something to scoop up on this pass. Probably not, as it flaps its wings faster and veers away from us to try a different patch of water.

As we go farther along the boardwalk out into the marshy areas, we are continually scanning the edges of the reeds and other plants. We see several Great Blue Herons patiently waiting for something to swim near enough to their legs to make a strike with their long bills. Each bird seems to have a personal hunting spot—they are spaced widely apart from each other. From time to time one gives up and flies off to try a new location, but when it lands it makes certain to not get too close to another heron. Great Egrets also looking for places to hunt fly over from time to time, and then we see one already standing in shallow water make a strike. The much shorter Cattle Egrets are easy to find, hunched over on low branches, their orangish breeding plumage outlining the edges of their white heads and shoulders.

As we amble along we talk about some of our birding adventures and our lives back home. His wife also enjoys birding, but she had other things to do this morning. He's going to be teaching biology this fall at a high school for the first time and might start a birdwatching club for the students.

We see some Double-crested Cormorants up ahead, then a Royal Tern flies past, quite close. Oddly enough, I spot a Rock Dove next, and I mention how confusing it was to me, when I first got interested in birds, to discover how the official common name for pigeons has changed over the years. We talk about how the science side of birding keeps us on our toes when we're out in the field observing birds.

The handsome little birds that fly by on our right are Least Terns, and I jot that down in my notebook. This place is turning out to offer a nice variety of birds and I'm glad to be here. And I'm also glad that this local birder struck up a conversation with me. Rambling along at a leisurely pace with him is adding to the pleasure of this morning among so many birds.

Some American Coots have formed a little raft nearby, bobbing and drifting on the water, and we pause to watch them for a short while. Then, as we walk very quietly along the boardwalk into an area of reeds, we have a real treat. We can look over the railing and down amid the vegetation onto a Tricolored Heron hunting in about six inches of water just a few feet away from us. Carefully I bring my camera up to eye level, adjust the focus, and get what I hope will be a really nice photo that will show the white skin around the bird's eye, the thin rim of white feathers visible at the shoulder, and a few wispy white feathers on the neck. I've never been this close to a Tricolored Heron before, and I consider this a wonderful treat. Already I'm convinced that this boardwalk is a great place to observe birds.

§

So far, we haven't come across any other people, and that makes it easy for us to go at our own pace, with no need to stand aside for through-walkers or stop and wait for a clump of people to move on in front of us. As we explore another section of the boardwalk, we have a better view of some sandy flats where several Black-bellied Plovers are gathered at the water's edge.

And then I see a much larger bird with contrasting areas of black and white feathers and a long, thick, reddish-orange bill. Although I've never encountered this bird before, I recognize it immediately from some recent photos on social media—it's another lifer for me, an American Oystercatcher. I think of the Gulf as a great place for shrimp, but apparently there are enough oysters in these shallow waters to make it a good hunting ground for this species that specializes in prying mollusk shells open to feed on the soft animal inside.

This section of the boardwalk leads back toward the edge of a reedy area, and when we get there, we lean over to watch a hen duck and her ducklings swimming on the smooth water. By now I've learned that my companion's name is Brandon, and I tell him about seeing a Mallard at the pond in the parking lot when I arrived earlier this morning. He smiles and says I should look again at the duck below us because, although at first glance it looks like a Mallard, it's really a different species, a Mottled Duck. Brandon points out two of the key differences—no black mark on the bill and no white feathers in the tail.

He mentions that for a long time it was considered a subspecies within the Mallards, but scientists have determined it really is a separate species, so it's fair for me to mark it as a lifer. Well, most of time it's a separate species. That is to say, sometimes Mallards will breed with Mottled Ducks, and those hybrids can be really confusing to identify. This hen is very attentive to her little ducklings, which, based on their size, I'd estimate to be less than a week old. She calls softly to them in a low murmuring voice to keep them close to her as they swim along on the water just below us by the boardwalk, then disappear for a few seconds under the boardwalk, and soon emerge on the other side to paddle off to explore another area of water.

Two women have walked up behind us quietly, and we all say hello to each other. They ask if we saw that great big white bird flap over a little while ago—they thought it was really cool. We agree, and tell them it's a Great Egret. They seem eager to walk ahead, so we wish them a good morning as they move on past us.

Soon we reach another section of the boardwalk with a good view of some sandy flats where a Wilson's Plover stands still momentarily. I tell Brandon about seeing my first one up the coast at Bolivar Flats just a few days ago, and how the single, thick black neckband is one of the things that helps me remember it and keep it straight from the larger but similarly shaped Killdeer, who sports two black necklaces.

As a group of Barn Swallows flit above us, chasing tiny little insects we can't see, I tell him how much I enjoy being in all the birding groups I've found on social media. He's not in any of those groups, but he's very well connected with the local birding community in other ways, and he recommends some places I ought to visit while I'm here in the Rio Grande Valley. He has a friend who's doing a survey of birds in the Brownsville area and he gives me the name of the place as a good spot to look for birds near sunset tomorrow.

A short while later we have a good view of a streaky, yet sort of spotted, black-and-white bird with long legs. The bill seems to curve upward just a tiny bit at the end, but the bright yellow legs are what get my attention. When I first got started in birding I had to learn the oddities of bird anatomy. And that's not so easy to do, because most field guides concentrate on the feathers, not the structure of the bird's body under those pretty feathers, or the way the legs and feet are put together. In field guides, one is much more likely to find detailed drawings of bird wings, with arrows pointing to the names of the different groups of feathers. Only rarely is there any explanation of the fact that there are bones underneath comparable to human fingers.

The legs of birds get even less attention, but their structure and colors often help with solving identification problems. Bird legs and feet are similar to human legs and feet, but the proportions are very different. On all the birds I can think of, the distance between the hip and the knee is very short, and the knee joint is hidden by body feathers. It's the bird's heel that we see below the body, not a knee hinged backwards. For most birds, the bone connecting this joint to the toes is elongated. The size and arrangement of the toes vary among bird groups, and they can do things with them that we can only dream of doing with ours.

We look very closely at the bird. Yes, it has yellow legs but that is not enough to know. We look some more. The heel joint appears to be very thick. We decide this must be a Greater Yellowlegs, yet another lifer for me. Brandon has another advantage over me because of his familiarity with the local birds. He can also tell that this bird is taller than a Lesser Yellowlegs, even though there aren't any of that species nearby. It's just something one gets a feel for, similar to the way I can tell the approximate size of so many of the birds back home when I see them, even when they are not perched among tree limbs and leaves whose size I know for comparison, and when there are no other birds nearby. It's just something I know after seeing them over and over again.

We've made an almost complete circuit of the boardwalks and are now heading back towards the building. Brandon points out a Common Gallinule just seconds before it disappears among some emergent vegetation, and then both of us spot four Blue-winged Teal paddling around on the water about fifty feet away. We stop to take good, long looks at several Black-necked Stilts foraging in another section, and then Brandon suggests we take a look at the water tower.

§

That seems like an odd suggestion, but I figure, why not? As we continue our walk we get a good view of a Green Heron standing at the edge of a concrete structure where water spills to another level of the marsh. This is mostly wild habitat, but in some areas humans do a little bit of micromanaging to keep the water at appropriate levels. I'm used to seeing Green Herons hunched below overhanging limbs along a slow-flowing creek or standing half hidden among drooping willow branches on the muddy bank of my own pond at home. Finding one mostly out in the open is a treat — and an unexpected great photo opportunity.

When we get to the section of the boardwalk near the water tower, Brandon says we should look up. I do, and see a typical, small-town water tank, perhaps seventy-five feet above the ground, mounted on sturdy legs. The tank's side features the words "Laguna Madre Water District," written in all capital letters, with an attractive painting of the local lighthouse in the center. He asks if I can see anything on the left, below the large D in the word "Madre." I raise my binoculars and get a tremendous surprise — what I thought was just a dark smudge is actually a Peregrine Falcon! I try to zoom in on it with my camera, but I'm not satisfied with the results and we move a few steps forward on the boardwalk to get a bit closer.

Brandon explains that this bird hangs out here a lot, and seems accustomed to people walking along below on the boardwalk. This superb hunter is not easily spooked from his perch high above us, where he (or possibly she, the sexes look alike in this species) watches for potential prey. Unlike the Red-tailed Hawk, who only takes an occasional nestling or other unwary bird, the Peregrine Falcon is a bird-hunting specialist, swooping down to snatch up birds wherever it can find them. This marshy area offers plenty of opportunities. Tired, migrating songbirds who've just come ashore from their flight over the Gulf might be on the menu this week.

If I were here by myself, I doubt that I would ever have done anything more than take a quick glance at the water tower. I don't think it would have occurred to me to search it for a perched bird, and certainly not for a bird that was removed from the Endangered Species list less than twenty years ago. But there it is, and I have Brandon to thank for this treat. Peregrine Falcons typically perch and nest on natural cliffs, but they've taken to using skyscrapers and tall bridges in big cities, too. I guess this water tower, which is the tallest thing for miles around, seems like a good cliff substitute to the falcon.

The boardwalk leads around toward the north, so that now we are on the shady side of the structure and I have a much better view of the Peregrine Falcon, resting on a ledge formed by the top of one of the tank's support legs. The bird is huddled up next to the side of the tank and just behind a safety railing where water company workers can walk around when they need to climb up there. I take a photo and trust that later I'll be able to zoom in tighter to see the bird's trademark facial markings better, a blob of dark feathers that make it look like it's wearing a hat with black, pull-down ear flaps. I study the bird for a while with my binoculars, hoping that perhaps it will make a dive on prey, but it seems to be content to simply rest right now.

As we walk on a few steps, the sun is at just the right angle so that, when we lean over the boardwalk railing, we can see a very large crab with orange front claws below the water's surface, swimming in the shallows. Brandon thinks it might be a blue crab, but I really don't know anything about crab species, other than the fact that most of them are delicious to eat. The herons and egrets hunting here would agree with me.

Returning our gaze to the boardwalk, we see a Eurasian Collared-Dove perched on the railing out in front of us, but it flies off as we approach. There are many other shallow ponds out toward the eastern part of this excellent birding area. We are now in the section that borders the busy main road, hidden from us by a picket fence, and we linger to examine each bit of water for bird activity. Sure enough, we spot some Pied-billed Grebes drifting lazily on the calm water in the distance. A sandbar stretches across a portion of this pond, and we discover several Roseate Spoonbills standing out there preening and generally loafing around. But wait, what's that other bird? I refocus my binoculars and see that it is a Reddish Egret, poised for hunting in the shallow water.

As we've walked along this section of the boardwalk we can see a different boardwalk to our south. Brandon explains to me that the other one, which is made of well-weathered wood, belongs to the convention center next door. He says that although the habitats over there are basically the same as what we've been exploring here, it's worth a visit if I have time, and it's free.

§

As we turn the last corner on our section of boardwalk we see more waterfowl in the distance and begin scanning carefully with our binoculars. I notice the black rump of an otherwise rather bland gray-and-beige duck and remember that is a key field mark of a Gadwall, a bird I haven't seen in a very long time. Brandon tells me they spend the winter here in great numbers, and he expects these stragglers will leave soon for their summer breeding grounds in the Great Plains and Canada. As we're watching these ducks paddle slowly along, I catch sight of a different beige-y duck, one with a black breast and pretty rust-colored head. That's an easy one to name—it's a Redhead, a duck that also raises its young a thousand or more miles away from Texas.

We are very close to the Gulf here, even though we can't see it. I would guess that the waves on the sandy beach are less than half a mile away as a bird flies—just over the fence, across the busy road, then two or three short blocks past the condos. And that's why I'm not all that surprised to see a shorebird with a long, straight bill poking it rapidly up and down in the sandy flats here, just like a sewing machine needle going through cloth. That motion and the overall body shape plus the length of the legs make it recognizable to me as a dowitcher, but which one? The bill is going in and out of the sand so fast I can't get a good notion of the size relative to the body, and this is where ambling along with a local birder once again comes in handy.

Brandon tells me that since we are so near the shore, which starts with the letter "s," that's an easy way to get the name of the bird, which also begins with that letter—we're looking at a Short-billed Dowitcher. That's a good trick, and I appreciate it, but he also notes that the other dowitcher species with a longer bill that spends the winter in this area, usually over on the mudflat side behind us on the Lower Laguna Madre, left a few weeks ago to begin journeying northward. Since this is already the end of the second week of April, the short-billed version is the species we're most likely to see here, and they'll be leaving soon, too. More excellent details from a local birder—this really is my lucky morning. As I think about what Brandon is telling me, I realize that this is the same kind of dowitcher I saw out on Bolivar Flats several days ago.

We spend our last few minutes on the boardwalk talking about how different bird species use this area at different times of the year. We also talk about how important it is as birders to return to the same areas over and over again, to get a feel for the way things change throughout each season of the year. I mention that one of my goals on this trip is to develop a better understanding of migration patterns, not just of the popular and colorful warblers, but of all kinds of birds. This morning's exploration with Brandon and all the waterfowl we've seen has certainly been a bonus.

As we reach the visitor center building, a pair of Mourning Doves flutter away from us, murmuring their distinctive, soft cooing sounds. I thank Brandon for roaming along the boardwalk with me this morning, and wish him well in all his new adventures. We shake hands and I go inside the gift shop for a look around.

§

In the gift shop, the first thing that catches my eye is a rack of greeting cards. I see one I like, but then discover that the same design is also available as a full-size poster, the Coastal and Wetland Birds of the Gulf of Mexico. It's more artistic than a formal chart and features full-color portraits of at least fifty birds. I look at the display model and can pick out at least three dozen birds that I've seen on my trip so far. Below the model is a rack of posters rolled into stiff cardboard tubes, which will solve my transportation problem to get it back home unwrinkled. I grab a tube to take to the sales counter.

On the way there, I discover that another section of the shop has books. And there on one of the shelves is a fresh copy of the field guide that Jane was using on our bird walks at Goose Island State Park. I won't have to wait until I'm back home to order a copy—I can buy it today.

Out in the parking lot as I unlock my car, a White Ibis, the one with black wing tips, flies over me. That's a good sign—it's one of the birds on the poster I just bought. I lift my binoculars and camera off from around my neck, then find what I hope will be a safe place behind the passenger seat for the poster tube. And my new book goes straight into the laundry basket on the front seat so I can use it right away, while I'm still traveling.

I pause for a drink of water then put the plastic bottle in the door pocket and start the car. I'm ready for lunch. Today in bright sunshine I have no trouble finding the restaurant I wanted to try last night, and now there are plenty of places to park. From this side, all I can see are bright blue awnings and palm trees, but no way in. I'm not sure I've chosen wisely, but I walk around the building anyway. Ah, here are the stairs leading up to the entrance to the Painted Marlin Grille. At the top I find a pretty open-air bar with umbrella-topped tables, and an excellent view of a small boat dock and the beautiful, blue, open waters of Laguna Madre.

Gazing at the water sparkling in the sunlight, I sip a mimosa, then enjoy a delicious lunch of grilled red snapper, served with lightly sautéed julienned veggies sprinkled with some herbs. While I'm eating, I study the changing shapes of the big cumulus clouds towering above the water. I realize now that I was lucky that I didn't find this place last night—in the dark I wouldn't have had such a pretty view.

I've had to learn some quick geography while I've been traveling. The original Padre Island was one long barrier island more than one hundred miles long extending from the Corpus Christi area south to about where I'm sitting now. But in order to improve navigation, humans cut Mansfield Channel through it decades ago. So now it's two islands, which are not connected by a bridge or ferry service. That's why I had to go so far inland to drive here. Since the division, this section, known as South Padre Island, is only about thirty miles long. What gets even more confusing is that the larger part to the north isn't usually called North Padre Island but simply Padre Island. Only the smaller section, where I am now, gets a directional name, and it's also the name of the town here.

The water on the west side of what are now two separate islands is a continuous string of connected bays and estuaries known as Laguna Madre. However, in some books, and on some websites, the place where I spent the morning birding, and what I'm looking at now as I eat lunch, is referred to as Lower Laguna Madre. Yes, it's challenging to keep all this straight, and the location of the Texas portion of the Gulf Intracoastal Waterway between the islands and the mainland, and right through the Laguna Madre, makes it even more of a puzzle for a landlubber like me. But it doesn't seem to pose any problems for the birds, so I am content.

After lunch I turn back to drive farther north past the birding center and up through the center of South Padre Island, away from the restaurants and bars and shops. I have about four miles to go to reach my next destination, and the road soon changes from multiple lanes to only one lane in each direction. And then I get a surprise—sometimes part of the road is covered with drifting sand! There's so much sand that in quite a few places it covers my lane and spills over onto the yellow center line and into the lane of opposing traffic. Several times I have to stop to let approaching traffic in the bare southbound lane pass me before I can cross over into what is—for me—the wrong lane, to go forward. This is a problem I've never encountered before in decades of driving. Every so often there are breaks in the dunes on my right where cars are lined up at the side of the road to go out onto the beach, and I have to watch for people on foot exploring the dunes, too.

§

Soon I reach the entrance to South Padre Island Adventure Park on the left. I'm not here to go birding, and I'm not here to try the zip lines, no way. I'm here for some traditional Texas fun—a horseback ride. Standing by my car in the sand-and-gravel parking lot, I pull on my favorite heeled riding boots, then walk over more sand to get to the stables.

I'm one of the first riders to mount up, and as I wait for the rest of the group to get settled, I think about all the other places I've ridden. Through woods and across farm fields back in Kentucky and Indiana, up and down steep paths in mountains in the western states, across all sorts of terrain—except sand. Riding along on the beach by the waves coming in from the Gulf of Mexico is definitely going to be a new experience.

My mount's a sturdy palomino quarter horse, a gelding of about fifteen hands, a steady fellow named Rawhide, and I'm eager to get going. But a lot of the other riders are first-timers. The wranglers are very patient with them, explaining neck reining and then demonstrating it for the folks who do not understand spoken

English very well, if at all. I get the impression that for quite of few of these folks, this is a fantasy come to life. Giddy-up cowboy or cowgirl, as the case may be. Yeehaw!

Finally, our little group of about thirty horses and riders is ready, and the three wranglers get us started on our ride. One wrangler rides lead, one outrider moves continuously up and down the edge of the group watching for problems, and the third rides drag at the tail end of our group, just like herding cattle.

To begin, we have to cross the paved road, then weave up, over, and through the dunes, then out onto the beach. This section of the beach is open to cars and trucks, people with dogs, and all sorts of distractions, but these horses are all well mannered and accustomed to noisy humans and their machines and their pets. As we walk along I find it fascinating to look down past my horse's blond mane to watch the small waves rushing up the sand to cover his hooves. The pattern of the rippling water is mesmerizing.

While birdwatching from the saddle is certainly possible, I did not bring my binoculars along. This afternoon is more about horses than birds. What I need to watch is the other riders, particularly the novices whose horses are not responding to unclear guidance from their riders. I keep a close eye on them, and have to keep making minor adjustments with my reins and my knees to keep my horse from getting bumped by the other horses, who are drifting this way and that. As we amble along at a slow, steady pace, I think about how this island might have looked to the early Spanish explorers and settlers, and what birds they might have encountered. I wonder what names they called them, and whether they hunted any for food. The only birds flying around us now are the ones we call Laughing Gulls.

All too soon it is time to turn around to go back to the stables. As we walk along the almost-white sand, I chat with Tammy, the outrider. She's been riding horses all her life and rode competitively in college. She figures getting paid to ride her own horse while guiding tourists is the perfect job for now, and I like her spirit. She's also good with cell phones, and trusts her horse so well she drops her reins, turns sideways in her saddle to take my phone, then snaps a photo of me seated astride Rawhide. With my phone back in my pocket, I give Rawhide the signal to move on and we head back to the corral.

§

It's quite late in the afternoon, but I still have enough time to do a bit of shopping before dinner. I drive back south to town and spend about an hour going from tourist shop to tourist shop. I choose some postcards to send to family and friends back home, and then begin the hunt for a good dinner spot.

I figure I might as well keep the tourist thing going, so I park in the lot at Blackbeard's, a well-advertised destination with a pirate motif. A lot of other folks have the same idea this evening, and there's a wait for a table. But I prefer a seat at the bar, anyway, and am lucky to get the last barstool available inside. The countertop of the bar is covered with a stylish pattern of Mexican glazed tiles in various designs of cobalt blue, gray, white, and sunny yellow. I like it a lot. A cold Corona Extra tastes just right.

The two young women to my right are deeply engaged in conversation between themselves, and only take a moment to acknowledge my hello. To my left a married couple who live here year-round know the bartender's name and order their favorite drinks while telling me how good everything on the menu is. After studying the descriptions and seeing the huge portion sizes being served to other diners up and down the bar, I choose the simplest thing I can find, house-made corn chips and queso, and order another Corona Extra. This is the perfect way to celebrate such a fun-filled day of birds and horses.

The sun's set by the time I get back to my hotel, and finding a place to park takes some time. The hotel must be sold out for tonight because I see cars and trucks tucked into any place that seems even slightly out of the path of traffic. Some are even parked across the fire lanes. I don't want to do that, so I wait for some folks walking towards their car on their way to a late dinner, and as soon as they pull out, I slide into the vacant spot.

The lone working elevator takes me up to my room. The housekeepers have done a nice job of straightening things up, and I'm ready to relax. There's a big-screen TV that I could turn on, but I'd rather catch up with my field notes. And that's when I realize that I've left one of my bird lists in my car, so I'll have to go back outside.

Down in the jam-packed parking lot, I'm just a few steps from my car when I hear, "Ka-bang!" What? Then I hear it again. "Ka-bang! Boom! Boom, boom, boom!" I look up over the palm trees and see a showering cascade of red and white fireworks. I watch, thrilled and fascinated, as burst after colorful burst explodes somewhere above the beach. When I stand just so, I can see each pattern in the sky between the palm tree fronds—and its reflection on the shiny surface of my car's hood. This takes good travel karma to a whole new level, to be here on just the right night for such a dazzling extravaganza. When the show is over about fifteen minutes later, I gather up my bird lists and head back up to my room.

I write out my postcards first, then update my travel notebook and life bird list. I take some time to check in with friends and family back home via text messages, then review the latest Texas bird info on social media. But I'm getting very sleepy. Planning the details of tomorrow's excursions can wait until in the morning. Time for lights out.

###

CHAPTER TEN

Brownsville
and the Rio Grande Valley

Resaca de la Palma, border birds, footprints

The Great-tailed Grackles are at it again this morning during my before-breakfast walk at my hotel on South Padre Island, whistling and buzzing and doing a sort of whiny hum. I don't think they ever get tired of making noise. I'm beginning to think of them as the soundtrack for Texas.

After a substantial breakfast in the crowded hotel, I'm in my car by ten, ready to begin planning today's excursion. The book I bought so many weeks ago about birding along the Texas Gulf Coast lists more than two dozen birding sites under the Ranch Loop heading in this southernmost section of the Rio Grande Valley. I can't possibly see them all, and I knew that when I planned this trip. But I did organize my trip so that I have this entire day to explore as far from South Padre Island as I want to drive, and still get back to my base by dark, more or less. Now I have to choose the most likely spots to go. I want to get a good mix of inland sites with different habitats than the ones I've been exploring along the coast.

It makes the most sense to go to the one farthest away first, and then bird my way back. I enter some options into my phone's GPS and choose to drive south through Brownsville and then west to another one of the World Birding Center ecotourism sites. The place I want to explore is at Resaca de la Palma State Park. I should be able to get there in about an hour, so I put my car in gear and pull out of the parking lot.

I've been listening to Western swing music again this morning and enjoying the changing scenery. The last mile of driving takes me through mostly flat agricultural land on the right, and then amid shady trees to my left I see the turn for the entrance to the state park. I follow the short paved road into the park and emerge in a small, almost empty parking lot. Two families with young children are enjoying picnics at tables under the trees, and then ahead I spot a building that must be the park headquarters.

Inside the building I find a friendly park ranger, a young woman about my daughter's age, and we talk about my best birding opportunities. This place is about as different from the World Birding Center on South Padre Island as it could possibly be. Although it's just a few miles out from Brownsville, it seems remote and wild and unimproved—and will, I hope, be full of hidden gems.

This park is set up not for vehicles but for people on foot or riding bicycles. Instead of a network of fancy boardwalks, the widely separated trails here are mostly dirt, although three are specially designed for wheelchairs and other mobility devices. Private vehicles are not allowed in the park past the headquarters building, but there's a free tram service that makes a loop on an old paved road through about one-quarter of the park's twelve hundred acres. Visitors can ride it to one stop, get off and explore various trails on foot, then come back to that stop or go on to another and be picked up by the next tram. There's also a short walking trail right here by the building. The next tram will leave at one o'clock, so I have enough time to do both.

It's quite humid today and getting warmer, too. I go back to my car to add my water bottle to a pocket, then start out on the walking trail with my binoculars, camera, and notebook. A Northern Mockingbird flashes its white wing patches as it flies from the grass up to a nearby tree, and a noisy little group of Great-tailed Grackles make a commotion about fifty feet away.

The Ebony Trail leads through an old-growth woods, and I'm surprised by how many butterflies are flitting around in the dappled shade. If I could spend all day here, I would study these handsome insects more carefully. There's one with beautiful purple stripes that I really like. I know the butterflies of the Ohio River Valley very well, but I don't recognize this Rio Grande Valley creature at all. I take some photos and promise myself that when I get home I'll try to identify it. But it might not be in any of my butterfly books, because they, too, are often divided into separate field guides for eastern species and western species.

§

Walking along on the wide dirt trail, I'm not seeing or hearing any birds, and that's a bit disappointing. But I keep going, and keep looking at the small trail map the park ranger gave me. When the dirt path makes a slight turn to the right, I discover a guy up ahead with binoculars. We say hello and chat a minute. He's flown in from California after retiring from a career that took him around the world. He's seen birds all over the globe, and he wants me to know it. His conversation is sprinkled with remarks such as "when I was in Costa Rica" and "when I was in the Mediterranean," with a lot of name-dropping about birds that do not live here and that I do not know.

We walk along together for a short distance and then emerge from the shady trees to step out onto an overlook, a simple wooden platform with a railing. We have a fine view of a resaca, the Spanish name for an oxbow lake, which is what happens when a river changes its winding course and a section of the original riverbed gets cut off from the main channel. They're often shaped like a giant crescent, but sometimes the body of water that's cut off is wiggly shaped, and that's what's happened here. Since the flow of water has been interrupted and no longer drains downstream, whatever rain falls just stays put, either sinking into the ground or spreading out into marshy areas. The water levels are not constant, but rise up and down with the rains. From this man-made platform overlooking the water, I can see a Little Blue Heron standing on the distant, marshy bank of the resaca, which is quite wide right here.

While I'm studying all this, the guy is still talking about other places he's been and other birds he's seen. I'm beginning to think of him as an extreme example of a competitive birder, and in fact, I now have a private nickname for him: Quest Birder.

I do not recognize the large, yellowish-beige bird with a dark tail edged in white that we catch a glimpse of as it makes a short flight from one tree branch to another. It is much bigger than a crow, almost like a skinny chicken, and then I lose sight of it amid the leaves. How a bird that big can suddenly disappear is quite a puzzle. Quest Birder tells me it is a chachalaca, or more properly a Plain Chachalaca, and I write that down in my notebook as my first lifer of the day. As we look for other birds, I realize that Quest Birder has a very broad and deep knowledge of Texas birds, as well as all the ones he's seen in other parts of the world. But I get the distinct impression that many Texas birds seem rather ordinary to him now, and he's eager to find a novelty.

As I scan the far trees with my binoculars, hoping to get another look at the chachalaca, I see something very unusual suspended from an outer tree limb. At first I think it's a big brown plastic shopping bag caught on a branch, but with my binoculars I see that it's a very long hanging nest, easily more than two feet from top to bottom. It's made of dried grasses woven together. I bring up my camera to get a long-distance photo and suddenly I see a flash of very bright yellow with a hint of orange. This bird has black wings, and it approaches the nest, lands on the rim, then hops down and disappears inside. I've just seen my first Altimira Oriole. Its nest is constructed on the same plan as the oriole nests that I occasionally see in the Ohio River Valley, except this one is huge. I'm fascinated with the construction of such a large nest, and wonder how many days it took to build it. As a slight breeze ripples through the leaves, the branch it's suspended from sways and the nest moves very gently to and fro. For me, this park is already turning out to be well worth the drive.

We turn to go back to the visitor center, and as I walk along I see a Northern Cardinal ahead on the path, then Quest Birder and I go our separate ways. I walk out to my car to see what I can scrounge up for a quick lunch before the tram ride and make a meal of sorts out of three mini Snickers candy bars, a handful of pretzels, and a few gulps of cranberry juice. Not much, but it's the best I can do here.

At the tram starting point, Quest Birder turns up again, and it looks like we're going to be the only passengers. The tram is very simple, rather like a large golf cart, with open sides and a flat roof. The tram driver, Mike, is a local Texas guy who has plenty of interesting information to share with us. Since there aren't any other vehicles allowed on this road, our guide can stop the tram anywhere he thinks there might be something good to look at and talk about.

Our first stop is near a guardrail. To our right we have a fine view of a long section of the resaca, with the water extending perpendicularly away from the road. From this angle, the viewing platform on the Ebony Trail where Quest Birder and I watched birds just a short while ago is hidden behind some trees. Mike tells us that these woods include honey mesquite, retama (a tree whose name I have to ask how to spell), lead trees, plus sabal palm, cedar elm, and spiny hackberry. My overall impression is many shades of green all jumbled up together. All of the trees here are leafed out, and spring is very well in progress.

§

Out on the water I see some Blue-winged Teal and, a bit farther away, the elegant white form of a Great Egret. As we look over the resaca, I hear a churring noise that sounds like one of the woodpeckers I know at home. We turn to look more carefully at the trees nearest us on the right side of the resaca and see a bird about the same size as the one I'm thinking about, but this one is slightly different. I can tell with my binoculars that the top of its head has a red patch, like the species at home, but the nape of this bird's neck, which I would also expect to be red, is bright yellow instead. I've found yet another lifer, the Golden-fronted Woodpecker. The "fronted" part in its name makes it sound like it might have a yellow breast, but its breast is white. The yellow feathers, optimistically called golden, are in a small area just between the bill and the white forehead, and it's only a very small patch of color, a bit difficult to see even with binoculars, but I do get one quick look. The red I saw on the top of the bird's head makes me think it might be the male.

In typical woodpecker fashion, the bird uses its stiff central tail feathers to brace itself in an upright position as it clings to the tree bark with its sharply clawed toes, which it can splay out in different configurations depending on whether it wishes to cling to the bark or move upward. The tail feathers are black at the outer edges, with just a little bit of white showing on the rump where the bird's wing tips rest. And then a second bird flies in to land on a willow branch just above the male. This one looks like a female because she has no red patch on her head, and we suspect they are a mated pair choosing a location to excavate a nest hole.

Before we drive on, our guide asks us to look into the woods on our left. Quite some time ago the park staff put up an owl nest box with great hopes, but bees have taken it over instead and nobody wants to challenge them. Thousands of them are busy buzzing in and out as we watch. Some Black-bellied Whistling-Ducks fly over us, and then I see a few Cattle Egrets in the distance, and another Great Egret.

As we ride along slowly, Mike tells us that this was once ranchland, but no matter what the rancher did to change the land, it just wasn't as profitable as the other places where his cattle grazed. The Texas Parks and Wildlife Department acquired the land in the late 1970s but did not open it for public use until about ten years ago. The park includes several different kinds of habitats, ranging from wetlands along the resaca, to subtropical woodlands, to native scrubland, and some grassy savannah areas. Although many sections are not pristine, virgin plant communities, much of what was formerly modified for grazing cattle is now slowly returning to a more natural mix of vegetation. It's an example of old field succession, similar to what happens to abandoned land back in the Ohio River Valley, but the mix of plants is different. Each part of the park supports different groups of birds. Other wild animals are beginning to thrive here once again, too, including bobcats, as well as a good mix of reptiles and amphibians.

At a pull-off with a view across another section of the resaca, we pause at the tram stop, but there's no one waiting to be picked up. We watch and listen to some Red-winged Blackbirds, and spot a Mottled Duck swimming nearby. It's been clear to me since about a minute after we met that Quest Birder is here on a mission to see a particular kind of bird, one that has been reported on a more remote foot trail a bit farther on. He doesn't say so, but I'm beginning to think he might be working on a big year, a self-imposed challenge to observe as many species as possible in a single year, and he might be competing with other people who are also doing a big year. Then again, he might just be trying to reach a milestone number on his cumulative life list. Either way, he seems impatient to get to the trail he wants to walk on.

Mike drives us to the place where that trail intersects with the road, and he and Quest Birder make a plan for what time he should be back at the edge of the road so that Mike can give him a return ride to the visitor center. Although I could certainly go along with Quest Birder in search of whatever his target Awesome Bird is, I decide that I'd rather continue the tram ride and see more areas of the park.

That's what's so appealing about birding—people can set their own goals. I have friends who want to see every kind of warbler possible each spring, and other friends who are fascinated by hummingbirds. And I know several people who will drive hundreds of miles just to see owls. I know birders who count how many different species they can find in a single county during a year, and others who don't keep lists at all. I know one bird photographer who only likes to take pictures of birds in flight.

As for me, during this trip I'm trying to understand which kinds of birds prefer each of the habitats I'm exploring, which are different in many ways from what I know in the Ohio River Valley.

After Quest Birder walks out onto the trail, Mike and I ride along alone, talking about the way the land has changed over the years, and how much he enjoys working as a tram driver and guide. There's no one waiting at the next tram stop, but we linger nearby just in case, and to watch the birds in the distant woods. We've made a loop far away from the water, and these fields still look a lot like ranchland to me.

A Snowy Egret flies over, then we get a tantalizing glimpse of what we both believe is a kingbird, but we can't decide on the species. It has a lot of yellow on the breast, but I cannot get a good enough look, even with my binoculars, to be able to describe any other field marks. There are at least three kingbird possibilities in this part of Texas, all very similar in appearance, and neither one of us can sort out what we saw so briefly. The bird seems very wary of us, and we decide to move on so as not to disturb its natural behavior. Considering how advanced the spring season is here, this could be a male trying to establish a territory, or perhaps an already mated bird with nestlings to feed, and we do not want to cause it any added stress.

Back inside the visitor center, Mike and the park ranger and I talk about how much I've enjoyed visiting this park, and the three lifers I've found here. Then I mention that I've been hoping to find a certain kind of bird that my books tell me is likely to be here. It's not a rarity, but southern Texas seems to be the only state north of Mexico to find it in. They know exactly where I should go—right outside on the path next to this building. They offer some suggestions on what to do to see the bird, and I go out the door.

Just a few steps along the concrete sidewalk, several feeder platforms have been set up near the trees. And there, right in front of me, is the gorgeous bird I've been hoping for—a Green Jay! Of course, it isn't all green. While its back and wings are a pale, almost lime green, the throat is black, the head is a deep, rich cobalt blue with black around the eyes, and the underside of the tail is yellow. Yellow! This is a wonderfully colorful bird to look at, and I manage to take several photos from various angles.

Mike had explained to me that this jay's behavior is very different from a Blue Jay. The Green Jay is much more at home deep in the woods, not out in the open or along the edges. It's often a much shyer bird than a Blue Jay, and that's why the staff here have put up feeders to bring them out in the open so more people can enjoy them. I really appreciate that. As I stand quietly next to the building, two more Green Jays come to visit the feeders. If I had written out a list before I left home of must-see birds, this species would have been on it, for sure. I am delighted to have such good, close-up views of a very handsome bird.

After the Green Jays fly back towards the trees, I take a few minutes to walk around past the low plantings that are meant to attract butterflies and see a very pretty, solid orange one. I take a few photos, and then realize that if I'm going to visit another birding spot this afternoon, I need to get back to my car and get on the road right away.

§

To reach my next birding spot I have to drive east a bit, go around the city of Brownsville, then head straight south toward Mexico. All morning I've been listening to a favorite collection of instrumental Western swing music, and every time "South of the Border, Down Mexico Way" comes up in my play list, I'm humming along, trying to remember more of the lyrics.

Driving slowly ever farther southward on a narrow road leading toward the Rio Grande, I see a tall structure on the left, a dark fence about twenty feet high, made of what look like wood slats with small gaps between each upright. As I get closer, driving on the aptly named Southmost Road, I see that the posts are really made of metal. There's a big gap in the fence, and a sign for my destination tells me that the Sabal Palm Sanctuary visitor center is exactly one mile ahead, and helpfully notes that I should go "through the fence, over the levee—no passport needed!" This strikes me as odd because I had figured that I would remain on United States soil, but perhaps the actual international border varies somewhat from where the riverbed is now. Perhaps the fence, which appears to be rather old, is placed in the most convenient location from an engineering standpoint and does not actually mark the real physical border. It doesn't matter which side I end up on because I always travel with my American passport with me, just in case.

The road narrows, and I pass through a typical low farm-style gate that's propped wide open, arriving at a parking lot in front of a huge white house with covered porches on both levels. It's very different from typical Spanish- or Mexican-style haciendas or ranch headquarters buildings. It looks much more like something in New Orleans. According to the historical marker, this historic plantation home, the Rabb House, was built in 1892. It now serves as the visitor center for a section of unique subtropical habitat owned by the Audubon Society. I see two other cars in the parking lot and no people.

But when I walk into the house, I hear a man speaking with a British accent—it's Jeremy, the birder from Oxford, England, the fellow I met a week ago Saturday, much farther north on the boardwalk at the Skillern Tract of Anahuac NWR. This is a fun surprise, and he recognizes me right away as the woman from Kentucky. Jeremy's wife is making careful notes of the driving directions the young man at the desk is giving her about where to see certain birds and reptiles in this part of Texas. A young woman is behind the counter, too, but she doesn't work here; she's visiting her friend, the guy who's giving directions. All of us are keen field naturalists, and together we have a lively conversation about all sorts of animals and plants that we already know about or are curious about in this part of Texas. I tell about my delight in finding a Green Jay earlier today, and the guy at the counter says I might see some cool hummingbirds here.

As I pay for a postcard of the handsome house, plus my admission fee to walk the trails, Jeremy tells me that he spent all winter back in England planning the details of his trip, and he has very specific goals about what he wants to see in the limited number of weeks he can spend here in the United States. He wants to make every hour and every mile count, which I understand completely, considering the different logistics he has to deal with compared to my more relaxed approach. He's had to cross an ocean with his birding gear, rent a car, drive on what to him is always the wrong side of the road, and he's now about five thousand miles from home. For me, anytime I want to visit Texas, all I have to do is pack my own car and start driving. Well, and find somebody to take care of my three kitties. I miss them so much, and I hope that when the cat sitter texts me today she will include some photos.

Jeremy and his wife have finished their visit exploring the Sabal Palm Sanctuary and are eager now to get back on the road. We say goodbye and once again wish each other good luck birding. Then the fellow at the counter reminds me that the sanctuary will close at five, which means that I have a little less than an hour available to explore. When I tell him that I certainly don't want to end up on the wrong side of a locked gate, he laughs and says he won't start closing up until he sees that I'm back at my car.

This sanctuary includes about five hundred fifty acres of land, which sounds big, but the original plantation covered more than twenty thousand acres at its peak. More than one hundred years ago, much of the land was cleared of its native vegetation so the rancher could raise crops and livestock. The Rio Grande was a completely wild river back then, with the water flow changing as snow melted far to the north and west in the Rocky Mountains. Back then, the water level often was high enough that steamboats could pull up to a wharf nearby, and trade was brisk. The rancher added irrigation ditches and pump stations to control water levels in the agricultural sections of his land. Somehow or another amid all these alterations, about thirty acres of native sabal palms remained untouched, and they're still growing here. That's where I plan to walk.

Printed paper maps of the trails are not available, but the guy at the desk and I come up with an easy solution—I'll just take a cell phone photo of the color map encased in a sleeve of plastic that he keeps on the desk. He recommends a route that I can easily cover in the amount of time remaining until he must begin locking up for the night.

I follow the trail markers to take a wide dirt path under the low tree limbs crisscrossing the trail. As I walk along, my cell phone starts dinging with a new message. Hah! It says, "Welcome to Mexico, free text messaging is available." I don't think I'm really in Mexico, but I am walking close enough to the legal border to confuse my GPS system and phone service provider. I wasn't planning on making any calls or sending any texts just now, so I put my phone back in my pocket and keep walking.

Soon I reach a small wooden building, which is closed up, and an open-air observation platform similar to a backyard deck. The wooden benches offer a good view into a feeding area with small wood platforms at different levels and with different foods set out to appeal to different kinds of birds. And right there, perched on a tray holding some orange halves, is my fourth Green Jay of the day! I take a good close-up photo—the bird is less than fifteen feet away from where I'm sitting.

The Green Jay soon flies off into the surrounding brush. A bright red male Northern Cardinal hops from branch to branch farther back, and then I turn my attention to the water drips and artificial nectar feeders. After a few minutes a hummingbird approaches. It looks kind of big to me, accustomed as I am to tiny little Ruby-throated Hummingbirds. This one hovers in such a way that I can see an orangish-yellow bill and a long, for a hummer, tail that shines rusty red in the light. The belly isn't white, it's beige. I'm looking at another lifer, a Buff-bellied Hummingbird. It moves much too fast for a photo, but I'm pleased to simply watch it.

In just a few moments a Black-crested Titmouse flutters in to perch at the same feeder tray where the Green Jay snatched a morsel to eat. The titmouse sits still long enough for me to get a nice photo. Then I catch some movement down at ground level where some cracked corn is scattered and see that there's a very plump dove with pink legs foraging there. I take a good look at the bird's eye. The eye is very pale and the skin around it is red. As I move slightly to get a better look, I accidentally make a bit of noise, and that startles the bird into a short flight. I see some white at the end of its tail and realize that I am watching a White-tipped Dove. The lifers just keep showing up right in front of me. I'm so happy with my choices of places to explore today.

A Gray Catbird makes a mewing sound nearby as I continue to watch the area in front of me. Just beyond the wooden feeders, there's a carefully arranged pattern of what, to me, looks like sections of concrete curbing. That seems weird. And then I realize that the rounded edges of concrete hold water at various levels on the otherwise dry ground. Something small is splashing at the edge of one of these shallow, man-made puddles.

I focus my camera and see a little bird with a striped head and rather plain body. I watch as it turns this way and that, ducking down into the water then rising up to stand tall while shaking its feathers. The light here is rather dim and shadowy due to all the trees and surrounding vegetation, but I am able to make out that, instead of brown, the bird's back is a sort of drab green. Ah, yes, that's the key—this is an Olive Sparrow, yet another lifer for me. From time to time it carries its tail cocked up, rather like a wren, but I don't know if that is just because it's bathing, or something it does away from water, too. I take some photos and hope that I get that subtle green color right. It's not at all like the lime green feathers of the Green Jay.

Reluctantly, I leave this close-up viewing area and walk along a different trail that leads to the actual resaca. At this old river cut-off a small wooden structure serves as an observation point to see across the marshy expanse of low vegetation. It's a good place to view birds, but I also have to be careful to avoid fresh spiderwebs as I raise my binoculars. Far in the distance, Blue-winged Teal and a small group of Black-bellied Whistling-Ducks drift around on the shallow water. A Killdeer calls as it flies over closer to me. I continue to scan the water and discover a Pied-billed Grebe. A dark shape in the sky flaps and flaps, then glides— yes, it's a Black Vulture trying to gain altitude. Other than the Killdeer, it's very quiet here this late in the afternoon.

At first I am puzzled by the little bird on the water near some green plant stalks that might be reeds or cattails. Its swimming style is similar to the Pied-billed Grebe, but this little fellow is much, much smaller, and gray, not brown. I look again and see that its eye is a bright, golden yellow. The little bird is really small, and difficult to keep in focus, but the more I look, the more I am certain I have discovered another lifer, a Least Grebe. It's only about two-thirds the size of its cousin, the Pied-billed Grebe, and looks almost like a toy. This little fellow swims about energetically, dipping below the water's surface from time to time, slipping in and out of the green shoots, clearly at ease in this little wet patch. This is his home year-round, and southern Texas is the northern limit of this species' range.

I scan the edges of the vegetation one more time, just in case I missed something, but find nothing else. Overhead a Turkey Vulture soars effortlessly. I, however, need to walk briskly back to the visitor center—it's almost closing time and I don't want to keep anyone waiting. And I'm hungry. What I ate for "lunch" was the poorest excuse for a meal I've had to improvise in a long time, and I'm beyond ready for a cold beer and real food.

Someone either today or yesterday mentioned a local family-owned restaurant in town that serves authentic Mexican cuisine, which seems like an appropriate choice, considering where my phone thinks I've been today. However, when my GPS tells me to turn into the parking lot, it's empty—the restaurant is closed today.

Well, there goes that idea. Maybe I can find something good over on the main highway through the center of town. I shut down my GPS and drive a few blocks to look around to see what's available. I'll use the hunt-and-hope method. Amid the jumble of national chains I spot one that I know serves beer and might have something with a Mexican flair on the menu.

Inside, the bar is empty and the music playing over the speaker system is jarringly loud, so I keep walking and go outside to sit on the patio. I'm still thinking about Mexican food so I order a cold Corona Extra and a simple quesadilla filled with chicken and cheese.

While I'm checking my phone for the latest messages and bird photos I keep hearing snatches of conversation from the people at the table a few feet away. Their voices are impossible to ignore since there aren't any other people out here. They're not drunk, but something is not right. Try as I might, I simply cannot stay focused on the images of birds on my phone's screen. In fact, the more they talk, the more uncomfortable I am about the situation and I am extremely uneasy sitting so close to them. I'm not sure what they're up to, but it doesn't sound good, and I don't want to hear any more of their schemes.

When I can finally flag down my server, I change my order from dine in to takeout, and request my check. I leave my beer unfinished, grab the check to pay indoors, and take my box of food out to my car. So much for my plan to enjoy a relaxing, sit-down dinner.

§

My challenge is to get to Oliviera Park northwest of here at about half an hour before sunset so I can watch birds come in to roost. I'll be cutting it rather close to get there at the proper time. But that's the time Brandon, the guy I walked around with yesterday morning, recommended, and I am determined to follow his advice. I re-program my GPS and resign myself to eating a lukewarm dinner when I get to the park.

When I hear my GPS announce "your destination is on the left," I can't believe it. I'm in the middle of an old suburban subdivision with single-story houses, a lot of overhead power lines, and the park isn't a nature preserve or artfully landscaped area—it's devoted to sports. I see playgrounds and swing sets, a softball diamond inside a chain-link fence, and soccer fields, but no games are in progress. I'm still hungry, still trying to shake off the disturbing conversation I overheard at the restaurant, and feeling quite grumpy because my good travel karma seems to have deserted me. I don't know if I'm in the right place at all.

When I get near the end of the curved road that makes a semicircle among the various sports fields, I pull into a parking space, back up, and reverse directions. I have the windows rolled down to listen for birds, but hear nothing. I roll forward another twenty feet and then a guy walking across the grass waves at me and says, "Stop, you're going the wrong direction on a one-way road."

Well, that does it! As much fun as I had in the morning and afternoon, I am so annoyed with the way this day is ending. And I am doubly annoyed with myself for being so careless, not noticing any traffic flow signs. If there were any. I really do not think there were any signs at the park entrance. But I don't want to be rude, and I'm glad he told me that I was making a mistake. Through the open window I say "thank you," and then I explain that I'm from out of state. I mention that this is a totally unfamiliar place, and I'm here to watch the birds come in to roost but I don't know where to park or where to look.

I am completely surprised when he says, "Pull in anywhere, and watch where I go. The birds will be here in just a few minutes." Oh! Maybe I haven't made a mistake after all.

I pull into the very next parking spot, get my dinner out, and stand next to the hood of my car to nibble at the practically flavorless—except for an excess of saltiness—quesadilla triangles, which are by now only vaguely warm. Not the dinner I wanted, but it's all I have. Laughing Gulls and Great-tailed Grackles make a lot of noise, and I catch a glimpse of a Northern Mockingbird flying towards the back of a house, but those are not the birds I came to see. I scarcely taste what I'm chewing, except for the salt, and halfway through the third triangle I give up, close the plastic box, take a swig of water, and grab my binoculars, camera, and notebook. Time to get back into the birding groove.

I click the door locks down, and stand by my car. Where is that guy who stopped me from driving any farther in the wrong direction? He had dark hair, and he was wearing a blue shirt. The light is beginning to fade as the sun sinks toward the horizon, and some puffy clouds are moving in. I have no idea where the birds will appear, if they come at all, but I figure my best bet is to walk away from the sports fields. I cross the pavement and onto some sandy ground with grass that's been mowed short. I'm looking around this way and that, and then I see a guy talking into his smartphone. It's him!

Just as I recognize the guy I'd been talking to, I begin hearing the strangest loud cries and calls—the first birds are already arriving. They squeal, they screech, they shriek in a crazy jumble that's piercingly loud. These are not just any birds; these are wild parrots, Yellow-headed Parrots, natives of Mexico who've established a little colony here in southern Texas. They continue to scream and shriek and squawk overhead as they fly in to find perches on the utility wires and in the tops of the leafy green trees, a flutter of wings as they find their balance. At first there are only a few birds, then dozens more materialize to swoop into this suburban neighborhood. The noise gets louder and louder. They like to form communal roosts at night, and this is the place they prefer right now.

And then from behind me I hear a familiar accented voice. "Hey, Kentucky—I saw your car tag. We meet again," Jeremy says as he adjusts the settings on his camera for some hand-held shots. His wife has the tripod, and we all stride across the grasses trying to guess where the most parrots will land above us and where we'll have the best views. I have my camera ready, plus my cell phone, but in this quickly dimming light I don't know if I'll be able to capture the rich greens of these pretty and noisy birds.

I hear another human voice and turn to see the dark-haired guy talking into his phone again. As I listen I realize that what he's doing is using the phone's voice-to-text feature to take notes. He's conducting an ongoing census of the number of each species of parrot here, something he does once a month on a certain Sunday, and I'm here on the correct evening—my travel karma is back to the positive side!

In the fading light I can barely distinguish the different head colors of the birds, but I finally see that there's another kind of parrot here, the aptly named Red-crowned Parrot, which does have a small patch of brilliant scarlet feathers on its forehead that's hard to miss.

More birds fly in and squabble about who gets to perch where, and I want to ask the bird-census-taker a few questions. However, he is too busy pivoting in a circle, naming off numbers and bird species at a fast pace as they arrive from all directions. But although he's focused on his task, he's friendly and says he will be glad to chat with me when the birds settle down after dark.

In the meantime, I'm snapping photos right, left, and center, especially of the birds perched on the utility wires. I laugh as two of them keep their toeholds but swing upside down like circus gymnasts on a trapeze. Jeremy's using his tripod closer to the trees to take photos of other parrots. The noises the birds make are incredible in volume and variety of screeches, and I use my cell phone to capture the chaos in a short video.

In less than ten minutes the birds are settling down in the tops of the tallest trees. Jeremy tells me that he and his wife are going farther west up the Rio Grande tomorrow, and I tell them I am going to turn northward, so we probably will not meet again. Well, at least not on this journey, but who knows? Maybe I'll go birding in Great Britain sometime in the future. Once again we wish each other good birding and safe travels, and part as friends.

I wait a few minutes to make sure that the bird census taker has stopped making verbal field notes, then introduce myself and mention meeting Brandon on South Padre Island. Sure enough, this is Carl, the friend Brandon had told me about, and we talk about what an interconnected world the birding community is.

Carl has been interested in parrots since he was a small boy growing up in the upper Midwest, and moving to Texas after undergraduate college is a dream come true. Now, as a graduate student working towards a Master's degree at a nearby university, he's doing original research on this colony of wild birds.

His monthly census project is going along very well. He's already gathered enough information to estimate that this Brownsville group regularly includes two hundred fifty to three hundred birds, and that a total of about six hundred parrots may live in this lower section of the valley. The Yellow-headed Parrots and the Red-crowned Parrots are the most numerous, but there are a few birds of a third species mixed in with them. He can recognize them, but in the dimming light I cannot, so I do not record them officially in my hand-written field notes. He saw two of them tonight, but it's just too hard for me to tell the difference, and now the light is gone completely.

I walk back to my car, and take a few minutes to put all my gear back in the laundry basket on the front seat as neatly as possible. I see a convenient trash barrel and dump the remainder of my dismal dinner into it. I settle into my car and program my GPS to take me back to my hotel on South Padre Island.

§

Driving over the causeway out to the island about an hour later, I realize that my route will take me right past the cozy bar where I had dinner my first night here. It's almost completely dark now, and I decide to stop in for a nightcap. I find a parking place on a side street, dress up my birding shirt with a patterned scarf draped around my shoulders, and walk upstairs.

There's a different bartender tonight, and fewer people at the tables, but overall it's still a pleasant place to unwind. I choose a bar chair over by the wooden railing where I can watch the colorful LED golf carts zip back and forth on the main street below, and order a Corona Extra. The guy sitting in a nearby chair is the owner of the bar, and when I tell him how attractive I find the PVC pipe design of the bar chairs he smiles. Then he tells me all about how sturdy they are, good in all kinds of weather, and how reasonably priced they are at a local outdoor furnishings store. He shops online then picks them up, and he's sure they would ship some to me in Kentucky. It's an idea, but I doubt that I'll do it. What looks good at night in a bar on the Gulf might not have quite the same appeal at home at my farm so far inland in Kentucky.

The baseball games on the big-screen TVs don't hold my interest for very long. Instead, as I sip my beer I'm thinking about the different habitats I explored today and all the birds I saw. The course of the Rio Grande has changed many times over the centuries, and political decisions about what country owns which bits of land on either side of the river have been the subject of wars and treaties. That's the human side of things—but the birds don't pay any attention to that. They don't care which side of the river they settle in, as long as they can find the foods they prefer amid the plant communities and a good place to raise their young.

I left my field guides and notebook down in the car, but I can make mental lists of the life birds I saw today. I begin to recite their names silently as I remember the day's events: Plain Chachalaca, Altimira Oriole. Golden-fronted Woodpecker and Green Jay. Buff-bellied Hummingbird, White-tipped Dove. Oh, and the little Olive Sparrow taking a bath, and the cute Least Grebe. And then the two kinds of parrots, the Red-crowned Parrot and the Yellow-headed Parrot. That's ten lifers in a single day!

It's no wonder that I've never seen any of them before. As different as their needs are, they have one thing in common. They are all birds of Mexico mostly, but whose northernmost range extends slightly past the Rio Grande into this section of southern

Texas. They don't migrate into the parts of the United States I explore most often, and this trip is my first chance to learn about them on their home turf. This is a delightful addition to my study of shore birds and migrating songbirds along the Gulf Coast, and I am so glad that I've come this far south.

I order a second beer and continue daydreaming about the sabal palms and the resacas and the chachalacas—the names all sound so exotic—and think about how much I've enjoyed this day. I take a few minutes to catch up with all the text messages and social media comments that came in on my phone while I was down by the border, post a few photos of today's adventures, then put my phone away.

Tonight is my last night on South Padre Island, and I have two puzzles to solve. First, I need to plan my morning activities in such a way that I can check out of my hotel at a reasonable time. I have now driven a little bit more than two thousand miles and will be turning north tomorrow. From this point on, I have no advance hotel reservations. I can zigzag inland and back out to the Gulf Coast in whatever way seems best for the rest of the coming week as I drive toward home. So the second puzzle is, how far do I want to travel tomorrow?

I don't have an answer right away, so I settle my bar tab and go downstairs to my car. Back in my hotel room, I realize that I am too tired to make any firm plans for tomorrow, so I race through my evening routine and turn the lights out early.

§

I'll be leaving South Padre Island today, but before I go, I want to explore as much as I can. While taking my usual morning walk around the hotel parking lot I realize that, although my horse's hooves got wet in the waves yesterday, I have not yet strolled barefoot in the sand here. I study the cloudy sky, check the NOAA weather website, and decide that I should eat a big breakfast in the hotel and then head over to the beach as soon as I can before the weather gets troublesome.

Back inside, I enjoy two big pancakes with lots of butter and syrup, and a generous portion of bacon, plus a glass of milk. After I finish I'm not sure how to get to the beach, so I ask the front desk clerk. "Oh, it's easy," he says. "Just go out the side door and follow the yellow footprints." Yellow footprints? I follow his instructions and there they are on the concrete—a stenciled line of lemon-yellow human feet, left, right, left, right, leading across the hotel parking lot, then between two condominium buildings, out to a sidewalk along a short neighborhood street. I continue walking past two more condominium buildings and arrive at the public beach access point. This section of the beach is for people on foot only, no vehicles allowed. A big sign explains all the usual rules about no glass, pets must be on a leash, and no overnight camping allowed.

I don't have to worry about any of that. This is purely a short pleasure stroll. I left my binoculars and camera in the car. I don't even have my pocket notebook. Any birds I encounter I will just have to remember without written notes. If I'm lucky, maybe I'll get a cell phone photo or two. A huge dark blue and gray cloud obscures the sun in the east as good-sized waves out on the Gulf roll and foam toward the beach. This may turn out to be a race against the storms that are offshore for now, but I will deal with that if and when I have to.

For now, I pull my ball cap down a bit more snugly over my forehead, then slip off my leather sandals and carry them in my left hand as I walk across the wet sand. I'm glad I chose to wear the capri pants with the straps and snaps that hold the folded cuffs in place this morning. I won't need to worry about them coming unrolled and dragging in the water. There's a stiff breeze blowing, and I'm glad I'm wearing a long-sleeved shirt, too, and that I thought to put my new palm tree scarf wrap over my shoulders. It's just thin cotton, blue with white batik palm tree designs, but it does help cut the wind a bit. Oh! The first wavelets that rush up across the sand and over my toes are colder than I expected.

I look up and down the shoreline at the all waves coming in, then look up to study the sky out over the Gulf again, and decide to go left, heading north along the beach. Way out in the distance the clouds are getting darker and darker, and I think it's raining about ten miles away. But I don't mind, the sand feels good under my toes and I like the way the water foams and bubbles as it slides up and down across my feet. I forgot to check the tide charts but it seems as though the tide is on the ebb, so I have plenty of room to walk on smooth sand between the breaking waves on my right and the line of low dunes on my left.

There are no sunbathers this morning, since the sun is behind the clouds, and I walk for quite a distance before I encounter any other people. When I see a young couple with their cell phones out, I make my usual offer. "Would you like for me to take a picture of y'all? And then I'll give you my phone so you can take a photo of me?" They agree quickly, and we pose for each other with the waves in the background.

As I walk along, I'm searching the sand for pretty shells to pick up, but they are few and far between. Up ahead I see a Willet striding purposefully across the sand. The bird would prefer living mollusks to eat, not the empty shells I'd like to have as souvenirs. Laughing Gulls swoop over and behind and in front of me, landing on the wet sand for a moment or two, then quickly dashing back up into the air. They seem unusually restless this morning, perhaps because of the rainstorms offshore. A few sandpipers dash along playing dodge 'em with the waves, but I cannot tell what species they are.

I keep looking up at the clouds, studying the colors on the undersides. Battleship gray, steely blue, purplish gray, all familiar signs of an approaching thunderstorm. I pause to study which direction the wind is blowing the fringe on my scarf, and take another look at the height of the waves curling toward shore. I think this would be a very good place to turn around and begin walking back toward my hotel.

The wind gusts get stronger and the air turns cooler. I walk a little bit faster, which is not easy to do on wet sand. More wind. The sky behind me darkens. I clutch my scarf to keep it from twisting off my shoulders in the increasingly blustery wind gusts. I look out towards the water and the waves hurtling toward the shore, then back to the dune side of the beach looking for a landmark. Ah, there's the pink condo building with the white porch railings near where I began my walk. When I'm about a hundred feet away from the beach access path, I feel the first raindrops splashing down.

By the time I step off the sand onto the paved road, the rain that began as a sprinkle is now a steady pelting of big drops. There's no point in putting my sandals on, my feet are completely sandy and wet, and I'd just as soon keep my sandals clean and dry. I walk on forward still barefoot, with my head ducked down a bit to watch for the puddles that are quickly forming on the road and in low spots on the sidewalk. My shoulders and back are wet through my scarf and shirt. As I walk between the buildings toward the hotel parking lot, the rain comes down faster. I get to the hotel's side door just as thunder rumbles. I manage to get my electronic key out of my pants pocket and into the card reader just as more thunder rumbles loudly, and this time it's directly overhead.

§

Walking through the hotel lobby I hear more thunder rumbles—and the lights flicker a few times. But the power doesn't go off completely. However, when I get to the one elevator that's been in service all weekend, I discover it is not operating. I turn around and go back to the front desk to find out what's happened. As it turns out, when the power flickers off and back on it takes the elevator's computer systems about half an hour to reset. I'll have to walk up to my room on the third floor.

I plan to pack and take a shower before checking out. When I arrived on Friday, I knew this would be my turnaround point, so I brought my big rolling suitcase up to my room along with my usual overnight duffel so I could reorganize my remaining clean clothes and decide when I will need to do laundry on the journey back north. While sorting through my clothes and looking for a plastic bag to put my wet scarf and shirt in, the lights flicker. And this time they stay off. Huh. Well, that's an unexpected development. However, my room has large windows, and pulling the curtains all the way back to the sides gives me plenty of light in the bedroom area to finish my task. From time to time I look out the windows to see what's going on with the rain. These are widely scattered thunderstorms and it looks like they will move on out of this area soon. I can already see thinner clouds and figure the sun will break through very soon.

While I'm waiting for the power to come back on, I realize that I could be cleaning out the interior of my car and getting my maps organized, so I walk downstairs. As soon as the rain thins out to a mere drizzle, I go out to the parking lot.

After neatening up the car, I go back inside the hotel and see that the power is still off. I really need to get going this morning, so I walk up the stairs again to my room. If I leave the bathroom door open, I will have enough light from the bedroom area's windows for showering and getting ready for the rest of the day. I can always put a flashlight on the counter in front of the big mirror to provide better light while I'm brushing my teeth and so forth. I won't be able to dry my hair, but that's alright.

Just as I plan all of this, the lights come back on. By the time I've finished showering, dried my hair, and am all dressed for the day, I figure the elevator will be back in service. I figured wrong. When I open my room door to put all my things out into the hall, I see people walking back from the elevator area and towards the stairs. Oh, well, I've dragged my stuff through plenty of airport concourses and up and down escalators many times, so the stairs shouldn't be a problem. I put the strap of my duffel bag crossways over my chest and shoulders, grab my suitcase by its telescoping handle with my right hand, then pick up my purse and the small tote bag with my birding notes inside with my left hand. Going down the stairs isn't that complicated, but it sure is noisy as my suitcase's wheels thump from tread to tread. Thump. Thump. Glide across the landing, thump down more stair treads, glide across another landing, then thump some more and turn in a descending spiral. Thump, thump, thump, all the way to the bottom. Whew! I made it.

When I check out and head to my car, the rain has stopped for good, the clouds are thinning, and the air is starting to heat up again. I get everything packed where it belongs in the car and drive half a mile or so north, past the World Birding Center and on to the convention center next to it to explore the Laguna Madre Nature Trail there. Brandon said it would be worth a visit, and so far his advice has turned out well, so I'm eager to see what this trail has to offer.

§

I find a place to park, gather up my binoculars, camera, and pocket notebook and walk past a little flower garden to step out onto the boardwalk. This is an old boardwalk, made the traditional way with real timbers, sideways slats, and a simple, sloping board for a handrail on top, no fancy posts. It's all weathered to a soft gray, some of the boards are warped, and I like it. From here I can see the more modern boardwalk where I walked around with Brandon on Saturday morning.

Although the two walks are of different construction materials, the habitats bordering each are similar, a mixture of mudflats, marshy bits, some freshwater ponds, and views out into the Laguna Madre bay. This section seems to include a few more shrubby trees, but perhaps it's just because this boardwalk is closer to them and I'm noticing them more easily. I recognize some of the plants—they are mangroves.

A crowd of Great-tailed Grackles are making noisy chatter, and then I see a White Ibis fly over. Its black wingtips are the key field mark for me. Several male Red-winged Blackbirds are showing off their yellow and red epaulettes and calling "onk-la-ree" loudly as they flit from perch to perch among the reeds. And who happens to be walking straight toward me? It's Jeremy from England, again, and his wife. As it turns out, they decided to stay in this area today before beginning their drive west. We laugh over meeting yet again, and then walk on in opposite directions.

Laughing Gulls wheel and circle overhead, and two perch briefly on the handrail before flapping off. I keep walking until I have a good view over the pale grasses to a shallow pond and mudflat between the boardwalk and the bay's blue water. I scan across the scene with my binoculars and can pick out some Cattle Egrets and then get a good look at a Reddish Egret. The birds have finished preening and drying off from the brief thunderstorm, and have resumed hunting for food, each species doing so in its own style.

This next section of the boardwalk runs through a very shallow marshy area, with clumps of what look like thick grasses emerging from the wet soil, but they might be reeds or rushes. There's a bit of an opening in the vegetation, perhaps ten feet across and fifteen feet wide. The water below me glistens in big, dark puddles. Suddenly I see some movement. Two large, mottled brown birds are stalking along from one grassy clump to the next. It's difficult to make out their shape at first, but my overall impression is of plump, round bodies, similar to domestic chickens' bodies, brownish feathers, long legs, and long bills. I bring my camera into position as quickly as I can without making any obvious, startling movements and snap three photos, hoping for good results in such a murky, shadowy environment.

I know they're rails, but before I can study them more carefully or re-focus my camera, they've melted away into the vegetation, completely disappearing from view. Rails seldom fly, going about their lives mostly in secret amid marshy vegetation. I put a big question mark about these birds in my field notebook, because I will need to study the photos later and compare them to the pictures and photos in field guides to see if I can name the species. For now, I'll make an educated guess, based on the habitat, their overall size, and the pattern of gray and brown on the individual feathers, that they are Clapper Rails, another lifer species.

I wait for a few minutes to see if I can get another glimpse of the rails, but they are too well camouflaged amid the marshy vegetation. A gleaming white Great Egret flaps over my head as I walk forward. A bit farther on I get a good look at a Tricolored Heron, but no photo today.

Soon I catch up with two women with binoculars. They notice my binoculars and ask if I've seen a particular warbler hopping around in the mangroves. I haven't, so I turn back a few steps on the boardwalk to look more carefully at the mangroves. I examine the limbs and peer intently amid the leaves. Ah, there's some movement. I stand as still as possible, and within a few seconds I get another look. Streaky black and white on the back and wings, with a mostly white belly. But then it's gone.

Silently, I will the bird to show itself again, to please come out into the open so I can get a better look. I wait. Another glimpse of a bit of streaky black and white. Then back into the leaves it hops to look for some insect prey. Wait. Wait some more. It's back out where I can see it—and the head has a black cap, not streaks. "Poll" is an old word for head, and that's how I remember the name of this bird. It's a Blackpoll Warbler, and I'm delighted to see it here, and somewhat surprised to find it so far west on the Gulf Coast.

This little species has an unusually long migration route, one of the longest known for songbirds that visit North America. Moving northward in the spring from their winter homes in South America, they fly over the Gulf and most come ashore along the Florida coast and in Louisiana. But quite a few do reach this part of Texas. But the more interesting part is that, when they finish nesting in northern Canada, they fly south in autumn by a completely different route, going way out over the Atlantic Ocean. They are very strong fliers and use the wind to their best advantage. When I catch up with the two women birders a few minutes later, I thank them for alerting me to look for the warbler in the mangroves.

On a distant stretch of water I see a little flotilla of Pied-billed Grebes. They don't seem to be actively hunting, just drifting around on the water, maybe getting ready to take naps. A Mottled Duck hen and her ducklings swim nearby, perhaps the same family group I saw on Saturday from the other boardwalk. Pretty beige-and-brown lizards scamper along the wooden boardwalk and up onto the side rails, keeping just ahead of my feet. I hear a high-pitched twittering sound and turn to the side just as a single Barn Swallow zooms past me, giving me a good look at its deeply forked tail as it goes past me at eye level.

I take a few more steps, and then I hear something. Or did I? There are frogs calling here from time to time, and I'm not sure whether what I heard came from a frog or a bird. I stop to look around among the reeds and down into the standing water. The area just below me is a confusing mix of dried gray and brown reed stalks, last year's growth now bent over into the water, then fresh, bright green leaves of weedy-looking shorter plants pushing up through the mats of reeds. I also see a bright blue cylinder, some kind of human trash, the remains of a discarded drinking cup, I think.

I look again very carefully and see a small, rusty-beige bird with huge yellow feet daintily high-stepping through the shallow water from a fallen reed to the mud and onto another fallen reed. The bird itself is only about twelve inches tall, but it's hard to tell its size exactly, because it doesn't stand up very straight. It's leaning forward to look into the water. It turns to the left, then the right, examining everything within striking distance of its sharply pointed bill. What wonderful luck to find this smallest member of the heron family, a Least Bittern, and another lifer for me. It's not paying the slightest bit of attention to me, either, so I can get several photos with my camera and my cell phone.

I watch it hunt for a while, but it doesn't make a strike, and I walk on. Soon I come to an area where I can see out to some mudflats in the center of a large, shallow pool of water where Roseate Spoonbills are gathered. The Great Blue Heron standing on the far edge is peering into the water in a similar way to the hunting technique of his little cousin the Least Bittern, but the heron would be a towering giant if they were to stand side by side. The Great Blue Heron would come up to about my shoulder, while the Least Bittern is much shorter, and his head would scarcely reach halfway up my shin.

Several pairs of Blue-winged Teal drift around lazily on the water to the left, and some Black-bellied Whistling-Ducks waddle around on the muddy edges of the sandbar to the right. The more I see these ducks, the more I like the neon pinkish-orange color of their bills and legs.

At the next place I pause, I see some Black-necked Stilts prospecting at the edge of a shallow pool of water and catch sight of a Redhead floating around, perhaps the same individual that Brandon and I saw on Saturday.

I continue my slow solo walk and get a good look at the red shield on the bill of a Common Gallinule. I stop for a moment because I hear the familiar "squark" of a Green Heron. There it is, just up ahead, perched on the wooden handrail. It turns around to face the marshy grasses, then lifts off into flight, giving me a good view—and great photo op—of its bright, rusty-orange legs. This is a male Green Heron ready for breeding. I watch to see where he's going, but quickly turn my attention back to the boardwalk when a second Green Heron flies in to perch on the opposite handrail. This one's legs are not such a rich orange color but rather more yellow, making me think it's not a rival but perhaps a female and a potential mate. I wait until it, too, flies off, then I resume walking.

What's that? Oh, a nice extra treat—it's a lizard with its gular patch extended from its neck in a red crescent shape as it pauses on the boardwalk just a few steps ahead. Slowly I raise my camera and manage to get one frame with the colorful patch exposed. A small tern swoops past me, slicing through the air at great speed. I cannot get a photo or make an identification, but that's okay. I can simply savor its fleeting beauty.

Walking at a leisurely pace this morning I've now made almost a complete circuit of this boardwalk and am standing opposite the fancier one I walked along on Saturday. I take a break to lean on the old gray wooden railing on my side. Looking at the water nearby, I soon spot a pair of Common Gallinules. Several pale beige-to-brown youngsters are following the more colorful adults around, begging and begging to be fed. The parent birds have little tidbits in their bills and lean over to pass the choicest morsels to the hungry youngsters. Nearby I spot an American Coot, and with these images in my mind, I'm ready to leave.

###

CHAPTER ELEVEN

North Padre Island and a national seashore

A walk on the sand, Aransas Pass, gulls

At my car I make a special note of my mileage. I've driven two thousand, thirty-three miles and will now be turning north and east to drive back home. I have an entire week to get there, and no particular plan, so I am in no hurry today. What I am is hungry for lunch.

I put all my birding gear back in the laundry basket on the front seat and start the engine. While I'm waiting for the air conditioning to cool things down, I look at my photo of the Least Bittern, using my camera's digital display, and compare that to the information in my field guides. Since the bird's plumage is soft brown and cinnamon, without a black crown, I know this one's a female.

Traffic is light on the approach to the causeway back to the mainland and I don't really need to slow down on the approach ramp, but I do, anyway. I want to get another look at the "Watch for Pelicans" sign. Apparently the birds like to walk across the pavement here instead of flying over. That would be an unusual traffic hazard.

On the other side of the causeway in the town of Port Isabel, I'm going to just roam around looking for a restaurant instead of picking something from a travel brochure or asking my phone for advice. I see one on the right that serves Italian food but I pass on by because I'm on the Gulf Coast and I'd rather eat a local specialty. I've learned that restaurants tend to be clustered on the shore near marinas, so I go up a few blocks, then circle back to make my way onto narrow side streets away from the main road and head towards the water. Sure enough, I soon find a place with a big, colorful mural featuring sea creatures on the front advertising Joe's Oyster Bar and Seafood Restaurant, with the slogan "the best little hole in the wall" under the name. From the outside it doesn't look like much, but almost all the parking spots nearby are full, so maybe the locals think it really is the best.

I park and go inside. The front room is also a mini-grocery and fresh seafood market. After studying the menu posted above the cases filled with fresh fish and other marine creatures I order a Corona Extra and the fried jumbo Gulf shrimp, which were probably caught this morning. For ten dollars, the lunch plate also comes with fries and coleslaw, and a roll. I sit at the tiny bar in the crowded, no-frills dining room and sip my beer. When my lunch arrives, the eight jumbo shrimp are piled up high in the center of the plate, and they are juicy and delicious under the crispy breading. I've found a Texas bargain.

After lunch, on my way back to my car I see an old-fashioned US Postal Service mailbox, so I get the postcards I wrote the other evening out of my car and drop them in. Back in my car, I take a quick look at the birding trail book that's been such a good guide so far and set my GPS for the town of Harlingen. Now that I'm moving northward, I am in sync with the migrating birds, but I do not know how this will affect the numbers of birds I see or the variety of species. There are some notable birding sites in that town, and I have to take Texas Highway 77 north anyway, so I'll stop there for a midafternoon break.

Driving at high speed, as usual, I arrive in Harlingen in only forty-five minutes. At a gas station on my side of the road, I stop to refuel and study my options. I set my GPS for a neighborhood park, but when I arrive, it doesn't seem like good bird habitat—not enough trees. Instead of taking a walk, I'm going to sit in my car and plan what to do next.

On the way southbound last week after leaving Fulton and Rockport, I skirted around Corpus Christi. This time now that I'll be back near that city I'd like to explore North Padre Island and other places in the area for a few days. My phone gives me the location of a Holiday Inn Express on the south side of Corpus Christi out on the island. I call, reserve a room for three nights, then reprogram my GPS.

§

Back on the highway and up to speed, relaxed and enjoying listening to Western swing music again, I begin seeing signs warning that dogs are in use ahead at the border patrol checkpoint. A few miles later I have to slow down and then stop as the lanes of traffic lead toward the checkpoint. Officers on foot are standing by to direct cars and trucks into various lanes or into the center parking lot where there are indeed dogs on short leashes, sniffing diligently as their handlers direct them around certain vehicles. I roll my windows down, turn off my music, and slide slowly forward.

The young officer standing at the checkpoint takes a look at my car and asks me where I'm from. In Texas cars and trucks have license tags front and back, but in Kentucky the only tag is on the back, which he can't see from his vantage point. I tell him about my trip, and although he's friendly and polite, he's only mildly interested in my birdwatching adventure and does not ask me for any identification. He wishes me a safe journey home and quickly waves me on through the checkpoint. That was sure easy.

A short while later, I reach the Sarita rest stop and park to see if it's more birdy this time through. Great-tailed Grackles are certainly abundant today. I watch an oriole, and make note of the parts of the bird I can see, its orange body, white bars on the black wings, black bib, and black tail, but that is not enough for an identification at the species level. No matter what I do, I can't get a clear view of the whole bird as it flits among the leaves. I do recognize the Eurasian Collared-Dove on the sidewalk easily enough. And the Common Grackle on my left is also easy to tell apart from the larger Great-tailed Grackles.

With about eighty more miles yet to drive, I don't linger. I'm ready for a different style of music, so I cue up a playlist of old-time fiddle music, the kind that's good to dance to, and pull out onto the highway. A mile or so up the road two Scissor-tailed Flycatchers fly over the grassy shoulder and drop down to perch on a wire fence, and that makes me smile.

§

I drive through some light sprinkles of rain, just enough to have to turn the windshield wipers on for a few minutes, and then the highway is dry as I circle around the south side of Corpus Christi. To get out to North Padre Island I must drive over another tall causeway. When I reach the island, my impression is that the town is spread out in a more open way than the one on South Padre Island, and this one is not so frantically focused on thrills. Instead of a jumble of gaudy souvenir shops crammed together, here the small shops and restaurants and other buildings are scattered about at intervals with plenty of space between them along the main boulevard, which has a grassy, green strip down the middle. Indeed, this doesn't seem like a tourist town at all, but has all the characteristics of an outlying, sprawling suburb instead.

On my way to my hotel, I pass several carefully landscaped condominium complexes, but there are still acres and acres of undeveloped land scattered among the neat and trim, low-rise mini-communities. My hotel is on a short, quiet street. I check in, pick up some tourist info from the rack in the lobby, and go up to my room to freshen up a bit.

I don't want to drive very far for dinner tonight, but the place just down the street that the desk clerk recommended doesn't appeal to me. I flip through a glossy travel brochure and see that there are several restaurants on the main boulevard. I'll go over there.

As I drive along, I see one of the ones that's advertised, a place called Costa Sur Wok and Ceviche Bar. Well, that's a combination I've never heard of. I pull in to a very small parking lot and sit in my car to look up the place online. Peruvian fusion cuisine? That's a new one, and I can't even imagine what that would include, but I'm here and I'm hungry, so I'll give it a try.

Inside I discover a hidden gem, a pocket of urban trendiness with lots of young men and women talking and drinking and eating. And in a side room next to the bar some are playing noisy games of foosball, crowding around the game tables, laughing and shouting at good plays and near misses.

I make my way across the tiny and jam-packed dining area—every table is full—and find the last open barstool at the bar along the back wall. Although there's only room for about ten barstools, the young woman who greets me at the bar is also fixing the drinks for all the customers in the whole restaurant. She is busy, busy, busy.

I order a glass of club soda and a glass of chardonnay, then ask for a menu. The food on the plates going out to the tables looks beautiful and artistic. But what will it taste like? I can't match up what I'm reading about in the menu descriptions with what I see going past me on the plates. I know I don't want anything especially spicy. When I mention this to the bartender she says the chef will make anything I want. I ask the young woman sitting on my right, who's obviously been here before, for some ideas. She introduces herself, and together with the bartender we figure I should try one of the grilled sandwiches with the salsa criolla on the side, just in case it's too intense for my tastebuds.

Melissa, the woman next to me at, has recently retired from the US Navy, at the age of thirty-one, and just bought a house as a dream come true to live on Padre Island. When I tell her about my birding adventure driving along the Gulf Coast she asks about the places I've been and what I've liked the best so far. I can't give just one answer to that because I've been to so many different kinds of places, each with its own special charms. Camping at Goose Island, horseback riding on the beach, and touring a sailing ship make the highlight reel for me so far.

When my Peruvian Asian sandwich arrives on a sliced French baguette—it is a fusion place, after all—it's delicious and the sauce is the perfect contrast to the flavors of the melted cheeses and the fresh tomato inside.

I have a second glass of wine for dessert, and keep right on chatting with Melissa about what Padre Island has to offer as a place to live year-round. Even though this is great fun, I have a lot of birds to look for tomorrow and I'm ready to leave.

Back in my hotel room I follow my usual nightly routine, then spend a few minutes catching up with my birding notes. My system of check marks and dots and asterisks is working fairly well, but I am not at all certain about exactly how many life birds I've discovered so far. The rough list covers forty new species but I'm not sure that I've included every bird. That doesn't matter, because the number isn't the point. For me, the fun is about learning something about each of the new ones—enough, I hope, to be able to recognize it if I see it again. Some are easy. There's no mistaking a Crested Caracara for anything else. Green Jay, American Oystercatcher, Great-tailed Grackle are all unique, too. But a lot of the shore birds are still hard for me to identify immediately, and I need a lot more practice. The same goes for the sparrows and doves. I have a lot of studying to do, but I'm getting sleepy.

I'm going to turn the lights out now.

§

I woke up when the sunlight glinting around the edges of the window shade became too bright to ignore. Now that I'm walking around the hotel parking lot before breakfast, accompanied by shrieks from Great-tailed Grackles, I've made an interesting discovery about the hotel building. About two inches out from the glass of each side of each window on all levels of the hotel, I see widely spaced single rows of wooden pegs, about the diameter of a pencil but only an inch long. They stick out from the concrete block outer shell of the building. They're the fastening points for plywood covers with holes drilled in them so they fit over the pegs, very necessary to protect the glass when a hurricane or tropical storm is approaching.

Back indoors in the breakfast area I choose a place to sit where I can look out the big windows as I eat, and then sip some decaf coffee as I consider my plan for today.

It's breezy and warm when I get in my car. I'm only a block or so away from the Gulf, but there's no main road over that way. Instead, I need to set my GPS to find the roads that will take me north to Mustang Island State Park. I drive back through the modest business district of the town, then turn onto a very good-quality, two-lane road leading toward the park. Along the way several low, flat bridges cross skinny bodies of water, but the only one that seems to cut all the way through to separate North Padre Island from Mustang Island is Packery Channel. I have no idea what that name means. I hope I can find out something about it later. As I drive north, Corpus Christi Bay is on my left.

Mustang Island is only about eighteen miles long. The entrance to the state park leads through low grasslands and a large parking area for campers and RVs. The building housing the park headquarters is tiny, and upstairs I cannot get much information about today's birdwatching opportunities because there is no naturalist on duty. After picking up a map and some postcards, and paying my entry fee, I'm ready to go exploring. This park includes several different kinds of habitats, a mixture of coastal grasslands, sand dunes, some marshy spots, and tidal flats and the seashore. I do not know much about the plants in each kind of community, or which birds prefer them.

Driving along I have the windows rolled down so I can hear any birds and smell the sea air. Laughing Gulls wheel and circle and shriek above me on my way over to the first camping parking lot. It's about half full with large RVs and pull-behind campers of various sizes and shapes, but there aren't many people in sight. Perhaps they've gone boating or fishing this morning. Sparrows forage for food on the short grass at the turnaround loop at the far edge of the campground, but even with my binoculars I can't get a close enough look to determine the species.

Cruising along very slowly on the short southern loop road reveals no birds, so I turn around and drive back to the main road, which leads east through the highest dunes I've seen so far. Some of the dunes are about as tall as the roof of my car, and some are a bit higher. This paved road leads to a parking lot that faces the Gulf of Mexico.

At the base of one of the dunes by the edge of the road a little animal scampers along by the short plants growing in the sand. I stop, put my emergency flashers on just in case someone comes up behind me, and get my camera out. The frisky little mammal on the sand is similar in size and shape to a chipmunk, but it doesn't have any stripes. I don't know what it is, but it's cute, and I manage to get three photos before it dashes away out of sight. I'll figure out what it is later.

At the parking area I get out to walk around and look at the huge waves crashing onto the shore. The surf's definitely up here, and it's windy. A Black Skimmer glides along, trying to pluck something to eat from the foaming water. Sturdy permanent signs warn of dangerous rip currents, so apparently the water here is always a bit rough. More Laughing Gulls sit on the wooden piling posts nearby, but otherwise this area is not birdy at all and I give up on this park for this morning. If I want to, I can always come back later and try again at a different time of day.

Back at my car I search through the books and maps in the laundry basket on the front seat for fresh ideas. Maybe I'll have better luck farther south on the Gulf Coast. I start up my engine and pull away.

Retracing the route I took to get here I see many shallow bodies of water on my right, the bay side, and find a place to pull off onto the road's shoulder to scan for birds. There's an old, weather-beaten sign that says this is site number CTC62 on the central section of the Great Texas Birding Trail. I'm near the Packery Channel area, but I still don't know what that means.

The land and the water here are in a constant battle for territory, with washovers caused by hurricanes and other tropical storms changing what's wet and what's dry from time to time. Some of the water is fresh, some salty, and some a diluted combination of brackish water, depending on recent weather events. I cannot tell the difference between the salt content of the various bodies of standing water, I just know that many different kinds of birds hunt for food in them.

Walking across the sand at the edge of the road I have to watch where I'm going very carefully, picking my way between random bits of human trash and low-growing plants. Off to my left I see two pickup trucks and people standing out in the water fishing in the deeper water. The water near me is a gigantic puddle, stretching out very wide across a few hundred feet but very shallow, and there are some utility poles nearby. Up and down this bay side of the island are small areas with houses and condos, and the people who live there depend on these overhead power lines for their electricity.

A string of Brown Pelicans cruise over above the water in the bay, then a Great Blue Heron flaps over. A Great Egret stands motionless in the distance, its tall white shape unmistakable. There must be another big puddle over there. From time to time Laughing Gulls wheel about over my head. On the left of the giant puddle in front of me, some Great-tailed Grackles strutting around on the sandy soil make their distinctly weird noises.

In between scanning the water here, close and in the distance, for more birds, I've also been watching one perched on the utility wire that's the farthest away from me. The body shape is that of a kingfisher, but I'm having trouble getting details. It flies up to perch on a closer wire—ah, yes, a Belted Kingfisher. He, for the bird only has a gray neck belt but not the rusty bellyband of a female, studies the water below very carefully. Belted Kingfishers have excellent eyesight to be able to spot prey under the surface of the water. But they also have keen judgment, because they are able to discern the depth of the water and whether it is appropriate for their dive-bombing, bill-first hunting style. He does not attempt to make a strike. The water here is too shallow for him, and the bird soon flies off to the north.

The handsome little shorebird walking in the inch-deep water straight out in front of me has a single dark necklace topped with a white collar, a longish, solid black bill, and a V of white feathers that extends from the bill, back over the dark eyes. Its head is gray-brown, and so are its wings and back. The belly is white. I take several photos, pleased to have another chance to study a Wilson's Plover.

§

Back at my car, I make an unhappy discovery. Something seemed a bit odd about my camera when I was adjusting the focus just now. The view around the edges seemed blurry. Now I know why. Yesterday, or perhaps it was the day before, I remember that my grip on the camera's strap slipped just as I was putting it back in the laundry basket. The strap and the camera slid from my grasp onto the car's passenger seat and, before I could get another firm grip on it, it slid right on down onto a gravel parking lot's surface. It wasn't a great distance, less than two feet, and I thought nothing of it at the time. The lens cap was on, and when I picked up my camera I didn't think to remove it to investigate.

Now I see that the point of impact was the rim of the UV haze filter I keep on the zoom lens—and the filter is cracked in a sort of starburst pattern that extends from the lower rim in an array of straight lines radiating across to the other parts of the rim. This is not good. The cracks cross the filter slightly above and below the center so that when I'm focusing on something right in the middle I'm seeing a mostly clear image. But the cracks are affecting wide shots of landscapes. That's the blur I'm noticing at the edges.

This is beyond not good. It's terrible. I have spare batteries. I have spare memory cards. What I do not have is a spare UV haze filter. I have no spare filters of any kind with me. This is very bad. I will just have to remove the filter and use the lens bare.

I grab this way, I grab that way, but no matter what I do I cannot twist the filter off. It is stuck in position as if it were put on with cement. It is possible that the threads are damaged and that is why I cannot unscrew the filter. Well, there goes that idea. Oh, this is maddening. I'll have to leave the cracked filter in place for now. Later, I'll check to see if there is a brick-and-mortar camera store over in Corpus Christi. Until then, I'll just have to be very careful. I do not think there is anything wrong with the way the zoom lens itself is working or the way adjusting its focus operates, so this isn't the most horrible and potentially expensive disaster it could be, at least as far as I know right now. But it is definitely a major annoyance. This is travel stress I do not need, but I've got it anyway.

Clearly what I need is some chocolate, so I dig around in the laundry basket for my package of M&Ms. As I savor each little treat, my mood improves. I look through my birding travel guide and decide that I should give the Gulf side of the island another chance. Maybe I can find a place with better birding opportunities than I had at Mustang Island State Park. I program my GPS for a new location and start driving.

§

I drive south for a few miles, then east, then south again, retracing my earlier route from my hotel, backtracking, but then going beyond the area I know into a new section of the island. Padre Island stretches along the outskirts of the Texas mainland for more than one hundred miles, but only a small part of the northern tip, where I've been exploring so far, has hotels and houses and condos and businesses. As I drive along toward the Gulf I see fewer and fewer buildings, and then finally none at all as I reach the entrance to Padre Island National Seashore. When I arrive, I see that the "national seashore" designation is something of a cross between what I would expect to find in a national wildlife refuge or wildlife management area, but with some aspects of a national park thrown in for good measure. There are plenty of things for people to do here, but mostly it is designed to protect the wildness of the barrier island. And it's big.

On the Gulf side, Padre Island National Seashore protects and preserves seventy miles of beaches, more than two-thirds of the island's length. But the protected area isn't just a narrow strip of sandy beach and the nearby dunes, the sort of scenes that the word "seashore" brings to mind. The park also includes the tidal flats and grasslands beyond the beach in the center of the island, and extends all the way across the island to include the bayside habitats along Laguna Madre on the western side.

This morning road crews are repairing the asphalt on some stretches of the road leading to the visitor center on the Gulf side and I have to dodge orange cones and wait in a few spots to be waved forward by the workers.

The landscapes around me seem, at a glance, to be rather barren because there are no tall trees and scarcely any shrubs. But this is not a desert. It rains here often, and even though the plants are short in stature, this is a complicated ecosystem, with many kinds of habitats used by a lot of different kinds of birds and other animals. I just don't know which ones—yet.

When I reach the parking lot at the Malaquite Visitor Center, I don't have to worry about steering around other cars, because there are only three already parked, but I do have to maneuver through a large flock of Laughing Gulls. Fifty or so individuals are strutting this way and that way on the warm asphalt in the late-morning sun, then flapping up into the air briefly, then re-alighting on the pavement in completely unpredictable ways. I have the windows down and I can hear their repetitive calls, like crazed laughter, on all sides. They have a tendency to lean forward as they open their bills to squeal and yodel, adding a bit of body language emphasis to their raucous shouts.

I find my wallet, close up the car, and walk up to the building. A group of middle school students are here for a field trip today and they're eating their picnic lunches at tables under a shaded section of the pavilion. Inside the building I take a few minutes to walk through a well-chosen photo exhibit that highlights some of the key animals and the plant communities here. It's like a micro-museum presentation, and quite attractive because the photos are huge and the explanations beside them are filled with fun facts and interesting insights.

Before I came here I did not know anything in particular about Kemp's Ridley Sea Turtles. I know that most sea turtle populations are struggling to survive, but I did not know that these are the most endangered species of sea turtle. Year-round residents of the Gulf of Mexico's waters, they mate in the water, then the female turtles come ashore in Mexico and the United States in the spring and summer months to dig nests and lay their eggs. These Padre Island beaches are prime nesting sites. But of course, people like to use these beaches, too. Researchers and dedicated volunteers have been working for almost forty years to help increase the turtles' chances for survival on these shared-use beaches. Birds and other predators will dig up the nests to eat the eggs, and they'll also try to catch the hatchlings when they crawl down the sand toward the ocean. Now I have something else to watch for when I'm out on the beaches.

While looking around at the usual t-shirts and other merchandise in the gift shop side, I see a book I want to add to my collection—Stan Tekiela's *Birds of Texas Field Guide*, from Adventure Publications. These little books have started another revolution in nature-watching. The field guides in the Peterson series, the Audubon Society series, as well as books from the National Geographic Society and other publishers, present the birds in scientific sequence, grouped together by families. They include many hundreds of birds arranged in proper scientific order, and cover multiple states, in huge regions, and sometimes even the whole continent. The books about animals and insects in the Adventure series are more like wildflower field guides, with the birds grouped by dominant color. That's the first thing most people notice about a bird, so these little books are great for people just getting interested in birds. Many books in the series cover just a single state, and that makes them much more appealing and easier for beginners to use.

The book groups birds into sections based on their most obvious color, with color thumb tabs printed on the outer page margins showing the dominant color. Mostly black birds are in one section and mostly yellow birds are in a different section. The photos are of living birds, and the range maps show where they're likely to occur in each season, but only within the state covered by the book. If you see a bird with a lot of yellow feathers, you just go to that thumb-tab section and look at the pictures until you see one that looks the most like the bird you're watching. You don't have to know anything else. What's especially nice is that, when the male and female of a bird species have different feather colors, the bird appears in two places of the book, such as a male Northern Cardinal in the red section, and the female in the brown section, and then they are cross-referenced.

The books in the series don't include every single species found in a state, but they do cover a good cross-section of the most easily observed species. When I first began studying birds, I had to learn going the long way around, sorting through all the extra information in enormous multi-state field guides. I didn't need all that then, but I do appreciate it now. The way birds are grouped into families is interesting to me, and there are good reasons to know about those sorts of relationships. But I also like the concept of these new books, and I buy them not just as travel souvenirs from the states I visit, but because I always find a few fun new facts, too. I've been studying birds for two decades, and I'm still learning—I don't think I'll ever stop asking questions.

On my way to the counter with the book, I pick up a magnet featuring a Great Blue Heron, and get ready to pay. But before I do, I chat with the park ranger and the volunteer about birding opportunities. They give me the standard color brochure and map of the area, and some good ideas about where to go exploring. When it's time to get out my credit card, I have to pay the park fee at one register, and then pay for my gift shop purchases at another, because the money goes to separate entities. Oh, well, I don't mind, as long as my dollars help keep the place operating.

Walking back to my car I watch the Laughing Gulls in the parking lot. Almost all of them are basically gray-and-white birds with a distinctive black hood on their heads. But a few have white heads without the black hood, and some have pale brown bodies, and others are a combination of brown and gray. This is probably not a mixed flock of several gull species, though, but simply a group of all Laughing Gulls that includes birds of different ages.

I find gulls extremely confusing, as do most other birders, because they can take two to four years to reach adult plumage. On their way to sexual maturity they molt and molt again in a series of feather changes, any one of which can be maddeningly similar to the appearance of a completely different species. At this point in my bird studies, I'm hopeless at picking out anything except mature adult gulls of a few species, and often have trouble even getting that right. I don't see many gull species at home. So watching the antics of these birds as they strut and fly and waddle across the parking lot, and listening to their voices, is a treat.

Among the adults, I cannot tell the males from the females because the sexes look alike. Well, at least to my human eyes. But there must be some way for the gulls to know who's a he and who's a she. There might be some subtle visual difference that's not apparent to my eyes, or perhaps a difference in voice? I don't know, but right in front of me two birds have figured it out.

In many of the songbirds only the males sing, but I'm not sure that gull shrieks would count as a song to most human listeners. And it seems to me that both the male gulls and the female gulls make the same kinds of noises. Do the male Laughing Gulls put something special into their strings of squawks and wails that the females find appealing? Whatever it is, something has happened amid all the racket and movement that seems random to me, and one female has given her consent to mate with a nearby male. She crouches down slightly on the pavement and the male flaps his wings just enough to flutter up to perch on top of her. He balances on her back and they mate. It's over in a few seconds, and then he flutters back down to the pavement in front of her. The other gulls pay absolutely no attention to what's just happened.

Seems all rather casual to me, a one-afternoon stand as it were, and perhaps that is the usual way of things among these gulls. I do not know if she will accept another partner later, or if there is some long-lasting bond between these two individuals. And where will she lay the resulting eggs? If I had extra time, I'd set up one of my lawn chairs and sit still to study their behavior to see if I can figure out more, but I'd rather go exploring beyond the parking lot.

§

The drive on the paved road that leads from the visitor center to the nearest section of beach doesn't take long. The paving stops and it's up to me to figure out where on the sand to park. It looks stable enough, and I choose a likely spot. From my car I watch as a string of Brown Pelicans fly along in single file a few feet above the waves, then I see one perched on a wooden piling nearby. A nearby sign tells me that "this one-of-a-kind national seashore protects the longest undeveloped stretch of barrier island in the world."

The key word here is "undeveloped." While it is true there are no permanent human structures on the sand, I can see plenty of tire tracks. Driving on some sections of the beach is permitted, but with restrictions. Any kind of vehicle with a driver who's wise to the ways of the tides may go out on the sand in this immediate area, but to go further, certain rules must be observed. There are barriers and signs announcing where only vehicles with four-wheel drive are allowed to venture. A sure knowledge of the condition of the sand is necessary for any driver wanting to go beyond the barriers. I've driven on packed sand on the Atlantic Coast at Daytona Beach for a very short distance, and that pretty much cured me of ever attempting such a thing again. Besides that, my car is only front-wheel drive, not all four, and I know nothing about the state of the tide or the sand here. I'll be quite satisfied to leave my car where it is, and just get out and walk.

And I'll keep my leather sandals on, too. This beach is not pure sand. Stringy bits and clumps of wet seaweed and other natural debris have been flung up onto the sand by the waves, and there are some small pebbles and larger rocks jumbled in, too, plus a few shell fragments. And, of course, here and there human trash, mostly empty drink containers, litters the beach. Out on the Gulf, waves about a foot high curl over into white foam as they rush towards the beach at regular intervals. The rest of the water glitters a beautiful blue under partly cloudy skies. The breeze coming in off the water feels good, and smells good, too, a nice, fresh, slightly salty scent.

I pause to watch a group of Ruddy Turnstones. At first I think they are hunting for food at the water's edge, but that's not it. They are bathing in the oncoming wavelets. They flutter and jump and twist and turn like little kids playing. As I stroll slowly along northbound, I bring up my binoculars to get a better look at three Willets, and then notice some Sanderlings dashing along the wet sand. I cannot identify the small tern that flies past me, but I do recognize the big one with an orange bill and head feathers that look like a black toupee as a Caspian Tern.

A large group of about thirty Brown Pelicans have formed into a loose circle in the sky, taking advantage of a column of slightly warmer air to rise higher without much wing-flapping effort. I'm so accustomed to seeing them fly only in single file, I get my cell phone out to snap a photo. I've left my big camera in the car for now. Within a minute the pelicans slowly unwind from their spiral and begin gliding off, single file, to the north.

When I turn around to walk past my car and go south along the beach, I pause to watch some Black-bellied Plovers poke and prod in the wet sand. They are definitely looking for food and seem to be finding something they like.

Walking slowly along, I'm keeping notes of the birds I see but I'm also enjoying the beach for what it is, a pleasant place to enjoy the sound of the waves and the scent of the salt air. A small group of Laughing Gulls are knee deep in the water near a line of wood pilings whose purpose I cannot guess. This is one of the wildest beaches I've ever been on, with a wonderful variety of birds doing what they do best—flying, feeding, bathing, grooming their feathers, just being birds. I like it.

Up ahead I watch a young woman in a flowery-patterned bathing suit set up a lounge chair about fifteen feet from the waves at the edge of the dunes. She gets some carefully matched beach towels from her tote bag and takes photos of her instant relaxing spot with her cell phone. When I'm nearer I say "hello" and she asks me first if I'll take her picture. Kathleen is a kindergarten teacher with a rare day off and she wants her friends to see the fun she's having today. After I take several photos with her phone, I give her mine and she snaps several pictures of me with my binoculars raised looking off in the distance at birds, and some more photos without the binoculars up, just me smiling directly at the camera. It's easy enough to do—I think I've been smiling ever since I got here.

Walking back to my car I make a mental note. If I ever return to this section of Padre Island, I want to find a small tour company that will drive me out where only the four-wheel-drive vehicles can go. I'd sure like to see that even wilder section of the Gulf Coast.

§

As I drive inland to explore more of this huge park, I stop at another small construction zone. This time it's not the road that's being repaired, but a bird blind at the edge of a good-sized pond. Workers are rebuilding the observation area with fresh lumber. I pull past their orange cones and park, then get out of my car with my binoculars and walk along the edge of the pavement to get as close as possible to the fresh water while avoiding their work zone. There are two little groups of Black-bellied Whistling-Ducks floating near the reeds, and some Mottled Ducks swimming in the center of the water. The pond is almost crowded. I see some Blue-winged Teal on the far left, and then study the movements of a very small little bird over on the right. It's a tiny little Least Grebe paddling this way, then that way, covering the same patch of water over and over again.

The meadowlark singing in the field beyond the road on my left sounds like an Eastern Meadowlark, and that's what I'm writing in my notebook. But this is an area where it could be the other kind of meadowlark, or a hybrid. I can't find it with my binoculars to examine its feathers, but it sure sounds like an eastern one to me, and that's all I can go by when I make my notes.

As I drive the rest of the way across the island to the Laguna Madre side to check out what's going on over there, I'm nibbling on my favorite birding snack, pretzels and cranberry juice. Soon I reach a boat ramp with a big parking lot and a pier, plus a primitive restroom. There are quite a few pickup trucks and empty boat trailers in the parking lot, so this must be a popular and convenient access point for fishing enthusiasts.

When I walk toward the pier I find a very plump Brown Pelican settled in quite determinedly on the top of a wooden piling. As I look at him, or perhaps her, as this is yet another bird species that we humans cannot tell the males from the females easily, I notice a cluster of a dozen or so American White Pelicans drifting around in a ragged group out on the water far beyond the pier. The folks at the visitor's center seemed to think that all the white ones who spent the winter here had already left to go north to their breeding grounds, so this is a nice surprise. Walking around to the best vantage point, I get a nice photo of the two pelican species together, the brown one in the foreground, the white ones in the background.

By the time I reach the end of the short pier to return to the parking lot, three of the American White Pelicans fly in and settle on the water close enough for me to see the strange protrusions on the center of their upper bills that indicate they are adults ready to breed. That weird knob will eventually disappear after the adults begin incubating eggs. But first they need to fly north and build a nest. Perhaps they'll leave later this week.

When I'm almost back to my car, a chittering sound and a flutter of swooping birds get my attention. It's a little band of Barn Swallows snatching up tiny insects as they fly over the water and the nearby fields. More Laughing Gulls show up behind me.

I get in my car, start up the engine, and roll down the windows. Driving along the outer edge of the parking lot, a large bird glides down into a field and stands on a slight rise of sand. It's a Crested Caracara and I take several photos with my digital camera, hoping that the cracked filter will not affect the quality of the images. The big bird is very alert, gazing to the left and right, not at all concerned by the row of pickup trucks and campers and RVs a few hundred feet across the way in a different section of the park.

As I drive along the road leading away from the parking lot, I spot a Tricolored Heron standing by some reedy green stuff, at the edge of what must be yet another shallow pond. Although the ground here looks uniformly flat, it isn't. There are little rises of sand maybe eight or ten inches high like the one the Crested Caracara stood on, and little depressions that fill with water from time to time, so there might be something good to eat wriggling or crawling around down there where the heron is searching so patiently. Some Turkey Vultures soar in lazy circles far ahead to the left, so there might be something dead out there. Anything dead would also be of interest to the Crested Caracara. A lone Cattle Egret flies past.

As I inch along ever so slowly, gently moving my foot off and on the brake, just barely touching the accelerator from time to time, and watching all my mirrors for any cars in a bigger hurry than I am to come up behind me, I get another surprise. There's a bird walking behind me, crossing the pavement from left to right. I can see it quite plainly in my driver's-side mirror. I put the car in park and shut off the engine to stop any vibrations. I pick up my camera out of the laundry basket. But instead of turning around, I continue to face forward and carefully focus my camera not on the bird, but on its reflection in the side mirror. This is one of those tricks that I've learned during decades of photography and birdwatching. If I were to open the car door to try to get a direct shot in the correct direction I would risk frightening the bird into flight, and I'd rather not take that chance. I've got the reflected bird in sharp focus. Click, click, click, and I have what I hope will be three very nice images of a Whimbrel crossing the double yellow center lines on the pavement behind me.

I re-start my car and drive over to another campground area, which is also where people can try windsurfing out on the waters of the Gulf. The Tricolored Heron has moved over here now and is dashing about, trying to stir up something to eat in the shallow water by the road's edge. There are plenty of Laughing Gulls and more grackles over here, too.

It's hours past noon now, I'm ready to try someplace new, and I'm thinking about food. Pretzels and cranberry juice only go so far. I'd like a real lunch.

§

It only takes me about fifteen minutes to drive back the way I came to reach the main boulevard and the business district. I pull off into a parking lot the first chance I get and use my cell phone to research independent camera stores in Corpus Christi. Well, there aren't any. There are national chain stores that sell electronics with some camera gear mixed in, but no place that specializes in cameras and specialty photography gear. I will just have to muddle along with my cracked filter, and deal with the problem at my local optics store when I get home. I'll keep my fingers crossed that the filter doesn't shatter into a gazillion pieces before then. I'm being extra, extra careful how I handle it now.

I drive on, and around the back of some businesses that seem to have something to do with boating, I find the entrance to Packery Channel County Park. From this gravel parking area it looks interesting, with a boardwalk and some interpretive signs. But instead of exploring it now, I'm going to have to drive back out on the boulevard to find lunch.

There's a Subway sandwich shop in a little shopping center next to a big tourist beach store. How am I going to get to it? I figure out a way to cross the median of the boulevard beyond the shop and then double back. It's hot and humid today, so I eat my sandwich indoors instead of taking it with me, and spend a few minutes catching up with friends through social media and text messaging.

Back at the park I drive along the side road that borders some houses and condos. This gets me to an area where people can put kayaks into the water, and while hunting for a place to park, I watch a guy pull his kayak out of the water and load it onto his car. I find an open spot and get out to scan the water and the shore for birds. I see a Snowy Egret's black wingtips as it flaps along above the shore, fifty feet or so beyond me, then a Great Blue Heron standing in the water on the left, then some Brown Pelicans fly past in single file. The wild noise of Laughing Gulls is a constant soundtrack. I can tell that the small birds coursing this way and that way in the air are terns, but I cannot decide on the species. Oh, what's that walking slowly over there? I refocus my binoculars and watch a Willet carefully stepping between some small rocks.

That seems to be about it for birds in this area, so I'm going to drive back toward the section with the boardwalk.

The first thing I find at the entrance to the boardwalk is a historical marker with a long section of text, which solves the name mystery for me. For a short time, just about two decades in the mid- to late 1800s, the easiest way to make money from all the cattle roaming on this island was to butcher them, not for the meat, but for their hide and tallow. That was before commercial refrigeration had been invented, and fresh meat didn't stay fresh for long. But the other products didn't spoil, so they were packed up and sent from the bay here on the Laguna Madre side of Padre Island to markets elsewhere via boats traveling through the pass—the channel—and into the Gulf of Mexico and beyond. That explains the name Packery Channel.

Lots of other parts of the carcasses were rendered into other products, including buttons, combs, and fertilizer, and the factories where this was accomplished smelled terrible and made an awful mess. By the late 1870s, weather extremes and changes in cattle markets made the work unprofitable, and the businesses closed.

Another historical marker tells me that the last cattle on Padre Island were not removed until 1970, not quite fifty years ago. But the damage to the natural environment and the habitats was immense and long-lasting.

The next sign I see provides more insights. This park is part of the Nueces County Coastal Parks System. Working in partnership with the Coastal Bend Bays and Estuaries Program, the ongoing Packery Channel Nature Park Habitat Restoration Project, funded by a grant from the Texas General Land Office, is making good progress towards making these acres more attractive and useful for resident and migratory birds again. They've already removed invasive Brazilian black pepper trees from the park and are beginning to re-seed the land with native wildflowers.

It's hot, it's humid, and it's getting late in the afternoon, not exactly the ideal time to see land birds, but I want to walk along the boardwalk anyway. A Northern Mockingbird flashes his white wing patches in some shrubby growth in the oak motte near the park's entrance as I read the smaller signs along the handrails on this wooden boardwalk. They describe many bird species and explain the plant communities. I see some water drips, but no birds. I keep walking, and watching, then finally find a Eurasian Collared-Dove puttering around on the top and sides of a little stone construction that supports one of the water drips.

The weather's been too good for many migrant songbirds to have lingered here today, and when I finish walking along the big rectangle that the boardwalk makes, I'm ready to try something else.

Back in my car, I realize that I have about two hours of good daylight before sunset. I look in my birding trail book and figure that I have plenty of time to drive north again, past Mustang Island State Park, and up to the Port Aransas area.

§

After a quick twenty-minute drive, my GPS says my destination is on the left. I see about four parking spots and the entrance to yet another boardwalk. I pull in, gather up my binoculars, camera—gently—and my pocket notebook and pen.

The boardwalk leads in a zigzag fashion to I know not what. I step forward, ready to be surprised. And I am. Just in front of me, around a curve, stretches a wide, shallow body of water covering a few acres—and it's filled with birds. As I begin scanning the area with my binoculars, I hear men's deep voices coming up behind me. They're talking about birds, and we reach a little gazebo sort of place at exactly the same time. We exchange brief hellos and focus on the variety of birds in front us. I don't know where to look first, there are so many birds here.

The first birds I focus on are some Black-necked Stilts, a stand-out in any crowd, with that curiously yin-yang pattern of black and white feathers on the head. I walk a few steps back out onto the boardwalk and look slowly and steadily from left to right, studying each bird I see, and then notice something especially big perched on a wooden piling.

I look, and look again. The more carefully I look, the more details I see of this large bird. Hook-tipped bill, white on the head and at the shoulder, white curving partway down the side, a longish, dark tail, a stocky, plump, dark body. Oh, wow! This is really special. It's a juvenile Magnificent Frigatebird. I have only seen one adult Magnificent Frigatebird in my life, soaring several hundred feet above me at J. N. "Ding" Darling National Wildlife Refuge on Sanibel Island, Florida, and that was more than ten years ago. And now to find a juvenile, perched, of all things, instead of soaring in flight, about seventy-five feet in front of me is very exciting, an extremely lucky find.

I can tell by their conversation that the two guys are well-experienced birders, and I describe which piling the young bird is perched on. Why, yes, yes, it is a juvenile Magnificent Frigatebird, they concur, and we talk about the pattern of white feathers on the youngster, and the thrill of watching the adults soar.

I make a note of several Roseate Spoonbills sweeping their spatula-like bills back and forth through the water farther away, then notice a Brown Pelican floating all by itself a little farther back and to the right. I also see a Great Egret, the tallest bird around so far, and then a smaller Reddish Egret nearby.

From time to time we point out interesting birds to each other and finally get around to introducing ourselves. When I hear the tall guy's name and put that together with the much larger, more complicated, and way-more-expensive-than-mine camera setup he has with him, I realize that I know who he is—he's one of the photographers whose work I see so often in posts in the Texas birding group I belong to. Greg's a local, and Stanley, the guy with him, lives up in Austin, and I recognize his name, too. Greg, the tall guy, is a professional fishing guide, and knows the habits of birds as well as he knows the habits of fish. Stanley is visiting, looking at birds, and generally having a good time today.

I spend a few minutes watching some American Avocets looking for food, their general body shape similar to the stilts' but taller, and the avocets' bills curve upward at the tip instead of being straight. The reasons for the different curves of bird bills, up or down, is something I do not know, but I'd like to find out more. A Tricolored Heron moves about in the shallow water to stir up something to eat but doesn't have any success so far. I often wonder how long these birds go between mouthfuls, how difficult it is not just to locate prey, but also catch it. Every day I come up with fresh questions about birds.

Laughing Gulls wheel and tilt above us, then a little band of Barn Swallows come sweeping through the air, jinking and slanting and swooping over the water in search of a totally different kind of food than what the birds hunting for something edible in the water are interested in. This wide but shallow wetland is sandwiched between a busy main road behind us and some commercial buildings to the west, including a huge boat-storage warehouse. Beyond that three oil rigs brought in for repair or storage jut above the building, their towering grids of metal struts silhouetted against the pale blue sky.

A Snowy Egret flies in, then I notice a Double-crested Cormorant near the young Magnificent Frigatebird. The cormorant has a hooked bill tip like the frigatebird, good for snagging slippery fish, but the resemblance stops there. The cormorant has a short, stubby tail, very useful as a rudder when it dives down into the water and swims through it to catch fish. The young frigatebird's much longer, though still somewhat raggedy, tail will eventually be a beautiful, deeply forked pair of streamers. These will be useful in a different way as it soars and steers through the air currents above the water, then glides lower to barely skim along the water's surface to find its food. The frigatebird sometimes steals already-captured prey from other birds, too, rather like a pirate.

There are so many different kinds of birds gathered here before sunset, tucked away from view on the main road, a hidden gem well worth taking the time to explore. This is a marvelous spot to observe the diversity of species, and that's one of the reasons I find birding so satisfying. Yes, I like to learn the names, and make lists. But even more than that, the distinct animal image and lifestyle details that each name brings to mind is what I treasure. And over on the left I find another example of comparative anatomy. A White Ibis, with white plumage and brilliant red face and white eye, is just a few feet away from a White-faced Ibis, its cousin with gleaming brown feathers and a ring of white skin around its red eye.

In the far distance I study some Blue-winged Teal paddling around slowly.

Greg and Stanley begin discussing the bird standing in the shallow water near us on the right. The three of us note the bird's field marks, and Greg explains to me why it is obviously—well, to him, at least—a Long-billed Dowitcher. I will have to take his word for it, because I have only the vaguest recollection of what Brandon told me just days ago about the distinguishing field marks of the Short-billed Dowitcher we saw. I take a photo to record this latest lifer. Then Greg and Stanley and I talk about the trouble we've had identifying birds whose names start with "lesser" or "greater" or some other comparison, which is fine for side-by-side dead museum specimens, but not so good for real-life studies. As if on cue, the next bird we all notice is another example of the kinds of problems we were just discussing—a Lesser Yellowlegs.

The sun is sinking closer to the horizon, and making identifications is going to get even more complicated as the light fades, but I do not want to leave just yet. A Mottled Duck drifts lazily on the water, then begins paddling in a determined fashion, perhaps to meet others of its kind on the distant edge of the water.

We all turn to examine a bird that's closer to us and note its long, slightly upturned bill, which is orange near the face, but black for the half extending to the tip. Greg knows it right away as a Marbled Godwit, but I have to study the bird much longer before I can agree. I just don't know this bird very well, even after watching one and discussing the field marks with Brandon the other day. That lesson stayed with me longer than the one about dowitchers, but I still have a lot of memorizing to do, and I need more experience in the field. But the calls of some Killdeer circling overhead are easy for me to recognize.

While watching the birds move around probing for food, I'm taking careful note of the sizes of their feet and how far the water comes up on their legs. The water depth here ranges from scarcely an inch to about three inches, quite shallow overall.

There's some exposed sand off to the left, although mudflat might be the better word, and I watch some birds dashing along for a few steps, then stopping to poke in the wet brown stuff. The one with the black belly, black neckerchief, and black face, topped with a white head, is fairly easy to figure out. It's a Black-bellied Plover. The other bird is much smaller. I watch the little guy and make out the single black necklace and white spot above its bill—aha, it's a Semipalmated Plover. I'm getting a much better look at this individual than I did when I first saw this species about ten days ago, but I don't have any hope of getting a good photo because it's so far away and the light is coming in at a bad angle.

We search and search, first from one section of the short boardwalk then another, scanning in different directions for any other different kinds of birds. The guys spot the Dunlin before I do, and tell me where to look. This bird has a dark black smudge on its belly, not as dark or clearly defined as the plover, and the rest of the bird is speckled black and white, with rusty wings and a few black tail feathers. The bill curves down at the tip. I am trying so hard to remember each combination of field marks, and I think I'm getting better at it with practice. But I still have to actively think—for many of these shorebirds I still cannot just come up with a name the instant I see it.

While I'm studying the birds in the distance, a movement closer to the boardwalk catches the guys' eyes. Three birds have just alighted to stand in the water. Their bodies are of a similar size as the Dunlin, but they don't have the dark belly smudge, and I can't see any rusty feathers. Their legs are much longer than the

Dunlin's, too, and that turns out to be the key. They are Stilt Sandpipers, a good name as far I'm concerned, and they are lifers for me. I'm so glad Greg and Stanley are familiar with it and can help me learn the field marks.

Several Great-tailed Grackles arrive with a flourish of noisy screeching as they flutter down toward a nearby parking lot, but I don't pay much attention to them because I'm watching a duck out on the water. It's a rather nondescript beige and gray, then it turns sideways to show its black rump. It's a male Gadwall. I cannot find the female, but that's not surprising. Her plumage would be much drabber, and without the distinctive black feathers at the rear. He might be alone, but then again, it might be that I can't find the well-camouflaged female because the light is going. I can barely make out an Osprey as it flies over with strong wingbeats. I wonder where it will spend the night?

As we walk fifty feet or so to the end of the boardwalk and back to our cars, the guys suggest two places I might want to visit tomorrow, and then we go our separate ways.

§

Driving back south, again, I stop at a gas station in town to refill my tank and scrub more bugs off my windshield. I've seen some ads in the tourist brochures for a restaurant that sounds like it might be fun, so I program my GPS to drive over to Scuttlebutt's Seafood Bar and Grill.

Inside I chat with the bartender about Lorelei Brewing Company, a local place over in Corpus Christi. I tell her some of the beers I enjoy, and she recommends the Blonde Ale. It's delicious, and very refreshing after such a busy day.

One of the great puzzles of traveling, and especially solo with no one to split dishes with, is to choose something to eat that will be just the right portion size. I have no way to deal with leftovers, so I often turn to the appetizer menu. The bacon-wrapped scallops in orange liqueur sound good. I add a side of rice, and sip beer for a while, thinking about all the different places I've been today. So many different habitats, so many different kinds of birds, a very satisfying day. When dinner arrives, it's delicious, and I eat every last morsel, no leftovers at all. The rice was an inspired extra because it makes it easy to spoon up all the wonderful orange liqueur sauce.

It's already an hour after dark when I get back to my hotel, but I cannot put off doing laundry another day. Unfortunately, my hotel's coin washer and dryer are out of order. The desk clerk calls the hotel across the street, a full-size Holiday Inn, and makes arrangements for me to go over there to use their machines. Even though the hotels are different brands, they are part of the same international group, so it's an easy deal to put together.

When I get there, I discover that the larger hotel is in the midst of major renovations. I had no idea that spring migration for birds coincides with hotel remodeling season. I take a service elevator up to the floor where the laundry machines are and then have to dodge stacks of lumber and buckets of spackling compound. I take advantage of the waiting time while my clothes are washing and then drying to catch up with all the messages and posts and e-mails on my phone, and then update my handwritten notes while cross-referencing birds on my life list. And I've found out that the cute little critter I saw scampering across the sand dune is a Spotted Ground Squirrel.

Back across the street in my own hotel room, I sort through my clean clothes and repack my duffel bag and the big suitcase so that the things I think I'll want for the rest of trip are easy to get to. I'm running out of energy as midnight approaches.

Soon I'm all settled in the comfy bed, with the pillows arranged just so. My phone's plugged into my charger and that's plugged into a wall outlet. I'm ready to relax and fall asleep. I reach over to turn off the bedside light. Click.

Hmm. Why is there still light in the room? I try the switch again. Click. Click. The lamp next to me comes on, then goes off. But nothing happens to the light behind me. What? Where is the light coming from? I sit up and see that there is a concealed light fixture that produces a wash of pale white light down the wall above the headboard of the bed. How it got turned on I have no idea.

I get up and go around the whole room flipping switches to find the one I missed. Click, click. Click, click. I keep clicking and re-clicking. Nothing happens to the light shining on the wall. I look at the bedside table. I see a power strip with connections for rechargers. Finally, I decide to click everything I see, and when I get to the red switch marked "reset," that turns out to be the secret to darkness. Perhaps I hit it accidentally when I plugged my phone charger in to the other outlet. All I know is that all is dark now, and I can finally settle in to drift off to sleep.

###

CHAPTER TWELVE

In and around Corpus Christi

Paradise Pond, scrubland, marsh ducks

Great-tailed Grackles and Laughing Gulls call back and forth to members of their own species as I take a quick walk before breakfast. When I turn to go back toward the hotel I notice a Jeep with a flat tire in the parking lot. No, make that two flat tires. Somebody's going to have a long morning.

During breakfast I plan my day. The guys on the boardwalk last night recommended a place to go birding in Port Aransas, so I look that up on my phone. It will be an easy drive, and as soon as I've finished eating, I take the rest of my decaf coffee outside to consider the weather and decide which other places I want to visit today. Two men are busy changing the tires on the Jeep—they hit sharp debris on the beach earlier. I'm so glad I decided not to drive on the sand yesterday. I'm going to stick to paved roads today, too.

Once again I drive west, then north, past Mustang Island State Park, and past Wetland Park where I had such good luck birding late yesterday afternoon. I make the turns my GPS says to take, but when I arrive at my so-called destination, I cannot figure out where I've gone wrong. All I see is a bumpy, weed-edged, gravel parking lot behind an old, weather-beaten restaurant. I'm supposed to be at Paradise Pond, or, more properly, Joan and Scott Holt Paradise Pond, and this place looks distinctly ordinary, nothing even remotely ideal or idyllic, certainly not a paradise.

Where did I goof? I make a circuit through the crowded parking lot, then pull off at the edge of the road to study my directions.

No, I haven't made a mistake. I just need to go back and find a place to park my car, then get out and walk. There should be a narrow strip of concrete sidewalk behind the backyards of some houses that will lead to the boardwalk and paradise. Well, maybe not paradise, but at least a good spot to study birds.

Once again, I really don't know what to expect, but I'm willing to give it a try. I gather together my notebook and camera and binoculars and walk between some pretty flowering plants. Ah, here's the beginning of a fresh wooden boardwalk, the totally flat kind with just a low edging as a curb along the boards, but no handrails. And I see other birders up ahead. I cannot see a pond, just a sort of brushy, boggy area, perhaps the streambed that feeds the pond. If there is one.

Laughing Gulls and Great-tailed Grackles make a racket from the parking lot behind me. I stop near some women peering intently at the leafy trees by the stream, which is little more than a giant mud puddle this morning. I look in the same direction to see if I can see what they're watching. A flash of cantaloupe orange, a black hood, white streaks on the wings—I put all these marks together as I get quick, partial glimpses of the bird as it moves among the leaves—it's the first migrant of the day, a Baltimore Oriole, a handsome bird I always enjoy watching. This one's a male, and he's poking around the leaves searching for some tasty caterpillars to eat to refuel after his long journey flying across the Gulf of Mexico.

I wonder, does he feel tired, the way I would after walking a great distance? Or is the sensation of extreme hunger more dominant? Will he eat as much as he can today, rest a bit, and then fly on farther north tonight? Or will he need to stay here another day or two to rest longer and continue eating to have enough energy to resume flying later in the week? Of course I cannot discover the answer to these questions and must use my imagination to dream about the strength he must have in those beautiful little wings.

Scanning the trees I discover a male Northern Cardinal and his mate, also foraging for food. But they would be resident birds, not migrants, and their hunger not as intense as the oriole's. Yes, they need food, but it's not a case of needing to gorge to refuel for long-distance flight. Nearby, a male Brown-headed Cowbird, then another, then a female hop along the branches, searching for food. They're year-round residents in this part of Texas, too.

The other birders ahead of me saunter along on the boardwalk, in no particular hurry this sunny morning. They seem to be a random assortment of men and women with binoculars and hats and cameras, not part of a special group. People speak in very soft voices, helping each other focus on first this bird, then that bird in a friendly way. I listen and turn my attention to another section of the taller trees and see what the others are discussing—a beautiful male Rose-breasted Grosbeak, his deep, dark, rich pink bib gleaming against his white breast feathers when he turns just so in the morning sunshine. He, too, is another migrant who's just flown hundreds of miles across the open waters of the Gulf of Mexico. Perhaps to him this leafy section of land with ample food really is paradise found.

More people have moved closer to me, and I realize that a group of schoolchildren are also exploring the boardwalk this morning. I sort of eavesdrop and discover that they're fourth graders. The teacher has divided them into small teams, and they're competing, a bit, with each other to identify the most birds this morning. Listening to the teacher, I gather that they've been studying a lot of the local birds in their classroom lessons, and today is their chance to use this information in the field. They're watching and looking and writing things down on a worksheet as they move along the boardwalk. And giggling from time to time. I get that. Birding is fun for me, too.

I walk on a few paces and then pause to watch a different oriole. This one has a brick-red breast and black hood, and a single white wing bar, the key features of another long-distance migrant, the Orchard Oriole.

Just past the next turn in the boardwalk I see a group of adults gathered in a clump. They're all looking at something down by the water's edge. I stop to look, too. We all agree that it's a waterthrush, but beyond that we are completely puzzled. The light down where it's skulking through the brushy leaves and weeds along the edge of the mud isn't very good, just dappled shade, and of course waterthrush plumage is designed to help them blend in amid that environment. This particular bird's camouflage is so good, all I can write down is waterthrush, without naming a species. I look and look, hoping to see the definitive field marks to be able to say one species or the other, since there are only two that I would be likely to see here. I'm about ready to give up when the bird makes the decisive move—disappearing completely into the deeper shadows and out of sight. Huh. Well, this will have to go in my notebook as today's unknown bird.

I cannot add it to my daily list, I cannot add it to my trip list, all I can do is think up a new symbol to put next to it in my field notes. I think a big fat zero with a slash mark through it would be about right. It will simply be waterthrush, species unknown.

Walking farther along I see tantalizing glimpses of what are clearly warbler-size birds hopping around in the leaves above the boardwalk, but I get no good looks. I'm beginning to wonder if my birding karma has shifted when I hear, then see, a Killdeer fly over. At least I can pick that one out with no uncertainty, so maybe all is not lost.

Finally I reach the pond. It's big, much bigger than I expected, with a railed observation deck where I can lean and relax while searching more than an acre of water for birds. The water close by seems to be about four or five inches deep in most places. Some Roseate Spoonbills and Black-bellied Whistling-Ducks are in the water very close by the deck. As I scan back and forth across the water, I see some Blue-winged Teal farther away to the right. Several male Red-winged Blackbirds are darting about in the surrounding vegetation, calling out "onk-la-ree" and flaring their red and yellow epaulets as they glide in to perches. But they don't stay in any one spot very long, seeming to play a sort of leapfrog game, struggling to find just exactly the right place to defend.

When I shift to lean against another section of the railing, I see a White-faced Ibis, its red eye gleaming like a ruby-colored marble above its shiny brown, slightly iridescent feathers. It's using its long, down-curved bill to reach the preen gland near its tail, intent on grooming its feathers. The sort of oily substance produced in the preen gland is an all-purpose feather conditioner. Birds gather a bit in their bills and then rub and stroke it onto their feathers to keep them flexible and waterproof.

Nearby a Roseate Spoonbill sweeps its bill back and forth through the shallow water, feeling for something to eat. A Snowy Egret flies in, its black wingtips barely missing some overhanging vegetation. This hidden spot, tucked away behind houses and businesses, is much busier with birds than I would have guessed, an oasis of wildness, and the name Paradise Pond doesn't seem so far-fetched to me now.

As people come and go to take a look over the water, some folks pausing only briefly, others lingering to watch more carefully, I hear talk of a certain other kind of blackbird and a particular warbler that have been spotted farther down the boardwalk. I have no idea if these reports mean in the last two minutes, or the last half hour, and I am determined to not chase after birds who could very well have flown off by the time I get there. I scan the pond again, just one more time, just in case I've missed something, and then decide to walk on. I'll take my chances on what birds will be ahead.

Ah. There's a White-winged Dove sidling along on a mostly bare branch near the boardwalk. Two of the schoolchildren and a small group of adults are looking at something on the other side of boardwalk. I move a few steps closer and see a bird with a sort of checkerboard pattern of black and pale orange. Those patches of contrasting colors on the upper tail and across the wings below the shoulders can only mean one thing, a male American Redstart who's recently returned from his winter home along the southern edges of the Gulf of Mexico. He's another hungry long-distance flyer who must be enjoying this safe haven of trees filled with good insects and spiders and who knows what else to eat.

As I move along another few steps, I keep scanning through the leaves and spot a Red-eyed Vireo who's just captured a caterpillar. He's come a long way from his winter home in the Amazon basin, which, as I understand it, is a treasure trove of insect prey. I wonder if the food tastes different down there? Or is one caterpillar pretty much the same as another? I suspect not, since most moth and butterfly caterpillars will eat only certain plants, and I would think that this would impart a special flavor to each species of caterpillar, sort of like the much-prized terroir of wines that many people can discern from just one sip.

I know that Monarch caterpillars, which feed on milkweeds, don't just taste bad to birds, but they're also full of noxious poisons. Birds learn to recognize certain markings on the bodies of the unsuitable caterpillars and avoid them, but do they actually prefer certain colors or shapes of especially delicious ones? That's something I might like to research when I get back home.

I'm ready to turn back now and see if I can find anything different on my way to my car. That might be a female oriole up among the little leaves in a large clumps of willows, so I take a quick photo, but at this distance I don't expect to get enough detail to determine the species.

§

Back at my car, I look at my guidebook again and see that it is only a matter of driving a few blocks to reach the birding center near the town dump and water treatment facility. The habitats there might be different from those around this pond, so I'll let my GPS get me there.

I drive through an old subdivision and past a tiny RV park, then see the entrance to a compound of buildings with shallow sections of open water near the narrow road and parking area. I don't know where the birding center is, but I find a place to park near the water and get out to take a look around. This doesn't seem to be a body of water involved in any way with the public water supply for humans, just a naturally low-lying section of ground that retains rainwater. It's basically another puddle. Looking across the water I find the biggest collection of Black-necked Stilts I've ever seen in one place, easily more than thirty individuals. Some Snowy Egrets and several Cattle Egrets are standing at the far edge, their white feathers a sharp contrast to the blue sky, which is also reflected on the surface of the water. I don't know if this water stands here more or less permanently, but today there must be tasty things to catch and eat here.

One side of the water is bordered with green grass, then farther away I see sandy mudflats where some of the smaller shorebirds are busy looking for food. I'm coming to understand that "shore" is a very flexible word, and doesn't necessarily have to be right next to the Gulf. Any body of water edged with exposed sand seems to be attractive to shorebirds. I get a good look at a Lesser Yellowlegs probing for food. They will soon be flying far north to the tundra in the upper sections of Canada, which isn't a shore but a vast expanse of treeless, flat soil with low-growing plants, to mate and raise their young.

Nearby a Willet seems about half asleep. I don't know what the usual etiquette is among the different shorebirds for how they interact with each other. At all the places I've been on this trip, the mixture of bird species has been different, and I've not been able to see a consistent pattern. The littlest birds don't seem to run away from the bigger ones. Big or little, their movements seem to depend only on whether they're finding food to eat or not. If a spot is teeming with their favorite food, they stay put, but if it's barren they move on. This Willett might already be full for the time being and isn't hungry right now. Or it could simply be waiting for the area to be less crowded before taking a turn hunting on the same patch of sand after the other species move on.

I scan around again and spot a White-faced Ibis. And then I realize that I've had exactly enough of shorebirds and migrants for this morning. I'm going to skip trying to find the birding center's boardwalk. This is my last full day in the Corpus Christi area and I want to explore some other places. I'd like a nice mid-day meal to make up for yesterday's ordinary un-Texas-style lunch, and I want to learn about some human history. I've picked up an ad for tours at the USS Lexington aircraft carrier, and this afternoon will be the perfect time to visit.

§

I look at my paper maps for a general idea of where I need to be, then let my GPS take over. I could go back the way I came, and indeed, according to my GPS, that's the first choice for the quickest travel time. But since I'm already at the northern tip of Mustang Island and not in any particular hurry, I'd rather continue going north instead of backtracking. I'll take the ferry that crosses from Redfish Bay to the mainland between Corpus Christi Bay and Aransas Bay, then drive along the northeast side of town. It's kind of the long way around, but since I'm here I might as well make a complete circle around the city of Corpus Christi.

The wait for this ferry isn't long, and soon a guy in a safety vest waves me to drive onboard. Laughing Gulls are perched here and there near the ferry landing, and others fly and squeal overhead above the ferry and the bay. This is a busy shipping lane, and the ferry captain has to time his crossings just so to avoid huge tankers and other kinds of cargo vessels.

In just a few minutes I drive off the ferry onto Harbor Island and onto a state highway with bridges that cross other islands until I reach the town of Aransas Pass on the mainland. The road then curves to the west, then turns south onto the Nueces Bay Causeway toward North Beach and the USS Lexington.

A few blocks from where the huge aircraft carrier is moored, I find a spot in a tiny parking lot next to a local restaurant called Pier 99. When I walk inside I see that sea turtles are a big deal here, with a life-size resin model suspended under the thatched roof over the open-air bar. While sipping a Corona Extra and enjoying my shrimp po'boy sandwich, I watch a handsome cat weaving in and out among the legs of the barstools. He's a light gray merle with four white feet, and clearly a regular visitor. He flops down in a shady spot under an empty barstool and watches the lunch crowd lazily. I wonder what my three kitties are doing at home? Probably taking a midday nap. I miss them so much.

After lunch I leave my car where it is and stroll over to the aircraft carrier. It's a long, steep walk up the concrete ramp at the pier to reach the admissions area where I buy a ticket for the self-guided tour. Aboard ship the next two hours are a fascinating introduction to the life and times of the servicemen, and later servicewomen, who lived and worked here on active duty during World War II and through the decades after that until she was decommissioned in November 1991.

I climb up, I climb down, I walk through passageways, I walk around and around throughout the public tour areas to explore the flight deck, the bridge, the crew's quarters, and the historic exhibits. This floating museum is enormous and fascinating, and I'm glad I took a break from birding to study the very different wings of the historic aircraft displayed on the flight deck.

Somewhere below—I've lost track of how many flights of stairs I've descended—I stop for a while to look at a case with colorful maps spread out underneath a pair of aviator's goggles. At first glance the maps look quite ordinary. But they're not printed on paper like the ones I carry in my car. These maps are printed on silk. A small card tells me this offers several advantages. Silk maps don't have to be folded carefully but can be crumpled and crushed any which way to stuff into a pocket. I'd sure like that instead of battling the accordion folds of stiff paper maps. Also, if they get wet they won't turn into a soggy mess and the colors won't run. Nice.

The displays explaining how aircraft are launched from the flight deck make me think about the different ways that birds get airborne. Many waterfowl can burst immediately straight up into the air from the water's surface, but others need to take a running start, their webbed feet pattering across the water until they get up enough speed to create lift across their wings.

On one of the lower decks, my favorite display case contains a pair of rather clunky-looking 7x50 binoculars used up on the flight deck to watch for aircraft during World War II. The same manufacturer, known then as the Square D Company, also made a different power binocular, 6x42s, for use on land. Modern binoculars feature high-tech optical coatings and other material improvements, but the basic technology is still the same. Any birder today would recognize the shape of these binoculars and be able to use such an old model immediately.

Back on land I check my maps while waiting for the air conditioning to cool down my car. I cue up the music from "Victory at Sea" again and reach into the laundry basket for my birding trail guidebook. It's sunny and hot in midafternoon, and after this history break I am definitely ready to look for birds again.

I plot a course to the northwest to visit the South Texas Botanical Gardens and Nature Center. It's far inland in a suburban area of Corpus Christi where there are remnants of the native scrubland habitats, so I might see some new bird species. I had pretty good luck when I visited the botanical gardens in Orange, so I'm willing to give this place a try.

§

Traffic is moving rather well even though there is major road construction along several miles of the road in front of the botanical gardens. In the visitor center and gift shop I find a pretty addition to my collection of refrigerator magnets, a very lifelike and life-sized representation of a zebra swallowtail butterfly, its painted china wings raised at a jaunty angle. When I pay for that and my entrance fee, I mention to the woman at the counter that I want to see the birds. She notices my binoculars and says, "I don't suppose you mean the caged parrots, do you?" Well, no, not really. She recommends the nature trail over by the lake, and gives me a map printed on yellow paper. I make some notes about which way to go and set off for a walk outdoors.

The ornamental plantings along the walkways are pretty but I don't stop to examine them carefully. Several Purple Martins swoop through the air, hunting for insects above me. When these birds get here, after flying across the Gulf of Mexico from their winter ranges on Caribbean islands and farther south, they are looking for holes in trees to build their nests in, but they will also choose man-made, apartment-style homes erected on poles. There might be one of those bird condos nearby.

A Northern Mockingbird dashes up to a convenient, low tree limb to get out of my way as I move forward on the path. I veer right to walk around the outside of the butterfly house and make my way to the hummingbird garden—where the only creature I can find is not a bird but a cottontail rabbit hopping nervously toward the denser shrubbery. When I get back onto the main path, a male Northern Cardinal flits from branch to branch nearby, then I accidentally startle a Mourning Dove walking in its pokey-headed way a few feet in front of me and it bursts into an abrupt flight upward.

I follow the signposts to the Brennecke Nature Trail and take the right-hand turn toward the observation tower. Weather-worn and somewhat uneven wooden steps take me to the deck about ten feet above the path. Almost immediately, I spot a Green Heron standing at the edge of Gator Lake. The map tells me that this habitat is called mesquite brush, a type of native forest that is just about gone in the Corpus Christi area, due to human activities. Indeed, I can see and hear the bulldozers working on the road over to my right, outside the boundary of the landscaped gardens and the natural wetland in front of me. I can also see the roofs of the houses crowded together in a subdivision on the other side of the lake.

I begin scanning the lake. The bright blue bill and jauntily cocked tail of a Ruddy Duck drake is unmistakable as he paddles to keep his position in the breeze that's rippling the water. He's part of a little flotilla of Ruddy Ducks trying to stay together. Closer to the reeds I find the dark shapes of American Coots, and then spot a Pied-billed Grebe drifting along. Right now, none of them seem to be the least bit bothered by the construction sounds and human activities out on the road. But they live on water amid reeds and cattails, and don't depend on forest habitats or grassy fields for their lifestyle.

The text on the map and signs along the paths warn visitors to be on the alert for alligators. I do the best job I can of searching in likely spots for them, but I haven't seen any yet. That's okay.

I begin to study another little group of ducks out on Gator Lake. Their bodies are sort of a beige-y brown, maybe kind of gray, and the pattern of markings on their heads has me puzzled. The bill is dark, almost black, there's a white patch on the cheek and a thin, dark eye stripe. Their tails don't seem to stick up very much, but then again they are tipping over to dabble and then popping upright, then dipping forward again quite industriously, so it's hard to say. Some sort of hybrid with domestic ducks? No. Wait. I know. These are the female Ruddy Ducks, who look different from the males. They won't pair up with the males until their annual courtship activities begin on their breeding grounds at the lakes on the western prairies later this spring. For now, they're not at all interested in each other.

I give the small tern flying over only a passing glance, and then focus my attention on the Red-winged Blackbirds in the brush next to the observation deck. Some Laughing Gulls barrel past overhead, and then I notice a Mottled Duck out on the water. That seems to be about it from this elevated spot.

I make my way very carefully down the oddly pitched steps and back onto the path. From the gazebo area, I have a good view at almost water level of some Blue-winged Teal couples drifting lazily nearby. Across the water some Northern Shovelers are drifting, then suddenly begin paddling to stay away from the reeds at the edge of the lake.

This boardwalk features informative signs about the various features of natural wetlands and why these areas are important wildlife communities. Oso Creek flows far off in the distance, but instead of taking that longer loop trail, I find a place nearby where I can look out over the wetlands and various sandbars and mudflats to search for birds. I see some Black-necked Stilts and hear a Killdeer calling as it flies over. Several Roseate Spoonbills are standing out on a sandbar in the distance.

The Brown Pelicans that fly over silently are easy to identify, but the various little birds poking and prodding in the wet, sandy dirt way out beyond the Roseate Spoonbills are just too far away for me to get them in good focus. As I turn around to walk back, I take one more look at the water and discover a Least Grebe half hidden in the waterside vegetation. They are so much smaller than the other waterfowl, they're easy to overlook.

Back at my car, I'm hot and sticky and uncertain where to go next. Great-tailed Grackles make a noisy fuss in the parking lot while I sip some water. I wasn't thinking about how the sun would shift when I picked this spot to park. The door pocket was shaded when I got out, but it's been in direct sunlight for quite a while, and the water's hot, not cool. Oh, well, it's wet, and that's what counts. I swish some around, swallow, and suddenly remember the name of a park the guys I met yesterday said was a good birding spot. I look it up in my guide, set my GPS, and get back on the road.

§

My route to the park goes into the center of old Corpus Christi during the afternoon rush hour. My GPS system takes me to a side of an old city park that is right next to what appears to be a soup kitchen sort of place. I don't see any people walking home from work or kids playing in the neighborhood, just what appear to be homeless people sitting on the sidewalk and in the shade of the trees. I don't see any birds on the short-cut park grass, either. I drive along as slowly as I can, considering the traffic, trying to make a decision. Should I go around the block to hunt for a place to park, or should I just keep on driving? I've had a busy day already, and I'm beginning to think about dinner. I'll keep going.

About three blocks away, near a high-rise apartment building, I pull over to the curb to adjust my GPS settings so I can complete my circuit around Corpus Christi and get back to Padre Island. As I cruise along on South Shoreline Drive in the rush-hour traffic, which is definitely not rushing, I have plenty of time to look at the beautiful old homes on my right and the open water of Corpus Christi Bay on my left. Traffic slows down even more. And stops. There's been a wreck in the center lane approaching the causeway that goes to Padre Island. Once I get past that, traffic speeds up to normal.

On the island again, I turn off the main road to check out a restaurant near the causeway that I've seen advertised. I walk up the steps. The view would probably be nice from this lofty spot, but the happy hour singer is off key, too loud, and beyond annoying, so I leave. I drive to my next choice. But it's karaoke night there. I've gone from bad to worse. I drive to my third choice, no place to park, same story at fourth choice, and I end up at the Padre Island Burger Company for a quick beer and, what else? A burger, of course.

Driving back to my hotel, I'm having a lot of trouble seeing the road. There are very few streetlights out here, and I like it that there's very little light pollution, but this is quite odd. I'm accustomed to driving on dark country roads where I live, and my night vision is excellent. Now I'm really straining to see where the left curb is, and I'm having trouble reading the street signs. When I pull into the hotel parking lot, I discover what the problem is—my driver's-side headlight is burned out. That's interesting. My car has warning lights and chimes and computer displays for a gazillion other things, but nothing to alert me to this safety problem. There's nothing I can do about it tonight, but in the morning I will have to figure out where to go to get a replacement installed.

Upstairs in my room, I'm going to make a tentative travel plan, update some of my birding notes, set my alarm for an early wakeup buzz, then get ready to go to sleep.

§

This morning I've got some logistics problems to solve, and the first one is figuring out how to make the fewest trips possible down to the parking lot to load my car. I re-packed my suitcase and duffle the night before last with clean clothes, so the big suitcase can go down with me now, on my way for my usual pre-breakfast walk. I've been quite satisfied with the way I've had all my stuff arranged in my car on this trip. Even though I don't expect I'll have to get anything out of the big suitcase on the way home, I'm going to put it in its usual spot.

A few Laughing Gulls shriek as they strut around the far corner of the hotel parking lot, then fly off as I approach on foot. This will be my last morning in Texas, and I'm going to miss those noisy birds when I drive north out of their home range.

I still have well over a thousand miles to drive. I have a general idea of the route I want to take today, but first I have to get my headlight replaced. At home that would be an easy job for the guys at my neighborhood car shop. I think a burnt-out bulb is the only issue here, but just in case there's a bigger problem I'm going to search my phone for a Ford dealership that will be easy to stop at along my route. I sure don't want to go out of my way to get the headlight fixed. For birds, yes, I'll go many miles off the direct path, but for a simple car repair? No.

Back upstairs after breakfast I gather my lists and maps and books, put them in a tote bag, grab my duffel bag, and head down to the front desk to turn in my electronic key. At my car, I put everything where it goes, set my GPS, and start the engine. To leave Padre Island I drive onto the causeway over Laguna Madre one more time to get back to the mainland and Corpus Christi.

This is a busy stretch of interstate-style highway with a lot of fast-moving traffic this morning, and I have to watch carefully for the right exit. At the Ford dealer, I get bad news. The service writer says I'll have to wait at least an hour before anyone can even look at my car to see what's wrong. Nevermind. I pull away, find a place to park, and check my phone for other options. As it turns out, I passed a larger Ford dealership a few miles back on the other side of the highway and didn't even know it. I reset my GPS, turn around and 'round, find the entrance ramp to the highway, and prepare to backtrack.

This Ford dealership has a separate quick-service center, and the guy and gal at the desk are really friendly, glad to help me right away. Unfortunately, they don't have my particular headlight in stock—but they can get it within ten minutes.

Instead of waiting in the lounge, I take a walk outdoors and think about what I want to do today. I will need to go inland to reach the best roads to go north towards Houston. But I'm not going to go into the city. I plan to skirt around it on the south and east. I'd like to get deep into Louisiana by tonight, but I have no hotel reservation yet.

Since I'll be sitting behind the steering wheel for much of the day, walking around now is a good alternative. This part of Corpus Christi is a dense corridor of many kinds of medium and small businesses next to the elevated highway, and there's more concrete and asphalt than dirt and grass. I'm not seeing birds, or hearing any, either. I might as well go on inside to see how much longer it will be before my car is ready.

It's ready now, and that sure was easy. And cheap, only nineteen dollars and twenty cents to solve this very minor travel glitch. I'm ready to get back on the road just after ten o'clock. Since this is my last morning in Texas and I'll be driving through more ranchland soon, I cue up a CD of cowboy songs, Riders in the Sky's "Public Cowboy Number One—The Music of Gene Autry," ready to sing along. I might even yodel.

###

CHAPTER THIRTEEN

From Texas
into Louisiana and Mississippi

Bluebonnet Swamp, owls, not exactly lost

I'm going inland, away from the Gulf of Mexico, and the land is getting hillier and greener as I drive north on US Highway 77. I smile when the song "Can't Shake the Sands of Texas from my Shoes" starts and then sing along to the lilting, blues-y rhythm of the tune. I think I'm bringing home a pound or two of Texas sand in my car—the floor mats are covered with it, and I'm sure there's more back in the liftgate section.

This is the same highway I used farther south, but I haven't driven on this section until today. It's a good road with one lane of traffic in each direction. Like so many such roads in Texas, the speed limit is seventy-five miles per hour. But that doesn't tell the whole story. There are three main driving speeds in Texas. Fast. Really fast. And then there's bat-out-of-hell fast! And that's sure what's going on here this morning. I'm doing the speed limit, and often a few miles above it—and I'm getting passed. A lot. That's okay, the other drivers are careful to watch for oncoming traffic before they zoom around me, and nobody's felt the need to blow their horn or flash their bright lights at me. My Kentucky license plate makes it obvious I'm not from around here.

I've noticed something else about the road signs. The most popular sign in coastal Texas is "No fishing from bridge." But people still manage to find places to pull over really close on the gravel or grass along the banks of whatever body of water the bridge crosses, and get out their tackle.

Although traffic is not bumper-to-bumper heavy here, there are plenty of folks coming and going, and I have to stay extremely alert, constantly shifting my gaze from straight ahead to checking all the rearview mirrors, and keeping track of who else is behind or ahead of me. But the road surface is smooth, the shoulders are wide, and the weather's fine. This is a good day to be traveling.

The road I'm on leads to Victoria, which will be a good place to take a lunch break. I find the center of town, park, and get out to take a short walk to stretch my legs. This town is old, with a long and significant history in the settlement and development of Texas into the dynamic state it is today. And it's high ground, for these parts, more than one hundred feet above sea level. Although I've driven about one hundred miles this morning, I'm only about forty miles inland from the Gulf, in the region of Texas known as the Coastal Bend.

Instead of asking my phone for restaurant recommendations, I want to do things the old-fashioned way by walking around the town square until I find something that appeals to me. I like the looks of this two-story red brick building with arched windows. The architectural details are painted in white and gray, a good choice to accent their features. Yes, the Rosebud Fountain and Grill on the first floor looks like fun.

Today's special is grilled antelope burger. I've seen antelope bounding across a meadow in the Rockies in Colorado, but I've never seen it on a menu and I'm curious to taste it. It's good! Not quite like ground bison, which I eat several times a year at home, and far different from everyday beef. But I can't exactly define the difference. I think it has to do with the texture. Antelope meat is firm, somewhat like venison, and seems to have very little fat. I like it, and I'm glad I found this place.

When I ask my server about things to see and do here, she recommends an artist gallery a few blocks away near the

Guadeloupe River. It will be an easy drive because the streets in this part of town are laid out in a grid, so I can wander a block this way and that way without annoying my GPS too much.

After lunch I walk back to my car and get ready to explore. The yards of the homes, some of which have elaborately crafted geometric designs in their brickwork, have plenty of trees and shrubs, and this is probably good habitat for songbirds. Some of the returning migrants might already be here. Although I'd like to hunt for them, I have a lot more miles to drive today, so I'm just going to make a quick stop at the Art League building.

When I arrive, I take a leisurely look around inside and come upon a pretty, laser-cut, wooden oval about six inches tall, featuring a silhouette of a pair of ducks flying up from a marsh. This is a great souvenir of my trip, and just the right thing to buy to support a local artisan.

From Victoria I'm going to drive on US Highway 59, which angles northeast toward Sugar Land on the southwest side of Houston, and then I'll skirt around below the city. I want to get past it before the major rush-hour traffic stacks up. I'd better get on the road right now.

§

As I drive along I'm keeping a close eye on my gas gauge and dashboard displays. My windshield is a splattery mess of insects, and when I pull into a truck stop to top up my gas tank, I spend more time scrubbing the glass than pumping gas. While I'm here I switch to a different playlist on my iPod, back to the one featuring Western swing music, but with no vocals to distract me, so I can concentrate on the crowded road ahead.

Near the town of Rosenberg I take the ramp up to I-69 and prepare myself mentally for a challenging drive south of Houston proper. Soon I reach the Sam Houston Tollway. I always keep coins and dollar bills in my center console, so I'm ready at the toll plazas. Since I don't have a sticker pass, I have to use the slower lanes. I'm surprised—they're not completely automated and there's a lane dedicated to cash payments. The clerks in the toll booths are friendly and cheerful, and at the third one, the last before a special toll bridge for sticker pass–holders only, when I ask the clerk about what to do as an out-of-state driver, she tells me which exit to take to get around the toll sensor. I really appreciate that.

I haven't been able to look carefully at the scenery here on this outer ring road around Houston because of the dense traffic, but my overall impression is a jumbled-up mix of industry and office buildings and suburban homes. At the intersection with I-45, which leads south to Galveston, I swing north instead. I like it that my car's dash display has compass readings, but I wish it also gave elevation. Maybe there's an add-on device I can get to mount on my dashboard that would tell me that. For now, all I can do is guess. I know that I've been going downhill, so to speak, since I left Victoria, and I must be very close to sea level again because I'm crossing Buffalo Bayou, which flows, somewhat sluggishly, into one of the smaller back bays connected to Galveston Bay.

Whew! I've reached I-10 and am now heading due east, but I'm still on the outskirts of sprawling Houston, near Baytown and the Port of Houston. Now I'm skirting Trinity Bay, yet another extension of Galveston Bay. The last two hours of driving have required my full and complete attention, and I deserve a reward. But what? I'll just keep looking for an idea.

At the exit for the town of Anahuac, which is many miles north of the wildlife refuge I explored during my first week in Texas, I see a fast-food chain restaurant that I've never tried, a Jack-in-the-Box. I pull over and go inside to order. The chocolate milk shake is creamy and flavorful, the perfect afternoon treat after such a long stretch of complicated driving. I sip about half of it inside the restaurant, then go out to walk around in the sunshine in the parking lot. I hear cheeping sounds in the shrubby landscaping along the edges of the lot. Stepping closer to look at the fronds of a low-growing palm species, I hear more cheeping. I look more carefully, and there, on one of the fronds closest to me, I spot a fledgling House Sparrow begging for a parent to bring it food. Although House Sparrows are quite bold around humans, I don't want to interfere, so I step back carefully and go back to my car.

I have about an hour and half of daylight left, so I study my maps to choose a place to spend the night. I call ahead to a Holiday Inn Express in Lake Charles, Louisiana, and begin driving east again. As I get closer to the last exit on I-10 and the Tony Houseman wildlife area, the first place I explored in Texas, I'm thinking about all the different kinds of birds I've seen in so many different habitats. My list of lifers is somewhere past forty new species, and I think I've seen more than one hundred fifty species of birds altogether. But I won't have a complete count until I'm at home and can go through all my field notes and look at all my photos carefully. I am already thinking about how much fun it will be to put all that I've learned into lists and review all the pictures.

§

While I'm considering those possibilities, the miles click away, and about half an hour later I cross the Sabine River, out of Texas and into the bayou country of Louisiana. I've left the Central Flyway and re-entered the Mississippi Flyway. I suppose when I get home I could make two new lists, one for the birds who use each of the flyways I've been exploring.

Ah, here's my exit for my hotel, and it's still daylight. That was good planning on my part because I am certainly ready to stop.

After getting settled in my room, I come back downstairs to ask the front-desk clerk about a good place to have dinner. She recommends Steamboat Bill's and tells me how easy it will be to find, a few blocks away on the main road.

I guess I'm tired because I passed the restaurant on the first go-round and have to double back, then make a left turn into the parking lot, which is full of cars and trucks. Inside, I study the menu, place my order at the counter, and sit down at one of the few open tables. A family nearby is celebrating somebody's birthday, and the smallest child, perhaps about three years old, keeps walking away from the table. She's a cutie, and I smile at her, and then smile at her mom who comes to get her. This scene repeats over and over until they're ready to leave, and then my food arrives. I nibble slowly and think more about birds. I want to explore Louisiana tomorrow on my way home, but I'm not sure where to go. One thing I do know—I am too tired to make a decision now.

Back at my hotel, I realize that I've been sitting way too long today. When I enter today's miles in my travel notebook, I'm impressed—three hundred ninety-six miles! I think I have just enough energy to walk around the parking lot a few times to stretch my legs. The lot is more than half full, but there's still plenty of space for me to pace along amid the cars and trucks. One of the pickup trucks has a miniature barbeque grill and smoker mounted in the corner of the bed—pretty convenient, I suppose, for a traveling worker or hunter.

What was that? I just caught sight of some movement near the tires of a car. I'll stand still to see if I see it again. Something black. Oh, it's little black cat, just about the same size as my Um-Yum back home. I call "kitty, kitty" softly. I keep standing still. "Kitty, oh, kitty?" The little one gathers courage and walks out from under the parked car and along the sidewalk, where I can see it prancing cautiously. I turn around to walk the other direction to see if it will follow me. Yup, and then it gives a squeaky little meow, just like the voice of my black cat. I sure do miss her. This little one approaches me close enough for me to get a cell phone photo, but when I lean down to try to pet it, it scampers off down the sidewalk.

I'm ready for sleep now, so I'm going up to my room. In the morning I can decide on a place to go birding on my way east and north toward home.

§

During my early-morning walk around the hotel parking lot, a Northern Mockingbird sings from a treetop, and I see two Blue Jays in the bushes. The morning sunshine strikes a male Northern Cardinal just right so that his feathers gleam brilliant red. Crest raised, he sings a short burst of "purdy, purdy, purdy," then flies to a different short shrub and repeats the song while looking this way and that for any rivals. I look for his beige mate but cannot find her. She might be sitting on eggs in a nest in one of these bushes. Really, now that I think about how late in April it is, and how far south I am, this pair might already have hungry nestlings to feed.

During breakfast I search my phone for some places to go birding between here and Baton Rouge, or possibly beyond. I'd like to get at least three hundred or so miles closer to home today, so I don't want to drive too far north or south of I-10. Hmm. Bluebonnet Swamp in Baton Rouge is the closest place to the interstate. I'll give it a try.

After I check out of the hotel, I have to go a little bit around the block to get back up on the interstate. It's sunny and clear, and I'm listening to some old-fashioned New Orleans jazz, the kind with fancy trumpet solos and perky drum beats. This is going to be a good morning for travel, and soon I'm rolling along at top speed. That's not the case for the folks who are westbound—a semi tractor–trailer rig has overturned, and traffic over there is backed up for more than three miles. Such a delay could easily happen on my side, and I am constantly watching ahead for any trouble.

When my GPS tells me which exit to take in suburban Baton Rouge, I end up in a densely developed area with medical offices, small businesses, and restaurants amid the trees along the main boulevard, and attractive condos and houses on the side streets, with carefully tended landscaping. Where's the swamp? My GPS sends me to an almost-empty parking lot, a sign for a library, and a chain-link fence. What? This is obviously not the entrance to a swampy natural area. But I do remember passing a very small road sign about the swamp a few blocks back. I ignored it because the GPS was telling me to go straight, not turn. Something's gone wrong, but I do not know what. I'll shut off the GPS system, turn around, and backtrack to see if I can find that sign again.

§

Three blocks later I find the sign. I'll turn left to see what happens. Hah. Here's the real entrance to the swamp, with towering trees shading the parking lot. I find a place to park, squirt on a few spritzes of Skin-So-Soft, gather up my binoculars and camera and notebook, and walk toward a big signboard explaining something. It's a map of the place. This is a new entrance to the nature center, only recently completed. Apparently my GPS system doesn't yet know about this change. The brand new sign tells about the habitats here. Nearby, there's a small pond with dragonflies flitting around. This swamp and nature center is part of a larger system overseen by a Louisiana agency that goes by the acronym BREC. It's dedicated to overseeing and maintaining many kinds of parks and recreational facilities in the East Baton Rouge Parish.

Amid leafy trees on the other side of the parking lot, the boardwalk entrance is wide and welcoming. This section seems to be mostly hardwood forest, and the shade is nice on this warm morning. I amble along slowly, listening to Northern Cardinals singing. Blue Jays squeal and squawk from time to time. So far, this sounds just like being in the woods at home. I'm going downhill a bit, curving this way then back, and then the boardwalk levels off, and I see a large building ahead.

This side of the building is a wall of tall glass windows, and I can see boys and girls sitting, not very still but not too wiggly either, on rows of wooden benches inside. I've found another school field trip, but what I'm looking for is the entrance to the building. At the far end of the glass, I see the doors and walk into a small gift shop area. While chatting with Bradley, the guy at the counter, I look around at the selection of items.

I don't really need another canvas tote bag. No, I really do not. But this one is so pretty. Block letters spell out Bluebonnet Swamp Nature Center, and above that, seven birds perch side by side on a single branch, each bird's dominant plumage in the correct color sequence one would see in a rainbow. I've not seen this design before, and I know each one of the bird species. Alright, I'll buy it. I can put my camera in it while I'm walking around here, and I'm sure I can find something useful to do with it when I get back home. I also see two strands of blue-and-gray sodalite beads that will be nice to wear anywhere, and they'll make a good conversation starter to tell about my travels.

While I'm at the counter to pay for my souvenirs and the very low admission fee, Bradley tells me that the school group will not be allowed on a certain trail this morning because they'd probably be too noisy. However, since I'm obviously an avid birder, I am welcome to go down there to look for the owlets. Owlets? What owlets? He gives me a paper map and uses a yellow highlighter to explain where they are, and says I should look for two local birders who'll be there taking photos.

Before I go outside I want to look around in this building. The children are paying very close attention to the young woman standing in front of the benches. I don't know if she's paid staff or a volunteer, but she sure knows how to talk with kids. She's holding a very handsomely marked yellow snake, about three feet long. As she tells about its life and features, the snake continuously writhes from hand to hand, and occasionally dangles down toward the concrete floor in an ever-changing series of s-shaped loops. The kids are fascinated, and begin asking questions as I step back to look at a tall display case along the back wall. Inside on glass shelves are row after row of classic Louisiana duck decoys. Many are carefully labeled, but unfortunately they are too high above eye level for easy reading. I do hope they'll be re-arranged soon in a way that makes them easier to appreciate, because the decoys are quite beautiful and very lifelike.

Outside, I walk along a trail going deeper through the woods down toward the swamp. I'm in a large expanse of woodland, with a high canopy of leafy, living trees and with standing dead trees, too, but not much shrubby undergrowth. But there are a lot of pretty green ferns amid the leaf litter on the ground. This whole place covers more than one hundred acres, and includes at least three distinct habitats, ranging from a mixed hardwood forest, plus a forest segment dominated by beech trees and magnolias, then the cypress and tupelo swamp.

Sunlight filters through the leaves, and suddenly I hear the distinctive pattern of laugh-like shrieks of a Pileated Woodpecker ringing out wildly. I can tell the bird is flying from my left to my right, and then I see a flash of black-and-white wings and a red crest. This beautiful bird is the largest living woodpecker species in North America, always exciting to see and hear. This old forest is the kind of habitat it prefers, and I'm glad to see this bird this morning.

§

Up ahead I see a guy in a floppy hat with a wide brim and a camera, and then a woman. These must be the birders Bradley told me about. We introduce ourselves, and Richard and Cassie and I begin to chat quietly. Suddenly the air is filled with a series of high, loud notes in a short series that really does sound like how birdsong is often represented in cartoon bubbles—"tweet, tweet, tweet, tweet." We stop talking and listen for it to repeat. "Tweet, tweet, tweet, tweet," the bird sings again, getting louder and more insistent toward the end. I haven't memorized very many warbler songs, and I'm kind of out of practice since last spring, but this one's easy—it's a Prothonotary Warbler.

This species spends the winter far to the south in Central and South America but is one of the first migrants to fly across the Gulf of Mexico to come north to breed. This male probably arrived here about three weeks ago. And indeed, Richard and Cassie, who visit here almost every day, know that he's found a mate and they already have eggs in the artificial nest box they point out to me. Most warblers make nests out in the open, but Prothonotary Warblers prefer nesting in tree cavities, often re-using ones abandoned by woodpeckers, but they will also use man-made substitutes.

Although the Prothonotary Warbler and the Northern Cardinal are not close kin, they do share something in common—the origin of their names. When the first European explorers saw the strikingly rich red feathers of the one bird, they thought of the scarlet clothing of a cardinal in the Roman Catholic church. There are a lot of warblers with yellow feathers, and when early naturalists saw the rich yellow of this kind of bird, they were reminded of the yellow vestments worn by prothonotary clerks who serve the Catholic Pope. In the days before photography or color printing presses, being able to tell someone else about the exact color of a newly found bird required some ingenuity.

Richard and Cassie walk down the trail a bit with me and point to the nesting tree where a pair of Barred Owls have raised two owlets this spring. The most exciting news is that the youngsters are no longer nestlings—now they're branchers! When young owls get too big for the nest but don't yet have enough feathers to fly, they step out onto a convenient branch and sit there where the parents can easily feed them. This dramatic development happened yesterday and is being closely monitored by several local birders. Richard's already taken many photographs. I sure did get lucky when I picked this place to visit today! Cassie offers to walk a few steps farther down the trail to point out the branch where they last saw one of the owlets perched so that I might get a photo, too.

Barred Owls are year-round residents in wooded areas along streams and swamps throughout the eastern United States and Canada, and they've extended their range into the upper northwest in recent decades. I know them well at home in Kentucky. They like areas with shallow creeks where they can hunt for crawdads or frogs, tadpoles, maybe a small fish. But they like the water for bathing, too. I've watched adult Barred Owls take a long bath in the same creek where they've been hunting. They splash into the water, then step out on a gravelly mud bar along the banks of the creek, all the while shaking their feathers out into a puffy silhouette, and they do this right in broad daylight. Then they do it again, over and over again. They seem to genuinely enjoy the sensation of water running into and between their feathers.

To come across this owl family here in Baton Rouge is an unexpected treat, and something completely new for me because I've never seen a young Barred Owl. In fact, I've never seen any kind of baby owl. I walk forward very quietly and slowly, and look up carefully. Oh! There, there's one of the branchers, perched right above me over the path, sitting patiently amid the green leaves and blinking its eyes. I look at the owlet, and it looks at me. The owlet is covered with dense, downy feathers, so fluffy and fuzzy it almost looks like a child's stuffed animal toy. As such a new brancher, this little one's flight feathers do not yet protrude beyond the down. And it doesn't have much of a tail yet, either. Although it cannot fly, it's good at hopping from branch to branch, something it will do for many days, clinging steadily with its well-developed talons.

I take photos with my digital camera and my cell phone, then after another minute I walk on. As much as I'd like to stay longer to keep watching it, I doubt that the parent birds will bring food to the owlet while I'm so close. So it's best for the youngster if I move on.

I'm only paying half attention to the sounds of songbirds in the other parts of the woods as I walk back toward the building and the parking lot. I'm so enchanted by my encounter with the owlet, I'm not even making any fresh notes in my little pocket notebook.

Just as I reach the part of the path that leads alongside an open meadow, I hear the rich, penetrating hoot of one of the adult Barred Owls from somewhere far behind me. "Who cooks for you, who cooks for you aaaallll?" it asks, with the last two syllables drawn out and quavering. Although Barred Owls are rather medium-sized as far as owls go, their voices are quite loud and carry very long distances.

I've heard this sequence of calls several times over the years on my own land, and elsewhere, and I still get goose bumps every time I hear it. The other parent replies, "Who cooks, who cooks, who cooks for you aaaallll?" It's about eighty degrees, hot, humid, and very sticky here, and yet I've got chills of wonder and delight going up and down my spine.

Those phrases are what we humans use to get the rhythm of the sounds right, but I think, for the owls, their conversation might be more along the lines of, "Have you found food for our children? I haven't yet, you keep hunting." Now the first adult calls out with another series ending in that descending vibrato, there's a pause, then another call-and-response series between the adults, then silence. I do hope they'll soon find something nutritious to bring to their owlet twins, who still have a lot of growing to do before they learn to hunt on their own.

Back at my car I take a long drink of water, then drive out to the main road to look for a restaurant. I see a local spot with a clever name, Roux 61, a combination of the well-known Cajun sauce base and the number of a major local highway. The sign's shape is clever, too, resembling the shield outline of a highway marker. The parking lot is still full of late lunchgoers, but I find an open spot and pull in.

Inside at the bar, I sip on a blonde ale from Tin Roof, a local Baton Rouge brewery, and chat with a guy on the barstool to my left. He's local, too, and tells me about the family who owns this restaurant. He knows a little bit about birds and I tell him about the owlets and my trip all the way down and back up the Texas Gulf Coast. He tells me he likes to watch for Great Blue Herons.

Soon we end up in a three-way conversation with the bartender, who also likes birds, but the main focus is choosing something for my lunch. I order the freshly shucked Louisiana oysters—I can see the guy at the other end of the bar swiftly levering open the shells—which are prepared on the half shell with butter, garlic, herbs, and then topped with a light sprinkling of parmesan cheese. Instead of baking them, the cooks put the opened shell halves right on the grill, cheese side up, and I can't wait to taste them.

When the six grilled oysters arrive, I pull the perfectly cooked, moist oyster bodies out of each shell with the little fork and savor them slowly. Oh, such sweetness! And the texture is perfect! The platter also includes two thick slices of grilled, crusty French bread, just exactly what I need to sop up the flavorful liquid remaining in the oyster shells. This might be the best lunch of my trip!

§

I don't need to use my GPS after lunch because I know where I'm going. Here in Baton Rouge, I-10 dips south. But I'm going to stay on I-12 on the interstate system to continue eastbound above New Orleans, just as I did heading south two weeks ago, until I can connect with I-59 north. This will be easy, and all I have to do is follow the big green signs on the highway.

However, I need to buy gas, and soon, so I'm looking for a convenient truck stop. I find one, pull in, and follow my usual routine of washing sticky bugs off the windshield while the gas goes into my tank. There's a good-sized lake over by the parking lot at the nearby Bass Pro Shop, and I might as well check it for waterfowl before I get on the highway. I zig and zag through the parking lots to get as close to the lake as I can, but only see Canada Geese and Mallards, two species that are quite at ease around humans and their buildings and activities. No migrant waterfowl are here today, so I'll get back on the highway.

I'm driving through the center of the Mississippi Flyway, and it would be fun to find a woodsy spot to look for returning songbirds, but I have a lot of miles to cover before stopping for the night. My travel routines are the opposite of most migrating songbirds. They like to eat and rest during the day, then fly at night. I'd rather eat and drive in the daylight, then spend the evening and night resting in one spot.

Two hours after lunch I cross the Pearl River and pull into the Mississippi welcome center rest stop. This will be a good place to take a walk and stretch my legs. My shoulders are a bit tight, too, so I'm going to wave my arms around and swing them up and down to loosen up the muscles and tendons. As I walk along windmilling my arms, I watch and listen to two Northern Mockingbirds as they flash their white wing patches while dashing from tree to ground, then up to another tree. Some Blue Jays shriek back and forth from the treetops, too. Turning back toward my car I hear cawing from some American Crows, then see four of them flapping along on the other side of the interstate.

I'm back on I-59 now and have at least two hours of good daylight left. But I'm not sure how much farther I want to drive. I'll aim for Meridian, but I might stop sooner. I'll make a decision later. Driving north I'm entering much hillier terrain, and the trees are rich green. Traffic is light, moving steadily and fast, so the miles are gliding by easily.

I see a sign for a Holiday Inn Express coming up soon and make a mental note of the exit number to take when I reach Laurel. I think that will be far enough for today instead of pushing toward Meridian.

When I get off the interstate, though, I cannot figure out what streets to take to get over to the hotel. I can see it, I just can't figure out which roads connect to it. I pull into a parking lot and program my GPS, then move back out into four lanes of traffic. I miss my left turn and end up going through an attractive old subdivision with lots of mature trees and pretty accent shrubs and small patches of garden flowers. I'm sure there are plenty of common birds here, maybe a few returning migrants by now, too, and I'd be willing to bet that there are backyard feeders hidden out of my sight from the street.

Well, I've found the hotel. But what I can't find are my reading glasses. They're supposed to be in the cup holder in the center console. I search in the laundry basket, I feel around on the floor mats, and still come up empty-handed. Oh well, I can squint if I have to read any really small print at the hotel desk. Inside the hotel, the clerk finds a nice room for me, so I check in, then ask for some dinner ideas. I tell her that I like local places, not national chains, and bistro or bar food is just fine. She recommends a spot in the old downtown area, only about a mile or so away.

Driving to the restaurant, I have to go around a couple of extra blocks due to one-way streets, then finally find a spot to park on the diagonal near the entrance to The Loft, a restaurant in an old, two-story brick building that's been prettied up with green and pale beige paint. Instead of sitting indoors at a bar, I ask the hostess to seat me out on the patio. It's a mild night, and being outdoors should be refreshing.

The patio, which runs between this building and the next one, is a recent addition, so new that the lumber of the upper decking is still bright yellow, no weathering stains from rain yet. I sit at a wrought iron table and sip a glass of chardonnay, and watch the people at the other tables. It's Friday night, and friends are meeting and talking and relaxing. The atmosphere here reminds me of just what I would be doing at home, at a restaurant where my friends and I like to gather outdoors at wrought iron tables to laugh and enjoy a spring evening. The patio here is separated from the building next door and the sidewalk out front by wrought iron fencing, each spike topped with a fleur-de-lis design, another reminder of home.

The waiter and I discuss some dinner possibilities and he steers me toward the pasta alfredo. Instead of seafood or chicken, theirs is made with beef. That's a combination I've never heard of, but I'm willing to give it a try. When the dish arrives, it's a generous portion and tastes good. I order a second glass of wine for dessert, and then drive back to my hotel.

After more than three hundred miles on the highway today, I'm ready for a walk around the hotel parking lot. As I pace around and around, I'm thinking about the owlet that I watched this morning. Its eyes were so large, and it moved its head so carefully from side to side amid the leaves to keep me in view. It didn't seem frightened of me, just curious.

§

Before going upstairs to my room, I stop by my car to pick up some of my field notes and lists, and search again for my reading glasses. I still can't find them. I'm not sure of the last place I had them. Did I use them in the restaurant at lunch? I think so, and I really do think I brought them back out to the car then. But what happened after that? I feel around some more, but it's dark, and I'm tired, and I can't make a very thorough search. I pick up my bird lists and notebooks and head inside. I can search again in the morning. I hope they're not lost forever. Oh, well, my usual evening routine is to take out my contacts when I'm back at my hotel for the night, and switch to my bifocals until bedtime, so I'll be fine.

Upstairs I catch up with one list of birds, but I don't want to stay up very late working on any others. I need to get an early start in the morning. I have a lot more miles to drive.

I make sure to put my bird lists and field notebook right by my duffel bag tonight where I cannot leave them behind, then finish getting ready for sleep. I might dream of owlets.

§

I don't remember what I dreamed about, but whatever it was, my time asleep was certainly refreshing. It's just after sunrise when I walk outside to stroll around the hotel parking lot, and a Gray Catbird is as excited to begin a new day as I am. He's mewing and jeering from the thick shrubbery above a retaining wall, letting all the world know this is his territory. It's warm enough here in Mississippi that he might be a year-round resident, but he could be a returning migrant. I'm just passing through, though, and eager to get on the road.

I race through breakfast, check out, load up my car, and drive over to the nearest drugstore to buy a cheap pair of reading glasses. I'm almost certain my favorite pair is somewhere in the car, but I still can't find them. Buying a replacement pair just about guarantees that the old ones will show up later today or tomorrow.

I'm enjoying the hilly scenery as I cruise along on the interstate through northeastern Mississippi. The trees here are green and lush with new leaves, and the sweeping curves bring pretty new vistas every few miles.

###

CHAPTER FOURTEEN

Exploring Alabama

Bad timing, Wheeler Lake, birding in the rain

My first stop when I cross into Alabama is the welcome center rest area. It's a beauty, with tall pine trees and leafy deciduous trees. A Northern Mockingbird greets me as I walk toward the building. Inside I pick up a map and some brochures about birding trails in Alabama, plus information about their state parks.

Back on the road some Turkey Vultures cruise and flap slowly above the trees, gaining altitude. They probably live here year-round, but as I drive along this morning, my direction of travel on the ground generally coincides with the path of many migrating birds who are flying northward to their breeding grounds. Some will stop here in Alabama to mate and nest and rear their young. Some will go farther and stop in Tennessee, some will keep going until they get to Kentucky. But many will only pause to eat and rest before flying on much farther north.

Two things tend to concentrate these traveling birds in predictable places, and both have to do with water. When the birds that spend the winter in the Caribbean and Central America and South America fly over the Gulf of Mexico, they have to do it nonstop, over hundreds of miles of open water. When they reach land again they are exhausted, and they stop at the first patches of greenery they see, including many of the places I've just been visiting along the Texas Gulf Coast.

As soon as they're ready to move again, they take off, but they won't fly for such long distances at a stretch after they leave the Gulf Coast. As they fly northward over the greening fields and woods of the North American continent, they can drop down from the sky just about anywhere that looks good to them to find food. They can rest during the day in shrubs and trees in parks and wildlife refuges, even suburban backyards. Some of them will choose woodsy spots and overgrown fencelines on old farms like mine. Some will forage along little creeks and streams, along the edges of farm ponds, and along the banks of rivers. Many will find food around the edges of the lakes in state parks and in and around the waters of national wildlife refuges.

Weather systems will influence how long they stay in any particular place. Heavy rain and winds blowing from the wrong direction will make them stay in one place a little longer, but soon they'll be flying again, dashing in nighttime spurts across the miles, then dropping down to eat, rest, and then fly again, over and over until they reach the place they want to settle in for the breeding season's activities. As they go, they'll have to avoid some man-made hazards, especially great expanses of glass windows on tall buildings, but mostly they will fly ever northward across the countryside.

As I drive the same direction now, and when I get back home, I'll be looking for these travelers every chance I get, and in all the most likely spots. But whether or not I find them is strictly up to chance. They'll be spread out across thousands of square miles, and the bush or tree I happen to be looking at on a particular morning might have a bird—or it might not. A bird may have been there yesterday, or one might turn up tomorrow morning.

Whether I see a migrating bird or not wherever I happen to be looking, I know they're out there somewhere, and that the ones who haven't yet reached their breeding grounds will keep on flying northward until they reach the other great natural water feature of this hemisphere, the chain of the Great Lakes that separate the United States from Canada. They'll have to stop at the edges of these huge bodies of water to load up on food before they fly across them.

In early to mid-May each year, one of the greatest concentrations of migrating birds with the greatest variety of species tends to occur along the shores of Lake Erie, just east of Toledo in northwestern Ohio. They'll stop at Magee Marsh and Crane Creek and in the surrounding areas, including Ohio's Maumee Bay State Park and the Ottawa National Wildlife Refuge on the southern shore of the lake. When they get there, the birds will pause in their journey northward to eat as much as they can find. Then as soon as weather conditions are favorable, they will begin the long, nonstop flight over the huge lake—from that area in Ohio they have more than fifty miles of open water to cross to reach Canada.

This predictable natural phenomenon and the splendid viewing opportunities for birders are now part of a festival called The Biggest Week in American Birding, sponsored by the Black Swamp Bird Observatory and other community organizations in the area. It's where I bought my favorite ball cap a few years ago. The event is such a big deal, it actually lasts ten days to stretch across two weekends, with special activities and tours for all the visiting birders who are watching and studying and photographing the migrants. And, after a few weeks at home in Kentucky, once again I'll be one of those birders journeying up to Lake Erie.

As soon as I can find a truck stop, I'm going to fill my gas tank and wash the windshield again to remove the latest smearing of juicy bugs that eluded the birds hunting for a meal. Then I have to make some phone calls. According to all the messages on my phone from my birding pals back home, it's my job today to make the campground reservations for our trip to Maumee Bay for the dates that the three of us are available.

The trip next month will be a different sort of adventure than this one. We'll travel together, and pitch our tents at one campsite just three hundred miles from home. We'll bring plenty of food with us, and I'll set up my camp kitchen. We'll share cooking duties for breakfasts and dinners, but eat tailgate lunches over in the other parks. The boardwalks we'll explore will be jam-packed with hundreds of birders from around the world, all eager to watch the migrants before they fly on northward across lake Erie.

But I'm still in Alabama. I see a Great Blue Heron over on the left, and a sign for an truck stop just two miles ahead. I'm ready for a break, and I've got work to do.

Gas tank filled, windshield clean, campground reservations made for next month—now I have one other thing to do. I need to figure out where I'm going to stay tonight. I've looked through the birding brochures I picked up at the welcome center this morning, and northern Alabama looks like a good area to explore. There's a state park very close to Wheeler National Wildlife Refuge, the place I drove past almost three weeks ago. I'm just a little more than one hundred miles away, so I can get there by midafternoon. There's a good chance of rain, though, and putting up my tent for just one night would not be an efficient use of my time. The state park brochure has pictures of a nice lodge with motel-style rooms, so I'll reserve one of those for tonight.

Back on the road, I'm listening to some British brass bands playing marches and up-tempo overtures from operas and ballets, but zooming along at top speed, I'm thinking about birds. Until I reach Birmingham. Oh, dear. There is a major construction zone on my side of the road, and traffic is clogged up, moving at a snail's pace. Will this ruin my plan for this afternoon? Going ten miles an hour doesn't look good for my timetable. Well, here's a nice surprise—the construction area is shorter than I thought it would be, and I'm back up to speed in just a few minutes.

In the northern suburbs of Birmingham I see a Cracker Barrel, and that sounds easy for a hearty lunch. When I get there, though, I decide to eat breakfast instead. I'm back on the road within an hour, and it's a good thing I didn't linger to shop—I keep having to slow down due to more road construction. I need to pull off again, anyway. I don't know what the dinner options will be in and around the state park, so I'm going to buy fresh ice for my cooler and a six-pack of a local beer. If I don't drink one tonight, it will be a nice souvenir to sample at home.

§

I'm really looking forward to exploring Wheeler National Wildlife Refuge for the rest of the afternoon. I've guaranteed my arrival at the lodge at the state park with a credit card, so I won't have to hurry. My GPS sends me to the closest access point at the refuge and I park, gather up my things, and walk up to the visitor center at a quarter past three. I can hear a Mourning Dove somewhere in the nearby trees, cooing and cooing, over and over, then I hear a Northern Cardinal singing and chipping to his mate, but they're all hidden among the leaves.

Inside the building I stop at the desk to get a map and some current birding information. The guy staffing the desk, a volunteer with the local park support group, gives me some terrible news. The refuge will be closing at four o'clock today. Oh, well, then I'll see what I can now, and come back in the morning. "No, that won't be possible," he says. "This time of year this part of the refuge is closed to the public on Sundays and Mondays. It will not re-open until nine Tuesday morning." I cannot understand why this should be so, but he explains that the refuge's hours changed in March, as they do every year, and this schedule will remain in effect through September. It has to do with the movements of the cranes, and the number of human visitors expected.

I am stunned by this information because it changes my plan completely. The volunteer is very apologetic about it all, and says he doesn't make the rules, but he gets all the fuming and fussing from visitors when he delivers the news. I'm not mad at him, far from it, but I will have to make some adjustments. And I have to admit, some of this is my fault. I should have looked up the hours and other information about the refuge when I stopped for gas this morning. Then I would have known to eat a quicker lunch. Oh, well, I didn't, and now I have to make the best of this situation. The volunteer tells me about the observation area upstairs and I reluctantly walk over to the stairs.

On the second floor I find a large room with huge plate-glass windows on three sides and expansive views across acres and acres of flat land. This visitor center is on a little bit of a rise, and the short, green grass growing next to the building slopes down a few feet to slightly lower ground and a large depression covered with a thin sheet of muddy-looking water. Beyond that, brown, flat fields extend to distant tree lines and woods. I do not know whether this is an intermittent puddle of many acres, or a permanently marshy spot. Beyond it are more brownish fields where I see the graceful, white shape of a Great Egret flapping along toward the trees. There may be more water beyond the trees. A small group of Canada Geese, flying in a typical V-shaped skein, make their way across my field of view, but do not descend to the water.

Closer to the building I see some Red-winged Blackbirds, their red epaulets showing boldly as they dash through the air. I walk across the room to look out the other windows and look down into a brushy garden with an assortment of manmade seed feeders. American Goldfinches are feasting here. The males are changing into their richest yellow plumage now, but their breeding season will not begin until much later, when they can take full advantage of summer's plentiful seed crop.

§

I turn to gaze out another section of windows to take another look at the brownish fields. What is that? Way out there? I bring my binoculars to my eyes and study the plump, gray body of a tall bird, with a bustle of feathers at the tail end. Well, the afternoon is not a total disaster after all—I am looking at a Sandhill Crane! The guy at the desk said the main flock of over-wintering birds left a week or so ago, maybe longer ago than that, but there could be a straggler or two. He's heard some reports but couldn't guarantee anything for this afternoon.

My travel karma has flipped from really bad timing to excellent luck. I know this bird species well, because, each spring and fall, the migrating flocks of Sandhill Cranes fly high over my house back home in Kentucky. I love to hear their distinctive, wildly exciting cries, a sort of drawn-out gargling, a rolling series that sounds kind of like "ga-roo-ah-roo-ooo" that gets my attention when they're still more than a mile away from my farm. Although sandies are only two or so inches taller than Great Blue Herons, in flight they seem much larger because their wingspan is a full foot wider. They fly differently, too, with their heads and necks stretched full out, making a distinctive shape overhead that I always enjoy watching.

I've also stood on the ground on partly flooded roads in south central Indiana near Muscatatuck National Wildlife Refuge amid thousands of them in early spring, scarcely knowing which way to turn for the best looks at them from only fifty feet away. And I've watched them walk sedately across a parking lot in Florida in winter, just twenty feet away from me, on their way to forage at a golf course.

This lone Sandhill Crane is standing still out in the brown field, and I wonder why it didn't leave with the others. Perhaps it has some minor injury that needs to heal before it can fly north. But I wonder, will it fly solo? I doubt it. It's much more likely that it will wait and join up with a flock of other stragglers coming from farther south. These birds like to travel in groups, with older birds showing the younger ones how to follow ancient paths to and from their breeding grounds. I take a few photos with my camera and my cell phone, then look at the time—oh, I need to go on downstairs before the volunteer guy starts to lock up the building.

Near the desk I stop to take a good, long look at a bird that I'll admit I've been trying to find for several years but still haven't connected with in the Ohio River Valley. I'll see reports on social media of this species mixed in with Sandhill Cranes, look at photos, some good, some blurry, and make plans to drive to this place or that place the next day, and then it rains, or something else comes up, and I end up not going. Finally, during the first week of February this year, when I was just beginning to plan this birding road trip, everything aligned and I had a free afternoon available to drive an hour south toward Cecilia, Kentucky to search for them.

With an endangered species, the directions given in public on social media are always a bit vague, to help protect these magnificent creatures from inconsiderate dolts. However, the gossip system among serious and ethical birders works wonders. But that afternoon, when I got to the place they were last reported, and equipped with solid information about street names and landmarks such as "behind the gray barn" or "near the fire department station" to guide me, I could not find them. They'd already flown away.

Now, here I am, at long last, face to face with a Whooping Crane. I am not looking at a photograph or a painting. I am also not looking at a living bird. I am standing in front of a glass case containing a taxidermied specimen. This bird, who appears to be almost as tall as I am because he's mounted on a few inches of dirt with dry brown grasses at his feet, is a mature male, known in the scientific community as 12-02. From inches away I can look directly at the ruby-red feathers on the top of his head and near his long bill, at his amazingly lifelike and completely accurate yellow glass eye, his snowy white plumage, and I marvel at his handsomeness. I try to speed-read the closely typed page of information nearby, and the guy at the desk tells me that I can take a printed sheet with all of that information with me to study later.

Right now, I know that that this bird hatched fifteen years ago in Maryland in May 2002, was moved by humans to Wisconsin as part of a recovery plan, and learned how to migrate by following an ultralight aircraft disguised as a giant adult Whooping Crane to Florida. He flew back and forth between Florida and Wisconsin several times, spent at least one winter in Georgia, and the winter of 2012 in Greene County, Indiana, with other stops in Alabama.

Oh, my goodness, he probably flew over Kentucky on one of those trips. I'd have to look at a map to figure out the flight path more accurately, but what exciting news! During his lifetime he had a least two different mates, and he and his consorts produced eggs, and sometimes raised chicks. He was found dead of natural causes, probably from disease, possibly a bacterial infection, in June last year, but at least one of the chicks he fathered is presumed to still be alive.

The small group of Whooping Cranes that wintered here among the Sandhill Cranes in northern Alabama this year flew north a short while ago—had I stopped on my way to Texas I might have seen the living birds. But I can't worry about that or waste time with regrets. I'm here today and I'll have to make the best of it.

I feel both somber and delighted by this story. I cannot put this bird on my trip list, but I can write his name in my pocket notebook as a reminder of the success of careful human intervention to bring these birds back from the brink of extinction. There were only about two dozen of them left alive when I was in grade school, and today there are nearly six hundred wild Whooping Cranes. I will be making more of an effort to see one as soon as possible. I know, I always say I do not chase rarities, but in this case I will continue to make an exception.

I only have a few more minutes here, so I'll take a quick walk through the outdoor gardens and habitats around the parking lot. As soon as I'm outdoors I hear a mixed-up jumble of raucous cawing from a little band of jet-black American Crows. They're flying with great determination and powerful wing strokes in a straight line toward some destination ahead and to my right. "Caw, caw, caw" they shout to one another, urging each other forward to their goal.

Here at the feeders at eye level, I watch first one House Finch then another snatch at the seeds on offer. The males have distinctly shaped, rosy-red bibs and more red feathers above their bills and are quite handsome, but the females are drab grayish brown, a camouflage pattern that is useful when they're sitting on their nests.

Mixed in with the finches, I see a perky little bird with a white belly and gray upper parts, and a small, shiny, black bill and beady black eye. Just above that black bill is a small patch of black feathers, topped with gray feathers to form a tiny crest. It's a Tufted Titmouse, the little guy I know so well who sings "peter, peter, peter" at home and whose cousin, the Black-crested Titmouse, I met so far south in Texas. The Tufted Titmouse closest to me turns to show the peachy wash on its side feathers just under its wings.

I hear another familiar bird calling "cheer-up, cheerily" and turn to see a little band of American Robins foraging on the grass nearby. Looking around I see that there are at least a dozen of them, hopping this way and that, cocking their heads to listen to noises in the soil, then stabbing with their bills to grab something to eat. These thrushes are the real worm-eaters, and doing a good job of it today. A bit farther away a Northern Mockingbird perches momentarily on a short bush, then flies away, flashing its white wing patches.

Oh! I hear a song I'd recognize anywhere—it's a murmuring, bubbling, quick set of notes, the last one rising as if asking a question, a rolling series of short sounds, the musical trademark of an Eastern Bluebird. And there he is, his rich blue head and wings and tail set off by a rusty breast with white under the tail. He's looking his best right now in full breeding plumage. And there's a female, with her softer, paler blue feathers, like a washed-out version of her mate. And there's a second and a third pair—they're fluttering around, duplicating each others' wing strokes in an aerial ballet that always amazes me. I don't see how they avoid hitting each other, but they do manage somehow to stay just far enough apart so their wingtips don't touch each other. Up and down, and curving this way and that, off they go, murmuring all the way among themselves, flying towards the trees, perhaps to investigate potential nest holes.

As I walk across the parking lot to my car, I hear the distinctive, rolling call, difficult to spell, but "kwirrrr" is often used in field guides, of a Red-bellied Woodpecker somewhere in the trees on the other side. I stop to listen more carefully, and, sure enough, he follows it with a sort of barking cough, "chiff-chuff-chuff," with the first syllable emphasized slightly. This time of year, these woodpeckers can be counted on to call back and forth throughout the day, with drumming their bills on hard surfaces thrown in for good measure, to establish and keep territories. Amid these familiar bird sounds I feel right at home myself, even though I'm just passing through today and tonight.

§

Here in northern Alabama this wildlife refuge sprawls along both banks of the Tennessee River, in a jagged, jigsaw-puzzle-piece shape, but the two banks are not connected to each other for drivers except in one spot, the interstate highway bridge. The map of the refuge boundaries and little access roads that meander through it shows several icons for boat ramps, but the only wildlife observation icon I can discover is for this building. I don't know what else is available.

As I study the map more carefully, I realize that I will not have enough time this afternoon to get across the river to try any of the little roads on the northern side. It's looking more and more likely that my best choice is to drive on over to the state park about forty miles away. Maybe I can walk some of the trails there before supper. Or not—I just checked the weather forecast again, and rain is headed this way. I'd better get on the road.

Arriving at the state park, I follow the signs at the edges of the roads through a forest to the lodge. The main section is a beautiful building combining wood, stonework, and glass windows in an attractive way. I register and get my room key, the first one of its kind I've had this trip. It's an RFID-type card, like security badges for controlled access buildings. Instead of inserting it in a slot, all I have to do is wave it next to the reader device on the door and it unlocks. Very cool. Must be kind of expensive, too, because there's a five-dollar fee if it's not returned at checkout time.

I've brought my duffel in, and the cooler. I open the curtains on the far side of the room and get a very nice surprise. I have a private, covered balcony that looks right out onto the lake and the marina. Happy Hour tonight will be right here! I open a can of Cahaba American Blonde Ale, my liquid souvenir, pour about half into a red Solo cup, and take it out onto my balcony. I've got some pretzels to munch, too, while I enjoy the view.

Wheeler Lake is an impoundment of a section of the Tennessee River. The lake has a surface area of more than sixty-nine thousand acres, but the parkland covers roughly two thousand, five hundred acres. The clouds are turning a darker gray, and I think they'll be dropping rain very soon.

As I look across the water, a very large, dark-brown bird with powerful wing beats, a snowy white tail, and a snowy white head crosses between me and the dark-green, well-leafed-out trees on the opposite bank—it's a mature Bald Eagle. It's landed in one of the trees at the edge of a little cove over there, but in the dimming light I've lost sight of it amid all the greenery.

The story of the recovery of inland populations of our national bird since the banning of DDT insecticide in 1972 is something worth thinking about during what will likely be my last happy hour out on the road. The range maps in my collection of field guides make the story clear. The sparse, disconnected dots of known Bald Eagles in the interior of the continent shown in my old Peterson's guide, printed in 1980 but based on much older observations, made it seem as though I'd have to go all the way up to Alaska to be certain of finding an eagle to watch. But in newer field guides, those dots have now been replaced by ever-larger blotches of solid color as the Bald Eagle population in the lower continental United States continues to expand.

For me, the breeding territories of Bald Eagles are not just blobs of blue and purple on tiny little field guide maps. They're real places. As I sip my beer—it's quite nice, crisp in a good, refreshing way—I'm thinking about the thrill of watching my first pair of eagles at an enormous nest in the crotch of a gigantic sycamore near Starve Hollow State Park in southern Indiana, back in late winter during 2014. Since then I've watched adult eagles bringing four-foot-long sticks to add to their nests at Magee Marsh. I've seen the parent birds bringing freshly caught fish to their nestlings there, too. And I've watched a whole family of adult and juvenile eagles flying above an old field near the Oxbow area west of Cincinnati. In the Louisville area I know the locations of three eagle nests on the Ohio River. And just last year, an adult Bald Eagle flew over my farm on its way to the creek in a park about four miles away. Adding another eagle sighting this evening to my collection of memories is quite a bonus.

Here comes the rain—and the wind. It's lashing down onto the surface of the water and blowing onto the edge of my little balcony in cold, wet gusts. I won't be walking any of the trails that lead off from the parking lot tonight, so I might as well go eat dinner. Fortunately, this motel section is connected to the main lodge by a series of covered wood walkways and stairs, so I stay fairly dry.

Tonight's dinner special is a seafood buffet, which is tasty, but nothing like the freshly caught bounty I've been sampling up and down the Texas coast. While I eat I watch the rain lash down onto the boats in the marina.

On my way back to my room, I laugh when I meet a young woman clutching a big pile of blankets and a sleeping bag, trying to keep them from getting drenched in the rain. When I smile and say, "You've got quite a lot to carry," she replies, "I have three four-year-olds with me and they each want their own blankie!" I wish her good luck and go on to my room.

I am completely surprised when I pull back the bedspread in my room and discover nothing under it except a sheet. Now I'm the one who has to retrieve blankies. I go out to my car in the pounding rain, pull out my red-and-black stadium blanket and the spare white cotton thermal blanket I keep in the liftgate section, then tuck both under my arms as best I can to keep them dry. Well, at least I didn't have to raid my camping gear to stay warm and cozy tonight.

After catching up on recording my expenses in my travel journal, I step back out onto my balcony to listen to the rain and the frogs calling on this side of the lake. I'm not sure what I want to do tomorrow. Since I couldn't explore as much as I wanted to at the wildlife refuge this afternoon, and this evening's rain has literally washed out my plan to hike here, maybe I can find some other places around here to look for birds before I begin to drive north.

If I get right back on the interstate first thing in the morning I can go straight home a day early. It's only about three hundred miles. Counting a lunch stop and rest stops, that's probably less than seven hours of travel time. But I would still like to look for birds in this area and perhaps in Tennessee.

I'll just have to wait and see what the weather's like in the morning before I make a firm plan. I'll set my alarm for about sunrise, check on the weather forecast again, and then make a decision. The rain is supposed to taper off, but there could be fog.

For now, it's lights out.

§

Sunrise in Alabama is a gray thing this morning, obscured by clouds. Mist drifts along the surface of the lake, and thin rain continues to sift down as I walk over to the lodge for breakfast. It's a buffet again this morning, and I see plenty of familiar southern breakfast foods I like. Scrambled eggs, strips of bacon, a biscuit with white cream gravy, and a big glass of milk—I'm ready for anything now!

A fine, misty rain continues as I load my duffel and other stuff into my car. While I'm shoving things this way and that to get everything mashed back where it belongs, I hear the nasal call of a Fish Crow. I think of Fish Crows as coastal birds and am surprised to hear the sound this far inland.

I look up, and there it is, perched on the roof peak of this motel section of the park lodge. Fish Crows are a bit smaller than American Crows, which can be hard to tell when they are not next to each other, but this bird is definitely not very big. It calls again, "uh-uh, uh-uh," and although young American Crows can make a similar sound, I am convinced this is indeed a Fish Crow. However, I will check with some Alabama birding pals later to make sure.

The Barn Swallows hunting in this wet morning air veer off from their insect chase for a moment to make a quick dive-bomb toward the perched Fish Crow's head, then swoop away to pass directly in front of me.

When I walk over to the main lodge to check out of my room and turn in that expensive key, I mention to Thomas, the front-desk clerk, how pleased I was to see a Bald Eagle yesterday. As it turns out, he's a birder, too, and he gives me directions to an active nest a few miles away. Then he tells me about some other places to go to look for other kinds of birds in the area. Walking back to my car, I hear, then see, a male Northern Cardinal. He's singing at the end of a very wet branch, whose leaves glisten and droop under the weight of the rain. A Northern Mockingbird has chosen a higher perch and gives a long string of imitations.

The rain has stopped now as I put my car in gear, but it's cold, only fifty-four degrees Fahrenheit. It's cold, it's gray, it's damp, but I have the front windows rolled down about halfway so I can hear birds as I drive out of the park. I have the heat and the defroster running at low fan speeds so they don't interfere with the sounds coming from the woods.

I'm driving through a lush, green hardwood forest along the shores of Wheeler Lake. Where the short-cut grass alongside the edge of the paved road meets the forest edge, I see a Brown Thrasher turning over leaves to look for insects. The places Thomas mentioned are to the west, so in a way I'll be going backwards this morning, but I don't mind. Just as I drive out of the park, I spot two Mourning Doves fluttering up from the wet pavement ahead of me.

This part of northern Alabama is a mostly rural area of small towns and farmland, with ragged pastures where cattle graze. Driving carefully on the wet roadway I see some Cattle Egrets in the short grasses beyond the fences, foraging for the insects the cows and calves stir up as they plod along in the wet fields.

I've got something wrong in the notes I scribbled while I was talking with Thomas. I've turned in at a park here in Priceland, but I don't think it's the right one. This place is called Veteran's Park, and it's a playground and community area, not near a body of water. It does have a lot of mature trees and grassy spots where American Robins hop along looking for something to eat. Above them, Blue Jays dash back and forth from perch to perch in the wet canopy of fresh green leaves. I seem to be the only person here this early on a wet morning, but I'll keep looking around.

As I scan around with my binoculars through the open car window, I spot a brilliant male Eastern Bluebird, then a Northern Cardinal. An Eastern Towhee flies in front of my car, a bird I seldom see out in the open. I get a good look at its handsome rusty brown and black and white feathers as it dashes back toward the trees. This park isn't a particularly wild spot, and I'd rather try one of the other places Thomas recommended.

I'll go back out on the main road to see if I can find the water treatment plant that he mentioned. It's still cloudy, but the drizzly rain has tapered off, so maybe more birds will become active. I turn left and discover a sign warning that access to the water treatment facility is restricted, which is exactly what I would expect. Many such places are favorite spots among birders, and we are careful to obey signs and check in with staff for permission to enter. However, here the rules don't seem to be especially rigid, as the chain link gate is wide open this morning. I pull in, prepared to show my binoculars to an official, but I don't see any people around. Even though there are plenty of Barn Swallows and Tree Swallows swooping through the air, I don't think I'll stay to investigate more carefully. I'm just not getting a very birdy vibe here. Driving slowly back out to the main road I see yet another Northern Mockingbird, then hear a Carolina Chickadee calling "dee-dee-dee."

As I go back through the open gate I see a sign on my right and pull over to stop to read it. It's the entrance to Seven Mile Island Wildlife Management Area, which is a joint effort between various agencies of Alabama state government and the Tennessee Valley Authority. This whole section of the Tennessee River was dammed decades ago for flood control and other purposes and is still managed by TVA. A huge transmission tower supporting high-voltage power lines stands just behind the sign. A smaller sign tells me that there's an ongoing habitat restoration project in progress here, although I cannot find any details when I search for it on my phone. This is primarily an area for hunters, and the bright yellow metal farm gate across the gravel road is shut tight. Another sign says no vehicles are allowed in the fields.

This looks like it would be a great place to go walking with a local birder, especially since it's unlikely that any hunting would be going on at this time of year, but I'm by myself and I think I will keep driving. But where should I go? I've been seeing signs for a place called Key Cave National Wildlife Refuge, so I look that up using my phone, and set my GPS. I'm still on the outskirts of the town called Florence, and the refuge seems to be about fifteen minutes away.

§

The fences here are mostly the post-and-wire kind, just the sort of man-made additions to the landscape that Eastern Meadowlarks like as perches. Sure enough, every few hundred feet I see a brown bird with a yellow breast and black necklace poised on the top wire, bill open, singing "spring of the year" and "I live right here" to all who will listen. They're the brightest things I've seen so far this gray, cloudy morning, and their songs drifting in through my open car windows make me smile.

As I continue on the smoothly paved country road, my GPS says that in so many feet I should turn left at such-and-such a road—but that doesn't look like a road to me. There's no street sign, and the brown gravel looks like an especially well-cared-for driveway, so I'll keep going. Maybe I didn't get the distance right.

Uh, well, apparently that really was the road, and now my GPS says I can get where I'm going if I turn left at this next bit of brown gravel. As it turns out, some of the county roads here in this rural section of Alabama are still gravel, not pavement. I put on my turn signal, out of habit only, as there is no other traffic around, and turn the steering wheel.

This is very nice gravel, freshly graded and flat, with no major potholes, but I'm going to go very slowly anyway. I won't have to worry about stirring up a dust plume, since it's been raining, but I want to go slow to avoid excessive vibration over the rocky surface, and to be able to see and hear any birds. A thick line of dark-green, leafy trees borders the right side of the road, with scattered bushes and trees on the left. In the distant fields on the left a few cattle are grazing. This is really pretty farmland.

As I drive along, scarcely faster than I can walk, I hear Northern Cardinals singing in the gray morning air. Every so often I also hear an Eastern Towhee's short "drink your tea-ee-ee" song. I pause here and there about every fifty feet to listen for anything more, and soon I hear the lilting "teakettle, teakettle, teakettle," song of a Carolina Wren. I roll along slowly, listening and looking. Ah, there's a Field Sparrow somewhere out in that field, his whistling, trilling song that seems to follow the rhythm of a bouncing ping-pong ball carrying far through the damp air. All the birds I'm hearing in this area probably established their territories many weeks ago, and indeed, may live here year-round. This morning's singing is their version of a fence, telling their neighbors and any migrants coming into the area "I already live here, keep going!"

The gravel is flat from side to side, but the road forward is not completely level. It glides up and down, dipping a foot or two here, then rising a foot or two a bit farther on, in long, shallow ripples across this rich farmland. As I come over one of these little drawn-out humps, I have a good view of the gravel stretching off into the distance—and there are birds on the gravel out there straight ahead.

I can see about half a dozen little brown jobs hopping along the gravel and into and out of the grass at the edges. Sparrow behavior for sure, but which kind? I stop and raise my binoculars to take a good steady look. I see black and bright white stripes on their heads, no yellow at all, and mostly pinkish bills. It's a little group of White-crowned Sparrows foraging for seeds and such, fueling up to leave their winter range and fly north to the upper sections of Canada for the summer. If these clouds clear off, they might take to the skies tonight.

I put the car in gear again to roll forward, but this is a mistake—the birds are extremely wary and fly up into the trees immediately. Okay, I'll just stop again and turn off the engine this time, then wait for them to come back out onto the gravel. While waiting I hear another Eastern Towhee, and more Northern Cardinals. This is a very birdy spot, and I'm glad I missed my first turn. Two of the bravest White-crowned Sparrows flit down to the gravel, and soon there are eight of them in sight. They're hungry, and apparently there's plenty to eat up there. I'll watch another minute or so because they're so full of energy, but then I'm going to have to drive forward. They'll dash away as I pass, but I'm sure they will come back down as soon as they figure the danger is past. That's what they do back at my place.

At the end of this gravel road, my GPS instructs me to turn left onto another county road, which is also gravel. An eastern cottontail rabbit bounds along in a zigzag path ahead of me and veers off to the left. The farm fields here are lush and green, with young soybean plants in row after row. I cannot see any farmhouses, but that's fine. I haven't seen any cars lately, either. It's a quiet morning in the country, a nice place to be looking for birds.

Here is the turn to the right to enter the Key Cave refuge. Well, this isn't much. In fact, I'm not at all sure I'm in the right place. The county road numbers on the signs do not match with anything in the birding brochure I picked up yesterday. This refuge includes about one thousand acres of land, some of it as forest, some as grassland, some as old-field successional habitat with young shrubs and trees growing up amidst the wildflowers, and some still planted with row crops. I seem to be in the abandoned farm field section, and I think I'm on the completely wrong side of the refuge. According to what little information I have about this place, there are no visitor services here in terms of buildings with restrooms or water fountains, but there is supposed to be a birding information kiosk and a walking trail somewhere. My GPS thinks there's a road across these fields to the other side, so I will drive on a bit.

This gravel is a mess. Grasses and weeds are growing up in the center in many spots and make me think of the maintenance I need to do this spring on my own driveway at home. I will have to go very, very slow here and be extra careful, as I don't know where the potholes are. I was going to listen to some music for a few minutes, but I'd better not. I need to concentrate on driving. I can't see around the curves, and I sure hope that this area is as deserted and empty of other humans as the places I've already been this morning. It would not do at all to meet another vehicle coming towards me on this narrow road. Road is too nice a word, it's more like a wilderness track.

I look from the woods on the left out over the overgrown fields in front of me and to the right, just in time to see a very pale Red-tailed Hawk flap up from the grasses and weeds. I cannot see anything in its talons, so that must have been an unsuccessful strike. It soars off to try again elsewhere.

I drive forward cautiously. The track is becoming more and more uneven. The gravel and clay is grooved with ruts, creating a series of bumps and ridges, with a generous collection of potholes in a variety of sizes. Oh dear. Just up ahead the track is completely washed out. And there's water standing in the lowest spot, perhaps the shallow trickle of a feeder stream. It's a muddy mess. With only front wheel drive and not an especially high ground clearance, I cannot go forward. I'm on a bit of a slope, and I don't know how I'm going to get turned around without bogging down. I'm going to have to think about this for a minute.

I set the parking brake and get out to look around. I walk off the gravel a few paces to see how firm the ground is. It's wet from last night's rain, but not too mucky, so I think I'll be okay. The remaining thin coating of gravel is about three feet wider than my wheelbase, and I should be able to get turned around without putting more than one wheel at a time into the sticky, wet, clayey soil.

I get back in my car, take a deep breath, release the parking brake, and put the car into forward gear. Ease ahead two feet, while turning the wheel. Put car in reverse. Ease backwards. Repeat. Jockey back and forth, back and forth, cutting the wheels to this side, then that side each time, oh, just keep moving. If I were to get stuck here, I'd have to rely on the kindness of a farmer with a tractor and a long chain to get me out, if I could even find another human being. One more forward-and-back series. Yes, yes, now I am completely turned around and can drive back the way I came. So far, so good, but I'm not out of trouble yet. I won't be able to relax until I get back to the real gravel county road.

As I drive slowly along, I keep watching and listening for birds, but there are none. I come around the last turn and get a surprise. Just ahead I see three people walking—and three dogs. The dogs are not leashed. The dogs decide to rush toward my car. They don't seem particularly ferocious, actually rather a bit overweight in the way of household pets, but they're barking, full of energy, and not all that keen about obeying the voice commands of their humans. The only thing for me to do is roll the windows up almost to the top, just in case they're jumpers, and stop. I will simply wait. I will wait as long as I need to, and smile toward the humans. Just keep smiling.

The two men and the woman continue to call to their dogs, but the dogs are not responding. Generally speaking, dogs, and especially ones off-leash, are not welcome at wildlife refuges. State parks are usually dog-friendly, but not areas devoted to wildlife. I'd guess from their two rather large pickup trucks that these are local folks just out for a stroll on a gray morning, but I don't know that. And they don't know anything about me, and are probably wondering what I'm doing here and why. We have a standoff. I continue to smile. Finally two of the dogs turn back toward the men, and the woman walks forward a few steps, scoops up the third dog to carry it, and they all go back toward the pickup trucks that are parked next to the refuge sign.

I drive forward, wave as I pass them, still smiling, and turn right onto the country road. I need to be somewhere else, and right now I don't much care where that somewhere else is. I take the first left, which is the road I was supposed to have been on earlier, the one I passed up trying to get here, and drive on. This road just leads between farm fields, with fewer trees, and isn't nearly as scenic as the one I took to correct my mistake. There might be more sparrows here, but I'm not going to stop until I get back to the paved road.

I think I've had exactly as much birding as I want this morning. I'm ready to leave Alabama and go north to Tennessee. But I have no idea where I am in relation to I-65 and will need help from my GPS to get there. Nashville will do for a destination, although all I really need is to reach the northbound lanes of the interstate and I can do the rest of the navigating myself.

###

CHAPTER FIFTEEN

The last miles, home again, and making lists

Familiar birds, a good surprise, fresh ideas

A fine, misty rain begins again as I drive up and down hills and around curves through rural Alabama. It's the kind of rain that makes choosing a speed for the windshield wipers a constant struggle. Too slow, too fast, back and forth, the raindrops come down in unpredictable bunches. The pavement is slick, there are no guardrails, and the road has a double yellow line in the center for miles and miles and miles. It's a good thing there don't seem to be any other people out and about this morning. Finally, I cross into rural Tennessee. It looks about the same as rural Alabama, and the interstate should be fairly close.

When I reach the intersection with the highway, I stop for a bathroom break and to buy gas at a tiny country place, then check my maps. I won't need GPS from this point on because I'm in familiar territory again. As I drive I'll listen to some traditional Appalachian fiddle music with claw hammer banjo picking and enjoy the scenery until I decide on a lunch stop.

In the suburbs south of Nashville I see a sign for a Cracker Barrel. I need a dependable, hearty meal, and a cup of decaf because I've made a decision. I'm going to go on and push for home this afternoon. Before I left, I arranged things so I wouldn't need to be back at home until noon tomorrow, but now that I'm so close I might as well drive the rest of the way today.

After an open-faced roast beef sandwich with mashed potatoes and gravy, I'm refreshed and ready for the road again. Before I go, though, I'll text-message the cat sitter to let her know that I'll be home tonight.

On the outskirts of downtown Nashville it's mighty nice to see the first green-and-white highway sign with the name "Louisville" on it, and arrows pointing the way north.

As soon as I cross the state line into Kentucky, I pull into the rest stop. The tourist welcome section is closed but the bathrooms are open. It's been rainy and getting colder all day as I push northward, so when I get back to my car, I take a minute to put on warmer socks and a different pair of sandals to finish the drive home.

Traffic is heavy, and I have to pay close attention. I've been thinking about a chocolate shake from McDonalds for the last few miles as a treat, but when I pull into the drive-up area a fuzzy voice says their shake machine is broken. Oh well, I still have some cranberry juice in my cooler, so I'll just pull out of line, find a place to park, drink that, and be on my way.

I need something perky to listen to, to keep me alert as I go farther north. One part of my mind is thinking back over all the birds I've seen, and another part is racing forward to what I want to do when I get home—cuddle with my kitties is tops on the list—and all of those thoughts racing around in my brain are interfering with watching the road. Before I left home I made a new playlist for just this sort of afternoon. Instead of instrumental music, I'm going bold and loud, with lyrics to give my mind something to focus on instead of careening around to the past and skipping ahead to the future. The songs I chose all have something to do with travel, from "On the Road Again," to "I've Been Everywhere," and a lot of other fun tunes in-between to entertain me as the miles click past. I'll sing along with Willie Nelson and Queen and Jimmy Buffet as I zoom across the miles.

I keep passing signs that warn of a lengthy construction project ahead. But this is my lucky day because, on this rainy Sunday, there's no work going on and I can keep up a good speed, singing as I go. After the construction zone, the rain stops just past Elizabethtown, about an hour from home.

In Jefferson County once again, I turn off at my usual exit and head not for home but the grocery store and wine shop. I also need to stop at the gas station to top up my tank so I can get an accurate figure for the gas mileage on this trip. One more stop at the post office to pick up three weeks' worth of mail from my box, and I'm really headed for home.

Driving past the familiar fields on the way to my place, I see American Robins foraging on the bright green grasses, then a small flock of European Starlings swoops over me near the creek. A male Northern Cardinal darts across in front of me, and angles up to a perch in a roadside tree. Two Mourning Doves sit side by side on a utility wire. A Turkey Vulture tilts and glides in the air above me, just a short way from the turn onto my road.

Here I am at last, driving on the narrow old road I love the best, even with its crumbling shoulders and bumpily patched potholes. Since I've been away the trees have leafed out to form a canopy of green over the road, a tree tunnel that makes me smile every time I drive through it.

I pull into my gravel drive and make my way slowly past the barn and on to my house. It's about two hours before sunset, and I'm tired. I've been away for twenty days on a birdwatching binge, and I've driven three thousand, eight hundred sixty-nine miles alone. I'm ready to play with my kitties, drink a glass of wine on my own deck, and get reacquainted with the birds on my own farm.

I'll just take my duffel inside—everything else can wait until tomorrow.

I'm home!

§

The Indigo Bunting who lived here last year got home a few days later in the same week that I did, and took up his usual singing perches on the lightning rods on the barn, filling the spring days with his cheerful, paired phrases. "Sweet, sweet, chew, chew, zwee, zwee, zweeta zweeta," he sings, stringing them together in ever-longer sequences, all day from sunup to sundown. Late in the afternoons, when the male Northern Cardinal, that same handsome red fellow who sang to me the morning I began my roadtrip, goes hunting for food down by my pond, the Indigo Bunting flies across the field to sing from the lightning rods on the house. He's so loud and insistent I can hear him as I work at my desk inside.

My first week at home was a blur of unpacking the car, washing clothes, and putting away my travel gear. Just as I had hoped they would, my old reading glasses turned up. I found them in the mysterious black hole between the center console and the driver's seat, wedged out of sight, and almost out of reach. At the carwash, it took three dollars' worth of quarters to vacuum all the Texas sand out of my car.

Dealing with my camera disaster wasn't too complicated. On the way back from the car wash, I stopped in at my local camera store to pick up a new UV haze filter. But when I sat down to fix things at home, I had to try three kinds of wrenches before I found one that would twist the cracked filter off the zoom lens. Fortunately, the screw threads on the lens were not stripped. I found no scratches on the lens glass, and the new filter fit right into place easily. I drank the last souvenir craft beer from Alabama that night to celebrate.

I put the beautifully crafted wooden duck from Louisiana on the table where I keep my keys at night. When I opened the cardboard tube and unrolled the Gulf Coast bird poster I bought on South Padre Island, it was uncreased and unwrinkled. I mounted it on a blue mat about the color of the Texas sky and framed it. It's hanging on the north wall in the kitchen, where I see it every day and smile. I rearranged some things on the refrigerator, and the new magnets I bought while traveling are right where I can enjoy them, too, and remember the birds I discovered.

§

Soon I settled back into the familiar responsibilities of work and the routines of home, filling the notebook I keep on the kitchen table with favorite bird names as more migrants returned to Kentucky. Throughout the rest of the spring and on into summer I've spent every available hour reviewing my field notes and the hundreds of photos from my trip to Texas and back.

Late one night I made a discovery. While traveling I'd been so careful to reset the time in my phone and on my dashboard when I crossed into the central time zone. But the one clock I didn't think about to re-set was the one in my camera. The time stamps on each image are an hour off from the times I jotted down in my travel journal.

As I cross-referenced my photos and notes about birds, I stopped to puzzle over that handsomely marked butterfly I photographed at Resaca de la Palma, the one with white and purplish spots on the upper sides of its wings. I was right about one thing—it isn't in any of my reference books here at home for eastern butterflies. I searched my usual dependable sources on the internet and discovered that it's a Mexican Bluewing, a butterfly that only occurs north of the Rio Grande in a few pockets of suitable habitat. I was lucky to see it.

I confirmed my only tentative bird identification when someone posted an excellent photo in the Texas birding group I belong to, an image made from the convention center boardwalk on South Padre Island. Yes, indeed, the bird in my rather dim photo is a Clapper Rail, most likely the very same individual that the other photographer captured in such great detail in just about the same area below the boardwalk.

Quite by accident, while looking for something else in a fifty-year-old book I bought at an antique mall years ago, I found out a little more about why the pretty, grayish-blue-headed warbler with the yellow wash across its breast is called a Northern Parula. The text in the well-worn pages of the National Geographic Society's *Song and Garden Birds of North America* says, "parula means 'little titmouse.'" Why I didn't think of that when I was looking at the bird I do not know, because the whole family of Wood Warblers is known scientifically as the Family Parulidae. Then again, Latin was the farthest thing from my mind when face to face with such a dainty little beauty.

My list of all birds identified during my birdwatching binge to Texas and back kept growing and growing as I worked on my field notes—and turned into just the kind of surprise I was hoping for. The final total for my trip is one hundred seventy bird species. Of course, two of them, Common Pauraque and Ladder-backed Woodpecker, are marked (h) because I only heard them but didn't see the birds. Forty-eight of the birds on the list are lifers, birds I encountered for the very first time. I have a footnote after the numbered list for the waterthrush that I could not see clearly enough to name. I still haven't found a living Whooping Crane, so it's not on any list. Yet.

§

As I think about my adventures amid such varied habitats so far from home I'm not thinking only of the birds. I remember the people I met, and how generously they shared their local knowledge with me. Danny, Jane, Brandon, the two ladies whose names I never did find out but told me where to look for the Blackpoll Warbler at Laguna Madre, and so many other friendly folks who enjoy birds. Exploring with them made the trip so much richer, so full of warmth and companionship.

Looking here, there, and everywhere for birds made the swatches of color on range maps come alive for me in new ways. And it reinforced an idea I've long understood. The marks on a range map show where a particular species might be at a particular time of year. But it's only a broad picture. The habitat at ground level must include the kinds of food that species is equipped to feast on, whether that's insects or fruit or seeds or nectar or fish or worms.

I checked with Alabama birding friends on social media, and found out that I was right about the Fish Crow at Wheeler State Park. They've been showing up more and more often along the edges of the lake there for a few years now. The range maps for this species in the next editions of field guides will show them farther north than the older books I have in my library.

I could easily make a new batch of lists organized by the kinds of foods the various birds I saw prefer. Or a list based on the shape of their bills, or the shape of their feet. Or which ones live in which states year-round, and which ones only visit temporarily. What I won't do is make a list of favorites. Yes, the young Barred Owl was a special treat. And the Least Grebe was such a cute little thing. But the Buff-bellied Hummingbird was cute, too. I often think about its whirring wings as I watched it so close to the Rio Grande. And then my thoughts shift to the Crested Caracara, a bird that looks like it's wearing a badly fitting toupee. I remember how unusual it was to find both kinds of pelicans within one hundred feet of each other. Then I think about all the shorebirds and the Scissor-tailed Flycatcher. All sorts of memories crowd in one upon another, each one exciting in a special way.

A pleasant side effect of the trip is that the birds on my lists are not just names. When I see the words, I see a mental image of the bird, and can recall where and when I saw it. I learned something about the new ones, some little tidbit of its life history, or a special field mark that sets it apart from all the others. As photos of them appear from time to time in social media I find that I can recognize them rather quickly now. And that gives me an extra little glimmer of satisfaction.

Those images, now so much easier to identify, constantly mix in with photos of birds I do not yet know. And that's making me curious. I keep seeing intriguing mentions of birdy spots along the Atlantic coast.

So I've picked up a stack of crisp new roadmaps from the auto club and I have two new bird travel books to study. I have a fresh pad of sticky notes and little purple flags are sprouting out from the margins of the books. There are some diving sea ducks I'd like to get to know, and some handsome geese, and a kind of puffin with a big, colorful bill and a unique fishing style. And there's jay of a different color that lives up by the Canadian border. But I'm not going to make a list.

What I am doing for now is chatting online with some new folks up in the New England states about the possibilities for good birding and the best time of year to visit. I'm already thinking about how to arrange things here at home so I'll be free to take another nice long solo road trip next spring. I'll need about three weeks, I think. I could drive northeast up through Ohio and into Pennsylvania on the first day. Then I could probably reach the Atlantic Ocean late on the second day...

###

Acknowledgments

While I was on the road alone, some very special people were keeping track of my whereabouts throughout each day and night. With text messages and phone calls, they knew in a general way what highways I would be driving, which parks I might visit during the daylight hours, and where I was supposed to check in to spend the night. And they had all memorized my car's license number in case I didn't. Of course, I did make it to every destination, although a few times I was several hours late getting there.

I extend special thanks to my far-flung base team during my solo journey: my friends Lori in Indiana and Jack in Kentucky; my daughter Jenn in Ohio; plus cat sitter extraordinaire Cindy. Cell phone technology is a wonderful thing, but it's the people at the other end of the signal who matter the most. Y'all are the best!

Trip list of birds
in order of their discovery

1. Red-tailed Hawk
2. Turkey Vulture
3. House Sparrow
4. Great Blue Heron
5. American Crow
6. Black Vulture
7. Northern Cardinal
8. Northern Mockingbird
9. European Starling
10. American Robin
11. Barn Swallow
12. Eastern Meadowlark
13. Mourning Dove
14. Common Grackle
15. Blue Jay
16. Canada Goose
17. Eastern Towhee
18. Red-winged Blackbird
19. Osprey
20. Tree Swallow
21. Mallard
22. Anhinga

23. Snowy Egret
24. Black-crowned Night-Heron
25. Black-bellied Whistling-Duck
26. Little Blue Heron
27. Green Heron
28. Great Egret
29. Double-crested Cormorant
30. Belted Kingfisher
31. Solitary Sandpiper
32. Red-shouldered Hawk
33. Blue-winged Teal
34. Yellow-crowned Night-Heron
35. Red-bellied Woodpecker
36. Fish Crow
37. Yellow-rumped Warbler
38. Great-tailed Grackle
39. Rock Pigeon
40. Carolina Wren
41. Red-headed Woodpecker
42. Neotropic Cormorant
43. Killdeer
44. American Coot
45. Black-necked Stilt
46. Sanderling
47. Semipalmated Plover
48. Laughing Gull
49. Common Gallinule
50. Cliff Swallow
51. Loggerhead Shrike
52. Glossy Ibis
53. Pied-billed Grebe
54. Northern Shoveler
55. Eastern Kingbird
56. Roseate Spoonbill
57. White Ibis

58. White-faced Ibis
59. Purple Gallinule
60. Boat-tailed Grackle
61. Cattle Egret
62. Willet
63. Seaside Sparrow
64. Ring-billed Gull
65. American Bittern
66. Scissor-tailed Flycatcher
67. Brown Pelican
68. Chimney Swift
69. Wilson's Plover
70. Western Sandpiper
71. Dunlin
72. Greater Scaup
73. Royal Tern
74. Piping Plover
75. Short-billed Dowitcher
76. Ruddy Turnstone
77. Northern Harrier
78. Lesser Yellowlegs
79. American White Pelican
80. Forster's Tern
81. Caspian Tern
82. Least Tern
83. Black-bellied Plover
84. Red Knot
85. Black Tern
86. Sandwich Tern
87. Savannah Sparrow
88. Summer Tanager
89. Blue-headed Vireo
90. Swainson's Hawk
91. White-throated Sparrow
92. Scarlet Tanager

93. Indigo Bunting
94. Hooded Warbler
95. Common Loon
96. Whimbrel
97. Tricolored Heron
98. Red-breasted Merganser
99. White-rumped Sandpiper
100. Ruby-throated Hummingbird
101. Black-and-white Warbler
102. Worm-eating Warbler
103. Yellow-throated Warbler
104. White-eyed Vireo
105. Black Skimmer
106. Lark Sparrow
107. Crested Caracara
108. Inca Dove
109. Lincoln's Sparrow
110. Brown-headed Cowbird
111. Gray Catbird
112. Eurasian Collared-Dove
113. Yellow Warbler
114. Yellow-throated Vireo
115. Northern Flicker
116. Red-eyed Vireo
117. Common Pauraque (h)
118. White-winged Dove
119. Black-crested Titmouse
120. Purple Martin
121. Brown Thrasher
122. Tennessee Warbler
123. Great Kiskadee
124. Blue-winged Warbler
125. Carolina Chickadee
126. Northern Parula
127. Orchard Oriole

128. Eastern Wood-Pewee
129. Ladder-backed Woodpecker (h)
130. Black-chinned Hummingbird
131. Marbled Godwit
132. American Oystercatcher
133. Mottled Duck
134. Greater Yellowlegs
135. Peregrine Falcon
136. Reddish Egret
137. Gadwall
138. Redhead
139. Plain Chachalaca
140. Altimira Oriole
141. Golden-fronted Woodpecker
142. Green Jay
143. Buff-bellied Hummingbird
144. White-tipped Dove
145. Olive Sparrow
146. Least Grebe
147. Yellow-headed Parrot
148. Red-crowned Parrot
149. Clapper Rail
150. Blackpoll Warbler
151. Least Bittern
152. Magnificent Frigatebird
153. American Avocet
154. Long-billed Dowitcher
155. Stilt Sandpiper
156. Baltimore Oriole
157. Rose-breasted Grosbeak
158. American Redstart
159. Ruddy Duck
160. Pileated Woodpecker
161. Prothonotary Warbler
162. Barred Owl

Nancy Grant

163. American Goldfinch
164. Sandhill Crane
165. House Finch
166. Tufted Titmouse
167. Eastern Bluebird
168. Bald Eagle
169. Field Sparrow
170. White-crowned Sparrow

And a Waterthrush, species undetermined

Trip list of birds in scientific groups

One way to understand more about birds is to know how they are related to each other. Scientists who study both living birds and fossils group them together into orders first, then into families. Within families, similar birds are grouped into a genus, which may include many species or only one. In the early days the groups were based on similarities in bone structure and other characteristics easily seen with the naked eye or a microscope. Advances in analyzing DNA with sophisticated new tools are revealing different relationships than were previously considered.

Scientists use common names for birds in their own country's language, but for accuracy around the world, each bird also has a Latin name consisting of two parts. The first word is the genus, sort of like a bunch of cousins. The second word is the species, a one-of-a-kind designation. In the United States, birders say "Prothonotary Warbler" when looking at a certain kind of bird with brilliant yellow feathers. In Mexico, birders looking at the same bird say "Chipe Dorado." In Latin, birders from both countries say "Protonotaira citrea."

The groupings and sequence of birds in this list, as well as their common names and their Latin names shown in parenthesis, represent what the scientists at both the American Ornithological Union and the American Birding Association considered accurate when I was on the road in April 2017. As more research reveals more similarities—and perhaps more differences—the groups may change over time.

Ducks, Geese, Swans: Family Anatidae

Black-bellied Whistling-Duck (*Dendrocygna autumnalis*)
Canada Goose (*Branta canadensis*)
Blue-winged Teal (*Spatula discors*)
           (formerly *Anas discors*)
Northern Shoveler (*Spatula clypeata*)
           (formerly *Anas clypeata*)
Gadwall (Mareca strepera)
           (formerly *Anas strepera*)
Mallard (*Anas platyrhynchos*)
Mottled Duck (*Anas fulvigula*)
Redhead (*Aythya americana*)
Greater Scaup (*Aythya marila*)
Red-breasted Merganser (*Mergus serrator*)
Ruddy Duck (*Oxyura jamaicensis*)

Curassows and Guans: Family Cracidae

Plain Chachalaca (*Ortalis vetula*)

Grebes: Family Podicipedidae

Least Grebe (*Tachybaptus dominicus*)
Pied-billed Grebe (*Podilymbus podiceps*)

Pigeons and Doves: Family Columbidae

Rock Pigeon (*Columba livia*)
Eurasian Collared-Dove (*Streptopelia decaocto*)
Inca Dove (*Columbina inca*)
White-tipped Dove (*Leptotila verreauxi*)
White-winged Dove (*Zenaida asiatica*)
Mourning Dove (*Zenaida macroura*)

Goatsuckers: Family Caprimulgidae

Common Pauraque (*Nyctidromus albicollis*)

Hummingbirds: Family Trochilidae

Ruby-throated Hummingbird (*Archilochus colubris*)

Black-chinned Hummingbird (*Archilochus alexandri*)
Buff-bellied Humingbird (*Amazilia yucatanensis*)

Rails, Gallinules, and Coots: Family Rallidae

Clapper Rail (*Rallus crepitans*)
                (formerly *Rallus longirostris*)
Purple Gallinule (*Porphyrio martinicus*)
Common Gallinule (*Gallinula galeata*)
American Coot (*Fulica americana*)

Swifts: Family Apodidae

Chimney Swift (*Chaetura pelagica*)

Cranes: Family Gruidae

Sandhill Crane (*Antigone canadensis*)
                (*formerly Grus canadensis*)

Stilts and Avocets: Family Recurvirostridae

Black-necked Stilt (*Himantopus mexicanus*)
American Avocet (*Recurvirostra americana*)

Oystercatchers: Family Haematopodidae

American Oystercatcher (*Haematopus palliatus*)

Lapwings and Plovers: Family Charadriidae

Black-bellied Plover (*Pluvialis squatarola*)
Wilson's Plover (*Charadrius wilsonia*)
Semipalmated Plover (*Charadrius semipalmatus*)
Piping Plover (*Charadrius melodus*)
Killdeer (*Charadrius vociferus*)

Sandpipers, Phalaropes, and Allies: Family Scolopacidae

Whimbrel (*Numenius phaeopus*)
Marbled Godwit (*Limosa fedoa*)
Ruddy Turnstone (*Arenaria interpres*)
Red Knot (*Calidris canutus*)

Stilt Sandpiper (*Calidris himantopus*)
Sanderling (*Calidris alba*)
Dunlin (*Calidris alpina*)
White-rumped Sandpiper (*Calidris fuscicollis*)
Western Sandpiper (*Calidris mauri*)
Short-billed Dowitcher (*Limnodromus griseus*)
Long-billed Dowitcher (*Limnodromus scolopaceus*)
Solitary Sandpiper (*Tringa solitaria*)
Lesser Yellowlegs (*Tringa flavipes*)
Willet (*Tringa semipalmata*)
Greater Yellowlegs (*Tringa melanoleuca*)

Gulls, Terns, and Skimmers: Family Laridae

Laughing Gull (*Leucophaeus atricilla*)
Ring-billed Gull (*Larus delawarensis*)
Least Tern (*Sternula antillarum*)
Caspian Tern (*Hydroprogne caspia*)
Black Tern (*Chlidonias niger*)
Forster's Tern (*Sterna forsteri*)
Royal Tern (*Thalasseus maximus*)
Sandwich Tern (*Thalasseus sandvicensis*)
Black Skimmer (*Rynchops niger*)

Loons: Family Gaviidae

Common Loon (*Gavia immer*)

Frigatebirds: Family Fregatidae

Magnificent Frigatebird (*Fregata magnificens*)

Cormorants: Family Phalacrocoracidae

Neotropic Cormorant (*Phalacrocorax brasilianus*)
Double-crested Cormorant (*Phalacrocorax auritus*)

Darters: Family Anhingidae

Anhinga (*Anhinga anhinga*)

Pelicans: Family Pelecanidae

American White Pelican (*Pelecanus erythrorhynchos*)
Brown Pelican (*Pelecanus occidentalis*)

Herons, Bitterns, and Allies: Family Ardeidae

American Bittern (*Botaurus lentiginosus*)
Least Bittern (*Ixobrychus exilis*)
Great Blue Heron (*Ardea herodias*)
Great Egret (*Ardea alba*)
Snowy Egret (*Egretta thula*)
Little Blue Heron (*Egretta caerulea*)
Tricolored Heron (*Egretta tricolor*)
Reddish Egret (*Egretta rufescens*)
Cattle Egret (*Bubulcus ibis*)
Green Heron (*Butorides virescens*)
Black-crowned Night-Heron (*Nycticorax nycticorax*)
Yellow-crowned Night-Heron (*Nycanassa violacea*)

Ibises and Spoonbills: Family Threskiornithidae

White Ibis (*Eudocimus albus*)
Glossy Ibis (*Plegadis falcinellus*)
White-faced Ibis (*Plegadis chihi*)
Roseate Spoonbill (*Platalea ajaja*)

New World Vultures: Family Cathartidae

Black Vulture (*Coragyps atratus*)
Turkey Vulture (*Cathartes aura*)

Ospreys: Family Pandionidae

Osprey (*Pandion haliaetus*)

Kites, Eagles, and Hawks: Family Accipitridae

Bald Eagle (*Haliaeetus leucocephalus*)
Northern Harrier (*Circus hudsonius*)
            (*formerly Circus cyaneus*)
Red-shouldered Hawk (*Buteo lineatus*)

Swainson's Hawk (*Buteo swainsoni*)
Red-tailed Hawk (*Buteo jamaicensis*)

Typical Owls: Family Strigidae

Barred Owl (*Strix varia*)

Kingfishers: Family Alcedinida

Belted Kingfisher (*Megaceryle alcyon*)

Woodpeckers: Family Picidae

Red-headed Woodpecker (*Melanerpes erythrocephalus*)
Golden-fronted Woodpecker (*Melanerpes aurifrons*)
Red-bellied Woodpecker (*Melanerpes carolinus*)
Ladder-backed Woodpecker (*Picoides scalaris*)
Northern Flicker (*Colaptes auratus*)
Pileated Woodpecker (*Dryocopus pileatus*)

Caracaras and Falcons: Family Falconidae

Crested Caracara (*Caracara cheriway*)
Peregrine Falcon (*Falco peregrinus*)

Lories, Parakeets, Macaws, and Parrots:

Family Psittacidae

Red-crowned Parrot (*Amazona viridigenalis*)
Yellow-headed Parrot (*Amazona oratrix*)

Tyrant Flycatchers: Family Tyrannidae

Eastern Wood-Pewee (*Contopus virens*)
Great Kiskadee (*Pitangus sulphuratus*)
Eastern Kingbird (*Tyrannus tyrannus*)
Scissor-tailed Flycatcher (*Tyrannus forficatus*)

Shrikes: Family Laniidae

Loggerhead Shrike (*Lanius ludovicicianus*)

Vireos: Family Vireonidae

White-eyed Vireo (*Vireo griseus*)
Yellow-throated Vireo (*Vireo flavifrons*)
Blue-headed Vireo (*Vireo solitarius*)
Red-eyed Vireo (*Vireo olivaceus*)

Crows and Jays: Family Corvidae

Green Jay (*Cyanocorax yncas*)
Blue Jay (*Cyanocitta cristata*)
American Crow (*Corvus brachyrhynchos*)
Fish Crow (*Corvus ossifragus*)

Swallows: Family Hirundinidae

Purple Martin (*Progne subis*)
Tree Swallow (*Tachycineta bicolor*)
Cliff Swallow (*Petrochelidon pyrrhonota*)
Barn Swallow (*Hirundo rustica*)

Chickadees and Titmice Family Paridae

Carolina Chickadee (*Poecile carolinensis*)
Tufted Titmouse (*Baeolophus bicolor*)
Black-crested Titmouse (*Baeolophus atricristatus*)

Wrens: Family Troglodytidae

Carolina Wren (*Thryothorus ludovicianus*)

Thrushes: Family Turdidae

Eastern Bluebird (*Sialia sialis*)
American Robin (*Turdus migratorius*)

Mockingbirds and Thrashers: Family Mimidae

Gray Catbird (*Dumetella carolinensis*)
Brown Thrasher (*Toxostoma rufum*)
Northern Mockingbird (*Mimus polyglottos*)

Starlings: Family Sturnidae

European Starling (*Sturnus vulgaris*)

Old World Sparrows: Family Passeridae

House Sparrow (*Passer domesticus*)

Fringilline and Cardueline Finches, and Allies:

Family Fringillidae

House Finch (*Haemorhous mexicanus*)
    (*formerly Carpodacus mexicanus*)
American Goldfinch (*Spinus tristis*)

New World Towhees, Sparrows, and Allies:

Family Passerellidae

Olive Sparrow (*Arremonops rufivirgatus*)
Eastern Towhee (*Pipilo erythrophthalmus*)
Field Sparrow (*Spizella pusilla*)
Lark Sparrow (*Chondestes grammacus*)
Savannah Sparrow (*Passerculus sandwichensis*)
Seaside Sparrow (*Ammodramus maritimus*)
Lincoln's Sparrow (*Melospiza lincolnii*)
White-throated Sparrow (*Zonotrichia albicollis*)
White-crowned Sparrow (*Zonotrichia leucophrys*)

Blackbirds: Family Icteridae

Eastern Meadowlark (*Sturnella magna*)
Orchard Oriole (*Icterus spurius*)
Altamira Oriole (*Icterus gularis*)
Baltimore Oriole (*Icterus galbula*)
Red-winged Blackbird (*Agelaius phoeniceus*)
Brown-headed Cowbird (*Molothrus ater*)
Common Grackle (*Quiscalus quiscula*)
Boat-tailed Grackle (*Quiscalus major*)
Great-tailed Grackle (*Quiscalus mexicanus*)

Wood-Warblers: Family Parulidae

Worm-eating Warbler (*Helmitheros vermivorum*)
Blue-winged Warbler (*Vermivora cyanoptera*)

Black-and-white Warbler (*Mniotilta varia*)
Prothonotary Warbler (*Protonotaria citrea*)
Tennessee Warbler (*Oreothlypis peregrina*)
Hooded Warbler (*Setophaga citrina*)
American Redstart (*Setophaga ruticilla*)
Northern Parula (*Setophaga americana*)
Yellow Warbler (*Setophaga petechia*)
Blackpoll Warbler (*Setophaga striata*)
Yellow-rumped Warbler (*Setophaga coronata*)
Yellow-throated Warbler (*Setophaga dominica*)

Cardinals, certain Tanagers, and Allies:

Family Cardinalidae

Summer Tanager (*Piranga rubra*)
Scarlet Tanager (*Piranga olivacea*)
Northern Cardinal (*Cardinalis cardinalis*)
Rose-breasted Grosbeak (*Pheucticus ludovicianus*)
Indigo Bunting (*Passerina cyanea*)

A scientific quirk: Four kinds of birds I saw while traveling have duplications in their names, in which the genus is the same Latin word as the species, such as the one for the Eastern Kingbird. Its scientific name is *Tyrannus tyrannus*.

Made in the USA
Middletown, DE
09 December 2022

17346988R00205